G.Gordinier
151 Lambtown Rd.
Ledyard, CT 06339

REVIEW COPY

THE COLLECTIONS OF THE
NEW JERSEY HISTORICAL SOCIETY,
VOLUME 17

For Want of Trade

Published by the Society as a
Thomas Alva Edison Study in
New Jersey Economic History,
with Funds from the
Charles Edison Fund,
Friends of the Society,
the Estate of Edward J. Grassmann,
and an Anonymous Gift
Dedicated to the Memory of
Delia Brinkerhoff Koster

For Want of Trade
Shipping and the New Jersey Ports,
1680–1783

James H. Levitt

NEWARK • 1981
New Jersey Historical Society

© 1981 by The New Jersey Historical Society
Library of Congress catalog card number 81-38352
ISBN 0-911020-03-9

Printed in the U.S.A.

Library of Congress Cataloging in Publication Data

Levitt, James H., 1940-
   For want of trade.

   (Collections of the New Jersey Historical Society ; v. 17)
   Bibliography: p. 224
   Includes index.
   1. Shipping — New Jersey — History. 2. Harbors — New Jersey — History. 3. New Jersey — Commerce — History. I. Title. II. Series.
F131.N62 vol. 17 [HF752.N5]   974.9s   81-38352
ISBN 0-911020-03-9   [387.1'09749]   AACR2

To the Memory of
Charles Edison,
Secretary of the Navy,
New Jersey Governor,
Businessman, and
Philanthropist

Contents

Preface, ix
Introduction, 1

1. THE COLONY OF NEW JERSEY, 7
   Commercial and Political Problems, 9 • Burlington and Perth Amboy, 13
   Smuggling and Other Illicit Trade, 18

2. EVOLUTION OF THE PORTS, 21
   New York's Early Dominance, 22 • War and Trade, 28 • Legislative Inaction, 34 • Problems of Geographic Location, 39

3. PORT ADMINISTRATION, 45
   Port Personnel and Procedures, 46 • Port Recordkeeping, 49 • John Stevens (ca. 1682–1737), of Perth Amboy, 52 • Charles Read, of Burlington, 54

4. PATTERNS OF TRADE, 57
   Perth Amboy Trade Routes, 59 • Shipping from Burlington, 64 • Regionalization of Trade, 66 • Comparison with Piscataqua, New Hampshire, 69

5. VESSELS, CREWS, AND CARGOS, 77
   Vessel Size and Cargo, 77 • Age of Vessels, 82 • Shipbuilding, 86 • Crew Size, 89 • Construction, Design, and Costs, 92 • Shipmasters and Sailors, 95 • The Navigation Acts, 99 • Cargo Trends, 102

6. MERCHANT-SHIPPERS, 107
   Maritime Bookkeeping, 110 • Versatility of Merchant-Shippers, 113 • Competition from across the Rivers, 119 • The Business of Agents, 123 Financial Difficulties, 130 • New Brunswick Merchants, 131 • West Jersey Merchants, 133 • Maritime Partnerships, 137

7. DARK AND DISMAL DAYS, 139
   Revolutionary Ferment and the Maritime Economy, 143 • War in the Ports, 146 • Attempts at Revitalization, 150

CONCLUSION, 153

COMPILATIONS FROM MARITIME RECORDS, 159
   List of Customs and Naval Officers in New Jersey, 159 • Cost of Building the Sloop *Catharine*, 161

TABLES DEVELOPED FROM THE CUSTOMS AND NAVAL OFFICERS RECORDS, 163
   1 Port Use at Perth Amboy, 1722–64, 164 • **2** Types of Vessels Using Perth Amboy, Selected Years, 165   **3** Volume and Region of Trade, Selected Years, 167 • **4** Percentage of Regional Trade by Vessels Entering and Clearing Perth Amboy, Selected Years, 169 • **5** Selected Samples of Voyage Patterns at Perth Amboy, 1722–27, 171 • **6** Tons — Guns — Men, 173 • **7** Types of Vessels Registered in New Jersey, 178 • **8** Types of Vessels Built in New Jersey, 178 • **9** Percentage of Vessels Built and/or Registered in New Jersey, Using New Jersey, 179 • **10** Shipbuilding Index, 180 • **11** Master/Vessel Relationship, 183 • **12** Types of Vessels Using Perth Amboy, 184

Abbreviations, 187
Notes, 189
Bibliographical Note, 213
Index, 219

Preface

"FOR WANT OF TRADE": this plaintive cry, expressed in many different ways, was echoed throughout much of the eighteenth century by New Jerseyans who struggled to develop maritime commercial centers at the official ports of entry. This work is in large part the story of that development. At the same time I have tried, through the inclusion of other small colonial ports, to place the ports of New Jersey in the broader context of colonial economic and maritime life.

The activities of New Jersey's colonial ports—Perth Amboy, Burlington, and Salem—have never been carefully investigated, for not only is there a paucity of material, but most historical studies have emphasized the maritime and economic activities of its great neighbors, New York and Philadelphia, which grew into commercial entrepôts and dominated much of colonial trade. New Jersey, we have been told, was like a keg tapped at both ends, and there most references to the economic life of the colony and state have ended. New Jersey's economic history, the story of the keg, is an exciting one in which New Jersey's ports played an important role. In relating that development it was my good fortune to have available a sufficient quantity of records kept by customs and naval officers to be able to reconstruct the inter-colonial, West Indian, and transatlantic trade carried on by New Jersey's ports. Herein was to be found a story of optimism, of agricultural development, of the rise of prominent families finding upward social and political mobility through the wealth afforded them by maritime commerce. Perhaps most impressive was the colonial New Jerseyans' determination never to be merely extensions of their neighbors, but to attempt to maintain, as their struggle for their ports clearly reveals, their own sense of identity.

For clarity, much of the information contained in the records was quantified. Data bases, requiring several years of preparation and containing many thousands of pieces of information on New Jersey's ports and other small colonial ports, were processed using the computer. The methodology that was developed formed a central part of this work.

This book, essentially an expansion of my doctoral dissertation, "New Jersey Shipping, 1722–1764," grew out of my firm belief that understanding our early development as a nation rests largely upon the firm foundation of our understanding of local history. That this work reached fruition at this time is attributable in large measure to the Charles Edison Fund's decision to encourage, through prize competition, research on New Jersey's economic history. At a time when the emphasis frequently is on publication of works that are broad or national in scope, it is gratifying to find such support for scholarly local histories. Again one is reminded that it is only through an examination and understanding of the parts that a sense of the whole may be achieved.

This work could not have been completed without the assistance of many individuals, the first of whom is Professor Larry R. Gerlach, of the University of Utah, friend and advisor, who launched me on this quest and encouraged me throughout the project. Quantifying the port records required the use of the computer and the development of appropriate software to accomplish this task. A special note of gratitude must go to Claude LaBarre, whose skills and insights in the area of academic computing made the methodological approach to this work possible.

To fill out the framework of quantification, I found the manuscript collections at Rutgers University and the New Jersey Historical Society essential to give this study both depth and breadth. I am indebted to all the librarians, archivists, and others at those institutions for their assistance in helping me to search out materials, with special thanks to Don C. Skemer, Editor of Publications, the New Jersey Historical Society, and Carl A. Lane, Keeper of Manuscripts, the New Jersey Historical Society.

I am grateful to *The American Neptune* and the New Jersey Historical Commission, respectively, for permission to use portions of my article, "From Whence or Where Bound—The Role of the Customs and Naval Officers at Colonial New Jersey's Ports," 37 *The American*

Neptune (1977): 262–75; and my pamphlet, *New Jersey's Revolutionary Economy*, New Jersey's Revolutionary Experience, vol. 9 (Trenton, N.J., 1975).

I also wish to express my gratitude for permission to use sections of letters, diaries, and other archival materials from the following repositories: Rutgers University Library, Special Collections, New Brunswick; the New Jersey State Library, Archives and History Bureau, Trenton; and the Historical Society of Pennsylvania, Philadelphia. I also appreciate the cooperation of the staff of the Public Records Office, London, whose assistance in obtaining microfilm copies of customs records vital to my research was invaluable.

Finally, I offer a special expression of appreciation to my wife, Viki. It is traditional to cite one's spouse for patience and understanding offered through the duration of a large project. But her contribution was far greater. Without her sound advice and editorial skills, this work would never have been accomplished.

Perth Amboy as it was known to the British on the eve of the Revolutionary War, in Thomas Jeffreys's American Atlas . . . (London, 1776). NJHS

Introduction

RUM FROM THE WEST INDIES for thirsty Jerseymen, wine from the Canary Islands for the more discriminating New Jersey customer; calico, linens, axes, and hardware from England to be delivered to a merchant's door, a local store, or a tavern, often came from the decks and cargo holds of sailing vessels that traded through New Jersey's official ports of entry. Vessels laden with such produce of the colony as wheat, flour, pork, beef, or timber products cleared New Jersey waters for places such as Madeira, Liverpool, Barbados, Jamaica, or Saint Kitts. During an active period at Perth Amboy, one of the colony's three official ports of entry—Perth Amboy, Burlington, and Salem—it was not unusual to find mariners such as Gerard Syere, Solomon David, or Peter Winants conducting business at a warehouse or having a drink at one of the local taverns with a merchant or fellow seaman.

Captain Syere was the commander of the *Samuel*, a dependable if not speedy fifty-ton brig that was more than a decade old in 1741. Its owners, James Leaterland and Bryand Blanding, had shipped from Liverpool to New Jersey's shores those European goods so much in demand—linens, hats, even bottled beer. By now the captain was probably well known around the harbor. Although it was probably not difficult to procure his export cargo, which consisted mostly of timber products, he had remained in the New Jersey harbor for more than three months before departing for Liverpool, and he would probably stop at New York for additional cargo before beginning the transatlantic voyage. In contrast was Solomon David, who captained a small fifteen-ton sloop, the *Two Brothers*, for John and Samuel Ogden. He had left port early in November for Rhode Island with a cargo of foodstuffs, principally flour, bread, and Indian corn, and had returned early in December with oil, molasses, and rum. He was likely to be impatient, however, for he had allotted himself less than a week to secure a cargo of Jersey cider, cheese, and other salables, such as a box of hatchets, for a trip down the Atlantic coast to Virginia. Earlier in the year Peter Winants had been in port with the sloop *Anne and Elizabeth*, which was registered in New York to a relative, Vinant Winants. The good captain had taken advantage of the onset of milder spring weather to make a quick run to North Carolina.

At a local store one might encounter Jeremiah Borden, a partner in the vessel he captained and a New Jersey resident. He might be delivering three brass kettles or sampling some of the rum that had been part of the cargo from his sloop *Good Resolution*, which had just returned from Rhode Island. Up the street a number of barrels of flour from a warehouse were on their way by wagon to the wharf where James Blain, master and sole owner of the sloop *Mary Anne*, waited impatiently for that cargo so he could depart for New England.[2] At another time one might even encounter John Parker, who had of late journeyed to Jamaica, Virginia, and Newfoundland as a supercargo and would have important information about markets.[3]

Here, as at most colonial ports, active periods alternated with long periods of relative inactivity when only local ships from New York or Philadelphia rode at Perth Amboy's landings and docks. Indeed, Perth Amboy, Burlington, and Salem, like so many of the twenty-eight smaller ports of entry along the Atlantic coast, were only modestly active compared with entrepôts such as Boston, Philadelphia, or New York. Even though many of these smaller ports, like those in New Jersey, suffered an eventual decline in the volume and scope of their trade, they are important for a more complete understanding of local history and of the nature of colonial maritime commerce.

Although New Jersey's rivers and coastline provided many harbors and landings, such as Raritan Landing, New Brunswick, Egg Harbor, or Cape May Landing, trade was almost exclusively local and largely undocumented. Perth Amboy, Burlington, and Salem, on the other hand, were the only New Jersey ports officially designated as ports of entry. Only from such ports could overseas and coastwise trade, other than from the neighboring provinces, be carried out, and the naval officer or customs officer stationed at these locations dutifully recorded such trade.[4] Because the records for the official ports of entry are more complete, this study focuses on these ports and the activities surrounding them, chiefly from 1722 to 1764.

A study of New Jersey shipping is not of merely local or regional value. Information about New Jersey's maritime trade, when combined with that from the lesser ports of Piscataqua, New Hampshire, and, to a more limited extent, Sunbury, Georgia, provides insights into the nature of the eighteenth-century maritime economy.[5] A comparison of the evolution of the New Jersey ports with Piscataqua provides important clues about why some lesser ports grew while others remained static or declined. Finally, when New Jersey's maritime trade is fitted into the larger context of all British colonies in North America, some additional insights, especially concerning trade patterns, are revealed.

It is unfortunate that attention has been too often riveted to the largest and most active ports, such as Boston, Philadelphia, and New York, or to the activities of merchant princes and their families, for that limited focus has produced an incomplete picture of maritime commerce.[6] Lesser ports and lesser merchants have often been neglected both in local histories and in studies of the overall development of colonial economic growth; such neglect was due in most cases to a paucity of traditional sources. In the case of the New Jersey ports, it is clear, their relatively modest activity and the lack of a large mercantile class has meant that merchant family papers, so plentiful for the study of many larger ports, are scarce. For example, there are only a few scattered references to shipping activities in the papers of the Hendrickson family and other prominent landowners who were occasionally involved in maritime enterprises. Little information on the activity of New Jersey ports can be found in the papers of merchant-shipping families that resided in New Jersey, such as the Stevens and Parker families at Perth Amboy and the Smith family at Burlington, for they conducted most of their business via New York and Philadelphia. Still less material is available in actual maritime records; only a few shipping ledgers are extant. In the end, the scarcity of manuscripts that describe port activities, shipping routes, merchant relationships, and cargos makes the task of reconstructing in a conventional manner the activities of New Jersey ports and those who used them, let alone the nature of the import and export trade, extremely difficult.

Among the sources for studying colonial shipping are the port records kept by the customs and naval officers. These records contain voluminous amounts of statistical materials that are rendered more intelligible through computer analysis. Unfortunately, only incomplete records are available for all three New Jersey ports. Perth

Amboy records cover the period 1722–64, but they are not inclusive; some months and even years are missing. Complete Burlington records are available for 1732–48, as are entrances and clearances at Salem for 1736–40.[7] A search of the customs and naval records and the treasury papers, conducted at my request at the Public Records Office, London, failed to produce any additional listing for Perth Amboy or Burlington. It is possible, however, that many of the records were never sent from the colonies to England, for it appears that throughout the period officials connected with the ports were notoriously careless in communicating those documents to England. If the records were sent, they may have been among those lost in the fire that destroyed the Plantation Wing of the London Customs House at the turn of the nineteenth century. One hopes, however, that more records will come to light.

Maintained as part of the legal machinery for the enforcement of the Navigation Acts, these records afford valuable information about each vessel—ownership registration, place of construction, cargo, and place of origin or destination. When processed by a computer, the records provide a vital link in our understanding of the nature of shipping, the merchant community, and the local economy.

Because so few customs records remain for Salem, and its activities were absorbed early into the commerce of Philadelphia, greater emphasis has been given here to the activities of Perth Amboy and Burlington. Analysis of the complete listing of some 1,103 cases at Perth Amboy and an additional partial listing of 1,411 cases[8] and all the data on the 105 existing cases of the port at Burlington has yielded a wealth of information about the nature and operation of these ports. Port growth and decline, the number of vessels, and tonnage passing through the port each year have been revealed. Technical questions about vessels using the port—type, frequency of appearance, amount of armament, size of crew—important for understanding economic development and growth in both a local and national context have been addressed. Compilations of registration and place of construction afford some knowledge of the extent of the shipbuilding industry in the colony, as well as the composition of the New Jersey fleet. A measurement of the ship's age of both New Jersey and non–New Jersey vessels suggests important national trends in the shipbuilding industry. Partial answers to complex problems of ownership and partnership, the role of the small entrepreneur, the frequency with which partnerships were employed, and the number of persons involved have been obtained. Finally, the quantity and type of imports and exports and the nature of trade patterns are more fully revealed.

Much of this work uses quantitative and statistical data developed from customs and naval officer records and from secondary sources concerned with merchants or maritime trade and commerce for this period. This type of data, especially shipping records, for the seventeenth and eighteenth centuries, often lack the exactness of similar data from more modern periods. Poor recordkeeping was endemic at eighteenth-century ports; vessel types were often incorrectly listed; tonnage figures are suspect both because of errors in listing tonnage and because of deliberate fraud and miscalculation on the part of owners who generally underrated tonnage to reduce port costs.[9] Ship destination poses another problem, for last-minute marketing information or other considerations might lead a captain who was reported cleared out for Barbados in the West Indies to go to Jamaica or even North Carolina instead. This and other kinds of problems suggest an inexactness in numbers for this period and indicate that quantification of data for this period produces not the answer but another means of examining the history of this period.

Statistical data, however, provide only the skeletal framework for understanding an important facet of New Jersey history that would otherwise remain hidden. Quantitative analysis answers only the "what" of history; it does not explain how or why such results come about. Herein lies the greatest limitation of the computer; the new method does not release the historian from the task of conventional research; the historian must still sift the manuscripts and use his or her own skill of analysis. My task, therefore, has been to combine the limited amount of information available from manuscripts with the computer data to arrive at a better understanding of New Jersey's ports and the activities surrounding them.

A Note on the Calendar

In transcribing the New Jersey port records, I have corrected the year to correspond to the Gregorian system. Months recorded numerically have been converted to the modern calendar. Thus the seventh month, Julian, often written *7ber*, has been recorded as September, not July. No attempt, however, has been made to modernize the dates or adjust months accordingly. If one wishes, one may add ten days to dates of the seventeenth century and eleven days to those of the eighteenth century.

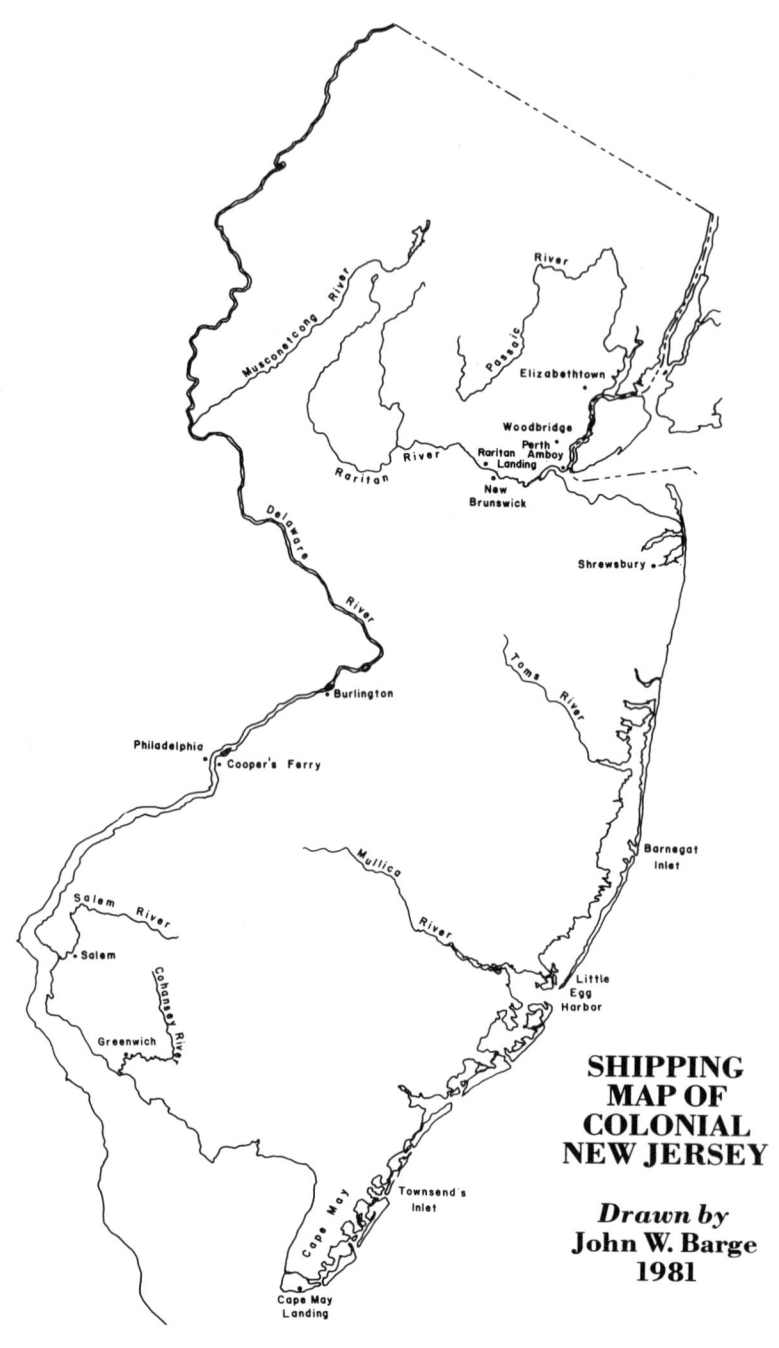

1
The Colony of New Jersey

ENGLAND in the seventeenth and eighteenth centuries attempted to adhere, if sometimes loosely, to a system of mercantilism implemented in part by a series of Navigation Acts regulating the nature of maritime commerce within the empire. In colonial America, as elsewhere, official ports of entry were established, where officials appointed by the Crown or its representatives oversaw the administration of these acts.

The proprietors of East and West Jersey hoped to entice potential settlers to a new land, where excellent and well-protected harbors on the Delaware and Hudson rivers would provide the nucleus for development of commercial ports. The successful development of city ports, however, was dependent upon many things beyond favorable geographical conditions.[1] Philadelphia and New York were a considerable distance from the sea. The latter required those unfamiliar with the river to use a pilot to reach its harbor safely; the former had a rival port on the same river that was closer to the sea; its harbor was better protected. Boston, at least in one aspect, was poorly placed for trade, as was the city port of Newport, Rhode Island: both lacked any significant hinterland.[2]

Far more critical than the location of a port was the manner in which it evolved. Essential to a port's life was the existence of a merchant community engaged in important economic activity; the development of complex trading relationships; an urban population with a large service factor in which from 20 to 25 percent of the population was made up of sailors, shipwrights, insurance underwriters, and others engaged in maritime commerce. This was the difference between ports that evolved into vital commercial centers and others, such as Perth Amboy, Burlington, and Salem, which languished or came to play a different role than that of the city port despite the civic aspirations of their leading citizens.[3]

The most crucial factor in the development of the port, however, remained the leadership and sense of direction and purpose that was most often provided by a viable merchant class committed to maritime trade as a primary means for capital development. The merchants were most successful when their efforts were enhanced by direct legislative support, or more often by legislative grants of city charters affording the petitioners substantial economic autonomy.[4] Success, however, was not assured even with the leadership of the merchant class and the support of government. Throughout the colonial period commercial rivalry was fierce between both nations and the urban centers of the British colonies. Boston, New York, and other major port cities, first in their evolutionary period and then as commercial entrepôts, attempted to apply the same mercantile principles that guided England in dealing with both its colonies and commercial rivals. Boston, attempting to follow the tenets of the time, tried to dominate the surrounding areas economically so that these regions would produce raw materials to be sent to Boston in return for finished products that Bostonians had imported.[5]

The relationship of Boston and other emerging seaports to the hinterland or back country, as well as to each other, mirrored the mercantile theories of the day. It also led to attempts by one colony to gain commercial advantage over another by means of local legislation.[6] Boston, in large part from the strength built on the absence of early competition, was able to dominate West Indian trade until around 1700 and continued to dominate the area of overseas imports until the 1730s, when New York and Philadelphia began to assert themselves in this lucrative area.[7] Growing as commercial centers, New York and Philadelphia also attempted to extend their sphere of economic influence over the surrounding hinterland, and wherever possible to encroach on the economic preserves of Boston or each other. In this economic maelstrom, New Jersey was ill prepared to advance its cause against determined opposition.

Commercial and Political Problems

Almost from its inception as an English colony, New Jersey was unable to achieve the cohesiveness necessary to develop its own commercial centers. The difficulty lay in the nature of its settlement, the subsequent problems over landownership, and endemic political turmoil. In addition, New Jersey's government lacked centralization. From 1702 to 1738 the colony had no governor of its own, and throughout its existence it maintained dual treasuries and sectional parity between East and West Jersey in the legislature, which met alternately at the twin capitals of Perth Amboy and Burlington. Thus, the government's ability to unite the colony was greatly diminished. New Jersey attracted little commerce and had no real merchant class, no sizable group of artisans, no newspapers. In fact, it had none of the usual assets with which to develop viable urban centers. Instead, the colony came to depend on other cities for its urban needs, furthering the process of decentralization and insuring a basically agrarian culture throughout the colony. Ethnically and religiously heterogeneous, markedly diffuse, and sparsely populated, New Jersey clearly manifested the characteristics of a provincial agrarian society.[8]

The Scottish settlement at Perth Amboy, which took place mainly between 1683 and 1685, marked the only clear departure from basic agrarianism. Earlier the proprietors had proposed to build "one principal town . . . for merchandize, trade, and fishery in those parts." The town was to be located at Amboy Point, "near adjacent to the place where ships in that great harbor, commonly ride at anchor."[9] That land, comprising 1,500 acres, was to be divided into 150 lots, two-thirds of them to be made available to those wishing to settle there. In addition, artisans, bricklayers, carpenters, tilemakers, and others were to be lured by the promise of aid in finding gainful employment and by the inducement of rent-free land to be available while working for the proprietors. Both the agricultural settlers and the artisans would form the town's nucleus. The town was to have roads, public buildings, and marketplaces. Three acres were specifically designated "for the publick warfage."[10] It was undoubtedly with these proprietary schemes in mind that the Scots attempted to develop a commercial city.

Such a radical departure from the norm gained little help or approval from the surrounding communities. The Puritans, in particular, were opposed to such ventures. Commerce on a large scale, they knew, brought with it an infusion of worldly goods and corrupting ideas, and the sanctity of Puritanism was best maintained by concerted resistance to changes of this nature.[11] Change would and did come, of course, but it was slow and painful, and Perth Amboy, while it awaited the transition, remained somewhat isolated from the mainstream of commercial life throughout the eighteenth century.

The nature of settlement and the demand for local autonomy inevitably gave rise to conflicts between towns and the proprietors who constituted the government. Even when the proprietors surrendered the right of governance to the Crown in 1702, the struggle continued unabated because they retained their title to the land. The question of landownership was a key element in the general unrest in the colony, producing a twofold conflict. First, the proprietors could not agree on the division line between East and West Jersey. Second, many landholders refused to pay quitrents to the proprietors, claiming clear title to the land based on prior grants by Colonel Richard Nicholls or previous purchase from the Indians. The proprietors then were forced into a long and arduous legal battle over landownership, a battle that had long-range political ramifications. Though the turmoil over land eventually subsided—with the proprietors victorious—it added to the alienation of many in the colony and helped produce a permanent alliance among those opposed to proprietary and later royal control and among the large landowners and commercial merchants who supported and were supported by this authority.

External challenges to the political power of New Jersey's governors arose almost simultaneously with the land disputes. The various governors of New York maintained that the rights of government could not be transferred by the sale of the land. The duke of York, they maintained, still retained the power of government over New Jersey, and the governors of New York, as his representatives, exercised governmental power over the latter colony.[12] At first no attempt was made to put this assertion into practice. But when it appeared that the duke was suffering financially by not receiving revenues from New Jersey imports and exports, his agents began to act against both East and West Jersey.[13] The conflict was heightened not only by the proprietors' denial of such assertions by New York, but by their insistence that a duty-free port be started at Perth Amboy.[14] The province of West Jersey, in the meantime, had solved the question of jurisdiction through a new grant made by the duke of York, conveying to Edward Byllings and his heirs and assigns the territory that had been purchased by George Carteret.[15] But the East Jersey proprietors fought a long and somewhat confusing legal battle against the duke.

In the interim, however, central authority in New Jersey suffered greatly. Already under challenge from opponents of the proprietors, the authority of the proprietors' agent, Governor Philip Carteret, was further diminished by his being temporarily arrested and forcibly removed from New Jersey to New York by officials of the latter colony.[16] New Jersey's attempt to expand commercially was an integral part of its political struggle with New York, and it suffered as New York governors used legal and occasionally illegal means to stifle New Jersey's commercial trade.[17]

During the proprietary era, East Jersey remained in a state of political and commercial confusion. Subsequent governors, lacking support either abroad or at home, seemed able only to dissipate rather than strengthen their office.[18] The result was that the legislature from the very beginning clearly dominated in colonial matters. New Jersey's predominantly agrarian economy was also evident in its elected assembly, where the rural element was dominant. The lack of legislation affecting commerce and the frustration of all attempts to increase the power of the governor or his council are testimony to the rural faction's success in preserving local agrarianism.[19]

Much different was the development of the rival cities of Philadelphia and New York. In 1685 the population of Perth Amboy or Burlington could not have numbered more than several hundred. Philadelphia by about that time had a population of about twenty-five hundred, including a significant community of merchants, shipwrights, ropemakers, and sailmakers. Philadelphia had a service sector crucial to port development. In addition, capital was available from a substantial number of merchants willing to undertake the construction of maritime facilities. The artisan class's small savings often went into commercial ventures in hope of more rapid monetary gain. The province across the river enjoyed none of these assets. After 1684 the city of Philadelphia began to move toward greater local autonomy, another requisite for commercial growth, and in 1691 the proprietors granted a charter of incorporation that proved important in Philadelphia's rapid development as a commercial center.[20]

New Jersey's other neighbor, too, was aided in its formative stages of maritime development by both direct governmental assistance and a high degree of local control that enabled New York City to deal with its own problems. New Amsterdam residents had battled the Dutch West India Company for greater local autonomy, achieving it to a limited degree in 1653 with the grant of a charter. Then, under English rule, Governor Thomas Dongan had strengthened the city's trade potential. He gave New York City, along with Albany, a monopoly on the bolting of flour to be exported and required that all foreign goods be loaded or unloaded in the city. In this way trade and commerce outside the province would be channeled through New York City in spite of economic hardships worked on other areas of the colony. For example, Long Island's trade with the West Indies and Boston was now subordinated to trade with the merchants in New York City. Finally, Dongan converted the older Dutch corporation into a charter for the city and in so doing enhanced its power. The major ruling body for the city, the common council, was given the power to make any laws and ordinances that were not contrary to the laws of the province or of England.[21] By the eighteenth century, New York merchant families such as Livingston and De Lancey alternately dominated all branches of government. But in New Jersey those representing commercial areas such as Burlington and Perth Amboy had only limited local strength; within the assembly they were an ineffective minority.[22] The commercial faction attempted to work through the New Jersey governor's council where they were stronger, with the result that the council was aligned against the assembly. Inevitably, schemes proposed by the council that might adversely affect the farmer were met by sufficient resistance from the other branch of government to render them ineffective. Typical was the legislation passed in 1717 to aid trade by restricting the export of flour, an act that was repealed the same year because of complaints by local farmers.[23]

The salutary effect of the merger of East and West Jersey into a single royal colony in 1702 should have been immediately apparent. With government officials now royal appointees and the government's composition theoretically determined by the governor's commission and instructions from the Board of Trade, self-government should have been greatly curtailed.[24] Actually such curtailment was somewhat offset by several factors. Among other things, a conservative rural Quaker faction bolstered local agrarianism; the designation of two capitals and the lack of a governor just for New Jersey weakened rather than consolidated the power of government.

From 1702 to 1738, New Jersey had no governor of its own, sharing one with New York. Under this dual arrangement, most governors preferred the latter province. Far larger and more active, New York required most of their time and ability. Except for Robert Hunter, governor from 1710 to 1719, the governors concerned themselves little with their less populous, less urban, and poorer charge.[25] Their absence from either of New Jersey's capitals for lengthy periods of time left the council, many members of which represented merchant interests, without guidance or direction and compounded their problems with the agrarian assembly.

William Cosby, who assumed the governorship in 1732 and held it until his death in April 1736, called only one assembly during this period. Minutes from the council during this period indicated that they seldom met and were able to do little of importance.[26] The resulting lack of focus was symptomatic of a long-standing condition that made it more difficult for East and West Jersey to develop commercially.

The connection between government and commercial growth was well understood by those at Burlington and Perth Amboy. While the legislature, impelled by pride and economic self-interest, sought a governor for New Jersey alone, the merchants were the motivating force in the demand for self-government.[27] Every petition to the Crown cited the increase in wealth that would accrue "in Trade and Navigation" if New Jersey had a governor of its own.[28] When a separate governor, Lewis Morris, was finally appointed in 1738, a grateful address to the king bore both the imprint and hopes of a commercial class long laboring for this objective; the merchants could now state, "From hence we hope to see Trade and Commerce flourish."[29] Yet having their own governor proved no panacea, for Morris had a long-standing disdain for commercial men who lacked the true gentleman's status as landholder.[30] What energies the governors did assert in the merchants' behalf were rendered less effective by problems such as challenges to governors' prerogatives, conflicts with the legislature over fiscal policies, and personal animosities.[31]

Burlington and Perth Amboy

Governmental efficiency, moreover, continued to be frustrated by the system of dual capitals and treasuries. Almost every governor complained about this arrangement.[32] Lewis Morris was particularly vehement, declaring in 1740 that "the holding of the Assemblies at Burlington and Amboy, and keeping two secretaries offices, proves very inconvenient both to the officers of the government and to the people." He went on to condemn both locations as being "Inconsiderable places likely to remain so" and implored the king to choose another more convenient place as the single capital.[33] The problem was never resolved, and no single centralized location was chosen during the colonial period. Yet had one been found, and had the royal governors worked diligently to aid commerce, New Jersey's trade would have been affected very little. By the time New Jersey was given its own governor, New York City and Philadelphia had already achieved dominant positions in commerce. In 1739 the ports of Burlington and Salem entered and cleared a total of five and fourteen vessels respectively. But the entries and clearances for Philadelphia three years later numbered 521 vessels. In 1741 its rival, New York, accommodated 530 vessels, while at Perth Amboy a total of seventy-six vessels, mostly small schooners and sloops, encompassed all harbor traffic.[34] As entrepôts New York City, Philadelphia, and other city ports were in control of most of the middle-man functions of commerce—banking, insurance, and marketing among others—and were already handling New Jersey's trade. At that late date it would have been impossible for New Jersey to reassert itself as a major port.

Faced from the beginning with an unstable government and a local population that not only did not support, but occasionally actively resisted commercial ventures, the proprietors nevertheless worked to develop both Burlington and Perth Amboy into major commercial centers. Those of a commercial mind saw in New Jersey's heavily timbered landscape "great plenty of Oak timbers, fit for shipping" as well as many other types of commercial lumber. There was also fertile land, which would soon produce an abundance of "wheat, barley, rye, Indian corn" for sale and export to the West Indies and Europe.[35]

An outstanding inland water system further enhanced New Jersey's potential for commercial development. In the western half of the colony a system of parallel streams, some of them, like the Musconetcong, large enough to be called rivers, flowed south and southwest into the Delaware. In this area the terrain rises so gradually that small creeks could be navigated as far as ten miles into the interior. In the eastern section the estuaries and creeks flowed mainly into the Raritan.[36] These waterways provided a source of power for the sawmills and flour mills, and they afforded small vessels access to the interior valleys so that farmers in the interior were linked with the commercial centers on the coast.[37]

The configuration of the colony, surrounded on three sides by water, was another windfall for trade and commerce. Almost a peninsula, it provided ready access to the sea. Although New Jersey's Atlantic coastline offered many landing places, the lack of sheltered areas made the coast too rugged for any permanent shipping facility. But at the northern end of the colony, the topography of the land was different. The Hudson and Raritan rivers flow into Raritan Bay, a relatively sheltered body of water. Both rivers offer access to much of the hinterland. At the other end of the colony, the Delaware River empties into a broad bay. This river, easily accessible and navigable to the falls in Trenton, offered many havens along its banks for vessels seeking harbor.[38] It was in these two areas that New Jersey's maritime commercial centers had their beginnings.

Burlington's founders were quick to appreciate the possibility of being a viable commercial port on the Delaware. Within a few years after the initial settlement, they were sending vessels loaded with local farm products to the West Indies and were predicting an expanding trade.[39] By the early 1680s the town had built a large public landing and a town wharf at the end of High Street; by the next decade funds were being raised by subscription for its maintenance.[40] In East Jersey local farmers and mill owners who resided along the waterways had already taken advantage of the natural highway system by building docks or clearing places for vessels to land, a practice repeated by towns such as Woodbridge, which built public facilities to insure the flow of commerce.[41]

At Perth Amboy a major effort to develop a commercial port was begun in 1676. Here the Raritan empties into the bay, and Staten Island, immediately offshore, provides additional protection against the elements. The depth of the water at that point was such that a three-hundred-ton vessel could dock within a plank's length of the shore, for the channel between Perth Amboy and Sandy Hook was four to six fathoms deep and nowhere less than three fathoms at high tide.[42] Under the guidance of the Scottish proprietors, a town was laid out, and, as at Burlington, a large public dock with three acres set aside for a public wharf played a prominent role in the design. The dock, about one hundred feet broad, was constructed between the highway and the river, an indication of things to come.[43]

After William Penn and others involved in the West Jersey scheme successfully disputed Governor Andros's right to set customs policies and duties at Burlington, the latter port began to grow rapidly, as did Salem, another river harbor.[44] In 1682 both gained official recognition as ports of entry. On the other hand, Perth Amboy, while declaring itself a port of entry in 1687, met such fierce resistance from New York that not until 1698 could it begin to enjoy the commercial advantages it had originally anticipated.

Highly optimistic that Perth Amboy would become "the greatest port," its merchants searched for means of offsetting the lack of public support. They sought, long in vain, for a stronger executive body through which to act. Undaunted, they found other remedies. In

The town fathers of Perth Amboy, confident of their port's bright economic future, commissioned a seal in 1718, which shows a full-rigged ship riding at anchor in the harbor and proudly proclaims Perth Amboy "portus optimus" (the best port). Engraving in William A. Whitehead's Contributions to the Early History of Perth Amboy . . . *(New York, 1856), p. 52.*

1718, John Johnston, Thomas Gordon, John Stevens (ca. 1682–1737), and other Perth Amboy merchants proclaimed that the port and town "hath many years languished under designed and unjust impositions to prevent its growth to the loss and detriment of the province." Still, it remained "the best situation for place of trade in our said province of New Jersey and has a harbor for shipping preferable to those in the provinces adjoining." They felt that the granting of the town charter in 1718 would be the means of rejuvenating that trade, because it would produce the centralization and focus on a local basis so conspicuously lacking on the provincial level.[45] This action apparently provided a much-needed boost to commerce, and for the next decade, Perth Amboy showed some gradual progress toward becoming a major port.

In the development of any New Jersey port, the amount of commerce generated by local farmers, either in the towns or on widely dispersed farms in the hinterland, was all important. The New Jersey ploughman, though basically self-sufficient, did not live in economic isolation, producing his own food, shelter, and clothing, while requiring only powder, salt, nails, and some hardware to sustain himself.[46] Even in the frontier regions the New Jersey farmer rapidly made the transition from mere subsistence farming to commercial farming, marketing grain and livestock or their by-products and using the profits primarily for the acquisition of more land. But as the population became more dense[47] and as the farmer became part of a community, he began to purchase from merchants finished goods that he could not produce himself.[48] In return, merchants sought farm produce for export.

The interaction between farmers and merchants was essential to the economic growth of ports. The trade thus generated helped develop and expand urban areas, which, unlike the agrarian communities, lacked any degree of self-sufficiency. The more sophisticated the city, the more it came to depend on interlocking services such as the import and export trade. Under these circumstances circular growth developed, with trade being generated by its own force.

But Perth Amboy's merchants did not realize that the network of river transportation, so vital to their concept of a developing urban center, also worked to its detriment. With few exceptions, the population settled, as it had in Virginia, on widely separated farms or in towns along the many navigable rivers and streams. There was thus no large concentration of people at any major geographical point.[49] Without such concentrations, the development of any location into an urban center was doubtful. Sufficient commercial activity might in part compensate for this. But many of the New Jersey farmers, flour mill and sawmill operators, and small shopowners, who might have thought of themselves as merchants, bypassed the colony's three legal ports. Using the Raritan and Passaic rivers, they carried goods to and from their docks and landings not to Perth Amboy but across the bay to waiting merchants in the port of New York.[50]

Shippers at Perth Amboy were powerless to act. New York, with its larger and more dependable markets and its commercial resources, provided a greater variety of purchases and credit. The tendency to ignore Perth Amboy could be countered only by the legislature, which, dominated by agrarian interests, was unwilling to act.[51] Although Perth Amboy was stimulated by its own efforts throughout the 1720s, it could not sustain or generate enough commercial activities for continued growth; in subsequent decades the port declined until it was hardly more than a sleepy little town.[52]

Burlington and Salem suffered much the same fate. Although they were active in the early part of the eighteenth century, the shift of Quaker settlement from West Jersey to Pennsylvania beginning in 1682 led to their demise as commercial centers. The rapid change in settlement patterns left Burlington stagnant, while Salem, whose surrounding areas were not particularly well suited to farming, had an insufficient population to conduct business on its own.[53] Although unable to expand, Salem had nonetheless managed to avoid collapse by the middle of the eighteenth century. As a satellite to the major port of Philadelphia, it fed goods between South Jersey and Philadelphia and occasionally entered or cleared vessels bound for some coastal, West Indies, or foreign port.[54] As Philadelphia grew, Burlington's importance as a Quaker community and as a port declined. Philadelphia was closer to the Atlantic and had all the geographical advantages. Vessels stopped first at Philadelphia and seldom continued the journey up the river to Burlington, which consequently became increasingly isolated. Philadelphia experienced phenomenal growth as its businessmen increasingly acted as middlemen in commerce. New Jerseyans usually preferred Philadelphia for trade and commerce, using the Delaware River and a primitive network of roads and ferries for inland transportation. On the river, shallops and other small vessels, as well as large barges, carried farm products and local manufactures to Philadelphia markets, while on the roads wagons performed a similar function. By 1758 it was reported that although "the ports of Burlington and Amboy are extremely well situated and both formerly had some trade, the growth of Philadelphia has well nigh deprived the former of its citizens and shipping."[55] Burlington, like Perth Amboy, had become a place of little growth and few expectations.

Smuggling and Other Illicit Trade

Throughout the eighteenth century, as the maritime commerce that flowed through New Jersey's three ports declined, a more clandestine form of trade was increasingly finding its way into and through the colony. For American colonial merchants, smuggling was a way of life. Most of the smuggling was done with the West Indies, which provided the means of converting goods unsalable in Europe into credits on English mercantile houses. Molasses, the major commodity of the Indies, had become "the engine for commerce." When molasses was converted into rum, it provided a medium of trade and as such was central to the colonial economy.[56] English possessions in the West Indies were able to provide only a portion of the needed supply of molasses, and merchants in the colonies came to depend on the nearby French islands. French molasses, however, was not duty-free, so the merchants, already in a highly competitive market, sought to circumvent the additional cost through illegal means.[57]

Smuggling, mostly of molasses but also of almost anything upon which there was a duty, was conducted by a variety of methods. Shippers employed false papers, altered cockets and affidavits (often listing molasses as flour), maintained secret dual ownership with foreign nationals, or frequently carried on their illegal trade with the outright connivance of customs officials.[58] New Jersey merchants undoubtedly employed some or all of these methods from time to time. But the sparse population and scarcity of commerce meant that such trade, as it directly affected New Jersey, accounted for relatively little. The colony itself, however, acted as a conduit through which an enormous amount of illicit trade flowed to both New York and Philadelphia.

New York merchants, almost as part of their normal business enterprise, engaged in illicit trade, and many circumvented the New York customs officials. They surreptitiously landed their cargos in New Jersey and then smuggled them into New York City as part of the large volume of unsupervised trade between the two colonies. As early as 1687, Governor Thomas Dongan had noted the propensity of merchants in his colony to use the neighboring province: "Last year two or three ships came in there [New Jersey] with goods and I am sure that that Country cannot, noe not with the help of West Jersey consume one thousand in goods in two years soe that the rest of their goods must have been run into this Government without paying his matys customs and indeed theres noe possibility of preventing it."[59] Such trade continued unabated, and as late as 1762 a New York merchant, John Watts, advised his captains arriving with slaves from the West Indies to avoid New York duties by landing the cargo in New Jersey and channeling it to New York from there.[60] Such operations were apparently made easier by the complicity of customs officials. Customs abuses were apparently so blatant that in 1760 Cadwallader Colden, acting governor of New York, complained to William Pitt about the conduct of the officers in New Jersey who were issuing false papers to unscrupulous shippers.[61]

The illicit trade into New York was slight compared with similar trade with Philadelphia. Sparse population and the ease with which vessels could land their cargos on the beaches made New Jersey's southern coast a haven for smugglers. Cargos were unloaded from ships and carted through New Jersey's southern woods, across the Delaware River by ferry, and into Philadelphia duty free.[62] With the connivance of officials at Salem, it was possible in the 1760s for large vessels to transfer their cargos to smaller craft that could easily avoid the watchful eyes of any honest Philadelphia officials. Some shipmasters were even industrious enough to secure fraudulent clearances from a friendly collector at Salem and then brazenly present them to the helpless customs officials at Philadelphia.[63] How much illicit trade was conducted through this means is difficult to ascertain. But if the reports of government officials can be believed, smuggling was a major, if unmeasured, source of trade.

Illicit trade, however, did little to aid the shipping merchants at New Jersey's ports. Caught up by forces they could not control, the majority of them fought, largely in vain, to maintain the viability of their ports. Their situation was occasionally made desperate by the currency problems that continuously plagued the colony. Specie, always in short supply, was quickly drained off into the neighboring colonies. Paper money provided a poor substitute because its issuance was restricted and its value fluctuated greatly. According to the Council of New Jersey in 1744/5, the shortage of specie was a condition that "lays the Merchant and Trader under very great Disadvantages for after they have sold their Goods at a Moderate Advantage (for which it is generally two Years after they receive their Pay) they are always Losers in Proportion to the sinking Credit of such a Currency."[64] Worst of all, acceptance of paper money and its current worth was uncontrolled outside the colony. Those who depended upon or dealt with their New York or Philadelphia counterparts found that New York merchants would manipulate New Jersey bills to their advantage and to the detriment of the New Jersey shippers. The lack of a sound, flexible currency was thus a further blow to New Jersey's maritime hopes.[65]

Faced with almost insurmountable odds, many of New Jersey's shippers bowed to the inevitable and abandoned shipping, becoming simply merchants who relied on the surrounding urban areas to supply them with goods for sale. Others retained their New Jersey residences but shifted their commercial shipping operations to a neighboring colony. They would occasionally bring a vessel directly to the New Jersey ports, but the venture was usually negotiated through their business concerns in New York or Philadelphia.[66]

By 1760 New Jersey had become a commercial stepchild of the larger urban areas developing around it. Because Nova Cæsaria, as it was sometimes called, remained almost totally agrarian during the colonial period, it became dependent on larger, more settled areas outside its own boundaries for services it could not provide and thus assumed a cultural and, to some degree, political dependency on neighboring provinces. The eastern part of the colony gravitated toward New York City while the western part looked to Philadelphia for guidance. The inability to develop urban centers left New Jersey without a focus to bring these diffuse elements together. The result was a colony without integrating influences and without a clearcut direction, purpose, or identity of its own.

2
Evolution of the Ports

DURING THE COLONIAL PERIOD, the American economy underwent considerable expansion. Development was uneven but continuous, and historians have attempted to assess the relationship between that expansion and the rate and nature of economic growth. Because colonial maritime commerce in all its stages was an important element in this development—the other major factor being agricultural changes—various studies of colonial ports and shipping have been undertaken to aid in understanding the nature of maritime commerce and in assessing the rate of economic advancement.

The earliest studies, most of them by scholars with limited economic training, drew heavily on contemporary accounts of merchants and Crown officials. In a relatively subjective way the early studies portrayed the entire colonial period as one of considerable overall economic rise. Periods of intermittent recession and depression resulting from the cycle of war and peace were considered minor fluctuations in an otherwise advancing economy.[1]

Other studies have both challenged and supported the earlier assumptions. They have involved a re-examination of the growth of cities, the use of factor analysis in assessing the population in relation to economic growth, and the use of more quantitative and statistical methods, especially in the study of maritime commerce.[2]

The latest evidence suggests that some, perhaps rather considerable, growth in the colonial period did occur, although its nature was sometimes obscured by short-range economic problems that often reflected the immediate military or political situation. Marc Engal, the economic historian, proposes that the economic period might be viewed in terms of two long swings that rested upon the interaction of population growth and an expansion of production. Real growth, he feels, was beginning by about 1720; it lasted for slightly over a decade before reaching a plateau that lasted until 1745. Then growth resumed for more than fifteen years before leveling off and remaining stable until the outbreak of the Revolution.[3]

New York's Early Dominance

Because large port cities such as New York and Philadelphia dominated regional trade, it is possible to examine fruitfully the growth or decline of their maritime ventures. By incorporating regional fluctuations into the calculations one can arrive at a meaningful assessment of the general economic trends. Lesser port towns, such as Salem, Burlington, and Perth Amboy, are less profitably studied as entities in this regard. New Jersey's ports, especially, were too limited in their regional effect. New York's volume of exports from 1768 to 1772, for example, was ninety-four times greater than New Jersey's; Philadelphia's was 176 times greater.[4] In addition, these ports lacked any significant volume of overseas trade. At the outbreak of the Revolution New Jersey's merchants had amassed no overseas trade debt to British merchants, not so much from frugality as from the absence of such trade, while New York's debt was over £88,000. Philadelphia's debt was greater by one-third.[5] New Jersey's ports were also largely reactive to the dominant ports. As we have seen, their development often depended upon external and internal institutional forces that infrequently responded to prevailing economic needs. The nature of economic growth that can be ascertained by a study of these ports is therefore illuminated by an examination of the vessels using these facilities. Through a study of the routes followed by the vessels, the commodities they carried, where they were built, how long they were in service, and similar information, we are able to place the lesser ports into historical context, as well as to address, to a degree, the questions of cost and capital in connection with the overall economic development in the American colonies. The evolution of New Jersey's ports in terms of trade volume is thus important to our understanding of the history of the mid-Atlantic region and warrants investigation. At the same time, there is only negligible understanding of national growth. But a study of the function of shipping within this realm, the means by which trade patterns were established and changed, may well have broader implications in the study of colonial economic development.

The creation of New Jersey's official ports occurred amid confusion and turmoil. The excellent harbors at Perth Amboy in East Jersey and Burlington and Salem on the Delaware River in West Jersey led the proprietary regime to attempt to establish at these locations ports of entry for overseas trade. Such aspirations did not suit those who governed New York. As we have noted, Governor Andros, representing the duke of York, feared a loss of revenue and a reduction of James's authority and refused to allow New Jersey to operate independently in the area of commerce. Instead, he required all vessels bound for New Jersey to clear first through New York, and he placed a temporary 5- to 10-percent tax on all goods entering New Jersey as a means of raising revenue for the duke, an action that incensed many New Jerseyans.[6]

In 1676, when New Jersey's Governor Philip Carteret attempted to break what he considered unwarranted dominance by encouraging direct trade to his colony, Andros's reaction was immediate and hostile. He ordered the seizure of all vessels engaged in direct trade with New Jersey and soon after dispatched a force to Elizabethtown to arrest Carteret and carry him off to imprisonment in New York.[7] Subsequent New York administrators, though less aggressive, remained fearful that the absence of royal tariffs and duties as charged at their port would draw trade away from that colony. So they continued to deny New Jersey's proprietors' claim to their own ports of entry and kept the policy that all vessels bound for Perth Amboy must first clear through New York customs and pay the local duties.[8]

Contrary to expectations, a concession gained a decade after the initial problem with Governor Edmund Andros (in which James, now king of England, allowed an officer to collect customs at Perth Amboy) provided none of the independence to establish the free port that East Jersey's proprietors sought.[9] New York officials appointed the specific individual and set the fees to be assessed. In subsequent years East Jersey apparently again began to operate as a free port in the hope of attracting more overseas commerce. But the volume of trade remained small; in 1686 only two or three vessels arrived loaded with goods. Even this trade elicited hostile comments from Governor Dongan of New York; having decided not to pursue the more aggressive policy of confrontation carried out by his predecessors, he suggested to English authorities that so many goods could not possibly be consumed by the neighboring province and New Jersey's port was therefore merely a conduit to carry goods into New York without paying royal customs. To prevent this alleged smuggling and guard against being "deserted by a great many of our merchants who intend to settle there," he strongly suggested that New Jersey be "annexed to this Government."[10]

Undaunted, the East Jersey proprietors managed, in November 1696, to gain some official recognition for their claim when they secured from the Commissioners of the Customs a collector for Perth Amboy. Thomas Coker was empowered "to be collector of all the Rates, Duties and Imposition, Arising and Growing Due unto his Majesty at Perth Amboy in East Jersey."[11] Burlington was also afforded status as a port of entry, and the surveyor general of customs in America, Edmund Randolph, was so informed by the commissioners.[12] New Jersey's victory was short-lived, for in a year New York secured from the Council of Trade a resolution giving it a firm legal foundation for its previous assertions that New Jersey trade should first pass through New York. By an Order in Council issued at the Court at Kensington, November 25, 1697, "Duties to be paid by Ships Trading in Hudson River [must] be continued to the Governor of New York for the time being who is not to Suffer any innovation within the said River in that behalf, nor to permit any goods to pass up the same but what shall have paid the Duties at New York."[13]

As governor of New York, a jubilant Richard Coote, earl of Bellomont, immediately issued a proclamation designed in part to convince those New York merchants wishing to relocate across the Hudson that such a move would not gain them economic advantage and might well work additional hardship upon them. The fear that neighboring free ports would ruin New York's commerce was more fanciful than factual. Yet in the age of mercantilism any advantage afforded the competition was to be resisted. Continual complaints from New York on this matter reflect the depth of concern that no economic advantage be afforded a rival.

The East Jersey proprietors, for their part, were for several reasons unwilling to accept this latest pronouncement. Not only was the legality of such an order in question, but, more important, the proprietors knew that their prosperity was endangered without their own ports of entry. Interestingly, their concern for the ports was grounded not so much in a desire to advance maritime commerce as in a guarantee of a high return on real estate. This factor has often escaped our attention. One must remember that the proprietors dealt not in commerce but in land, and the value of their American possessions, the fortunes they hoped to realize, were directly connected to a recognition of their colony's right to its own ports. Such a right, they were to tell the Lords of Trade, was vital to a proper return on their investments.[14]

With so much at stake it should come as no surprise that the proprietors were quick to refute New York's latest pronouncement. While it might be true that the Council of Trade had rendered a judgment in favor of New York on the question of the establishment of ports, those who guided the affairs of Nova Cæsaria maintained that the authority to establish ports was invested solely in the Commissioners of the Customs. It was that body that had declared, in the words of their agent, Governor Jeremiah Basse, "Perth Amboy in East Jersey is a port duely Established and Appointed."[15]

This paper battle of mercantilism continued, with each side calling upon historical precedent to support its contention. New York continued to express the fear that because Perth Amboy was half as far from the sea as New York was, and levied no local duties, the latter port, already well established and requiring considerable duties, would lose both revenue and trade. It is apparent that although the physical location of Perth Amboy was of concern, the real problem remained the duty-free status of New Jersey's ports, a condition that New York feared might prove ruinous. The extent to which New York was willing to protect its interest became readily apparent, for despite New Jersey's attempt at some form of reconciliation and a suggestion that the courts decide the legality of its claim,[16] New York abandoned this mere war of words in favor of its past policy of direct confrontation. This involved the seizure of vessels trading directly to Perth Amboy.

One such seizure became the focal point for another legal confrontation. The ship *Hester* had entered Perth Amboy directly and was loading a cargo of barrel staves in preparation for a departure for Madeira—an early example of a trade route that would become a mainstay for local merchants—when a contingent of thirty or forty men, acting under the authority of New York's governor, Lord Bellomont, seized the vessel and dispatched it to New York. There it was condemned for violating the Acts of Trade and sold at auction.[17] The owners of the vessel sought relief from this "illegal act" in the English courts, and all were aware that a favorable ruling would not only provide restitution for the loss of the vessel but strengthen New Jersey's claim as to the legality of their ports. Almost simultaneously, those representing New Jersey attempted to gain additional support in

England by professing a willingness to abandon the status of free ports and to charge fees identical to those of their neighbor. This move was calculated to weaken New York's claim and objections.[18] On still another front they pushed for the inclusion of ports of entry in any new charter for the province of New Jersey, for while the proprietors were prepared to surrender the right of governance to the Crown, they intended to maintain ownership of the land. As noted, colonial ports greatly enhanced the value of their landholdings.

In the end a compromise of sorts was achieved. Lord Bellomont might profess bitterness that the court judgment in the case of the ship *Hester* had gone against him and that the owner had secured, in his opinion, an exorbitant judgment against the king, predicated, he believed, on a fraudulent representation of the vessel's true value; Perth Amboy, Burlington, and Salem were now confirmed as official ports. But he gained some satisfaction in that economic protection had been achieved by the requirement that these rival ports charge no less a duty than was charged at the port of New York.[19]

A belated attempt on the Delaware River to gain economic advantage at the expense of West Jersey was more easily dealt with once the latter's right to maintain ports had been firmly established. In 1707 the lower counties on the Delaware, through an act of the Delaware assembly, decided to lay a duty based on tonnage against all vessels that passed New Castle on the Delaware. Such an act, of course, would have been detrimental to Burlington's commerce. Edward Hyde, Lord Cornbury, as governor of the colonies of both New York and New Jersey, responded forcefully.[20] The project was soon abandoned. From that point on there were no more overt attempts to control New Jersey shipping.

Prior to the eighteenth century little maritime commerce flowed through New Jersey's ports. This scarcity of trade is partly attributable to the resistance offered from the neighboring province. But the sparse population was a contributing factor. The earliest vessels, for example, to find their way to the colony (the ship *Griffen* in 1675, the *Kent* two years later, followed by the *Willing Mind*, the fly boat *Martha*, and the *Shield*) were involved not in maritime commerce but in transporting settlers to the new land.[21] From this nucleus, however, came the beginnings of maritime trade and commerce. The most prized trade pattern—trade with England and the continent—would always remain an unfulfilled dream for New Jersey.

A more realistic assessment of the most advantageous areas for trade was offered in 1681 by Sir George Carteret's executors in publicizing New Jersey's commercial potential. They asserted that agricultural produce and timber would find good markets in Nevis, Barbados, Jamaica, and elsewhere in the West Indies, while overseas the Canary Islands and Portugal seemed most suitable.[22] Available evidence seems to indicate that these two areas, on a very modest scale, did in fact attract much of New Jersey's earlier overseas activity. By 1680 several small vessels, among them a fifty-ton ketch belonging to Mahlon Stacy, were outward-bound to Barbados.[23] The instructions to Miles Forester, collector at Perth Amboy, to levy a duty of £2 per pipe and £1 per hogshead on wine from Madeira, Fayal, and other such islands suggest that there was some trade to the Canary Islands.[24]

Such areas of trade were not, of course, unique to New Jersey. The agricultural produce of the middle colonies dictated in large part the most profitable avenues of commerce. New York in the mid-1680s followed a similar pattern, sending as many as twenty small sloops and perhaps a large ketch or two to the West Indies, a far more active trade than was carried out by New Jersey.[25] New York also sent a considerable number of vessels overseas, and many undoubtedly engaged in the wine trade. The major—and very significant—difference between the trade of the two colonies was that by the mid-1680s New York had already begun to establish a direct trade of some substance with England and Holland, using nine or ten ships of eighty to one hundred tons.[26]

New York soon came to dominate overseas trade within the region. In order to conduct commerce in this valuable area of trade, New Jersey became increasingly dependent on New York. Almost from the beginning, New Jerseyans engaged in maritime commerce were forced to seek other more viable avenues of direct commerce. But this would be an evolutionary process. In the seventeenth century the function of New Jersey's ports was to provide safe harbors and potential town and market sites for a newly arrived and growing population; the ports also provided facilities for coastwise trade and served as the focal point for seaborne trade to the West Indies and the Canary Islands. In addition it was hoped that the ports, especially Perth Amboy, would attract a greater quantity of trade and a significant merchant community while gaining the designation of official ports of entry. This designation would help protect land values and facilitate the development of maritime commerce. Mercantilistic practices dominated the attempt to create, maintain, and strengthen a colony's maritime commerce. In the mercantile scheme, ports of entry within a colony were deemed essential. In addition, the proprietary nature of New Jersey and the relative value of land were strong incentives for establishing and maintaining legal ports.

War and Trade

By 1702, then, shipping activity at the New Jersey ports, which before had been conducted sporadically under adverse and uncertain conditions, as the venture of the ship *Hester* so aptly demonstrates, could now evolve with "official" sanction. A reconstruction of the activities at New Jersey ports such as Perth Amboy in the two decades following their official designation is rendered difficult by the loss (either in the Plantation Wing fire or by neglect) of the naval or customs records for the port. Fortunately, in the early 1700s, newspapers were introduced in the surrounding colonies, and a readership

The New Jersey ports were ill-equipped to compete with their powerful maritime neighbors such as New York, here depicted in a detail from a "Plan of the City of New York in North America: Surveyed in the Years 1766 & 1767," engraved by Thomas Jeffreys and William Faden, London, 1776. NJHS.

eager for news of any kind developed. These periodicals (the *Boston Newsletter* and the *American Weekly Mercury*, among others) often reported the events of maritime commerce, including the arrival and departure of vessels locally and in neighboring provinces. Unfortunately, newspaper accounts are notoriously unreliable: they constantly neglected the smallest vessels and were often careless about the details of arrival and departure, seldom mentioning owners or cargos and occasionally recording different names for the same vessels. Still, from such sources and from an occasional official pronouncement regarding the nature and state of the colony's trade, there emerges a sense of slow but continual growth, especially at Perth Amboy.

Queen Anne's War severely hampered maritime trade throughout the American colonies, and the effect on New Jersey's maritime commerce was devastating. The colony had almost no fleet of its own and depended for support upon its status as a port of call. New Jersey could offer little to make merchants risk their vessels against the French privateers who waited along the Eastern Seaboard in such great numbers that shipping moved primarily in convoys under the protection of the British fleet. If New Jersey was the recipient of any of this trade, it was undoubtedly through the occasional arrival of large vessels at New York—for example, thirteen merchant vessels arrived in September 1705, accompanied by three warships—that would also trade with merchants in the neighboring colony.[27]

The policy of restricted shipping applied not only to West Indies and overseas trade but on numerous occasions to coastal trade as well; it worked a greater hardship on the lesser ports than it did on the major commercial cities. As an additional protection against the seizure of English vessels by the enemy, an embargo of sorts was enforced in 1705 on ships departing for the Hudson River.[28] Maritime commerce in that region was further endangered when the warship *Tritons Prize* was stationed at New York with orders to cruise off the Sandy Hook. On occasion she ranged as far north as Rhode Island and as far south as Virginia. At least once the warship engaged a French privateer just off the New Jersey coast.[29]

New Jersey's smallest vessels, really boats, were active throughout this period in ferrying goods across the Hudson and Delaware rivers, joined sometimes by a sloop. But coastal trade languished with only a few vessels shuttling in and out. Articles in Boston newspapers offer a glimpse of this trade with New England. Almost monthly one or two small vessels, primarily sloops, would depart for the New Jersey ports, where they would seek out a cargo suitable for the New England market and then return directly home, the entire venture taking approximately eight weeks. Sometimes, as with Eleazar Darby's sloop out of Boston, a New England vessel might first go to a major port such as Philadelphia, unload a cargo there, then go to Salem in West Jersey to load before returning home. This New England shuttle trade saw an occasional Rhode Island vessel, but such trade was conducted primarily with Boston and carried in Boston vessels.[30]

At Salem, though the potential of the port was often noted, there was no significant trade. By 1707, New Jersey shipping was so depressed that Lord Cornbury reported to the Lords of Trade that no goods had been imported into New Jersey directly from England and that not a single vessel was registered in West Jersey. East Jersey was only marginally better off. Aside from wood boats, which brought firewood and staves to New York, only one small sloop was registered there, and this vessel was engaged in trade to the West Indies. What trade there was, Cornbury noted, was carried on almost totally between New Jersey and the neighboring colonies.[31] The depressed state of New Jersey shipping was perhaps the factor leading the assembly to consider laws to stimulate and improve maritime trade, doubtless at the expense of neighboring ports. The discussions brought a stern rebuke from their governor, who reminded the legislators that Her Majesty Queen Anne had decreed that the same duties must be charged for New Jersey imports and exports as were charged in the neighboring province of New York so that "her Subjects, there and here, may be upon equal foot."[32]

The larger ports fared only slightly better in the years from 1708 to 1714. Merchants and shopkeepers in Boston complained that their trade lay in ruins; Philadelphia merchants bitterly noted that "markets . . . were never worst."[33] Along the New Jersey coast, privateers remained active, seizing those unfortunates who sailed unprotected from Madeira or the West Indies, then often depositing their captives along the Cape May coast.[34] These activities and the apparent need to maintain an embargo on outbound vessels continued to restrict the flow of maritime commerce.[35]

The Treaty of Utrecht (1713) ended Queen Anne's War. Maritime commerce had been disrupted and contracted during the war, but many segments of the economy had artificially expanded. In the period of economic adjustment that followed the peace, a general recession set in. Over the next five years the natural recovery of maritime commerce was slow. In New Jersey the volume of shuttle trade with New England increased, although the increase appeared to have been largely the result of numerous trips by a few vessels, such as those commanded by a Captain Weeks and a Captain Wells, both of Boston.[36] Trade continued with both New York and Philadelphia, though little of it went through New Jersey's official ports. On rare occasions a vessel would be outbound from New Jersey to Madeira or an arriving vessel from the West Indies would drop anchor in the harbor.[37] This trade, though small compared with the volume at neighboring ports, represented sufficient growth for New Jersey's ports to warrant an official assessment in 1717 from Governor Robert Hunter. His New Jersey residence was at Perth Amboy, and he asserted that there had been an "increased Navigation and trade here in my time."[38]

In the following year merchants in East Jersey embarked on a course of action designed to insure a continuation and acceleration of this trend. The port town of Perth Amboy was incorporated and its seal, inscribed "*portus optimus*" (Latin for "the best port"), symbolized a spirit of revitalization. In the same spirit anonymous pamphleteers examined the previous state of trade and exhorted those most able to develop New Jersey's great potential.[39]

Governor Hunter was also caught up in the growing spirit of maritime expansion and suggested to the assembly that, rather than speculate on means to improve trade, it undertake a study of trade in other provinces and copy the actions of those who had been successful.[40] This renewed enthusiasm for trade in the early 1720s, coinciding with expanded shipping throughout colonial America as the colonies emerged from the doldrums of the past war years, meant a flurry of activity at New Jersey's ports. Ships and brigantines began to appear with some regularity in the harbor at Perth Amboy, most coming via New York and pausing to acquire a suitable cargo for a trip to the Canary Islands, Glasgow, or any overseas port where conditions warranted.[41]

An active and considerably larger trade again began with the West Indies. Barbados was the principal destination for the small fleet of sloops and an occasional brig from East Jersey. Coastal trade with New England continued, but for the first time a number of vessels from the South, primarily from North Carolina, visited the East Jersey port.[42] New Jersey's ports on the Delaware, with a smaller volume of trade than Perth Amboy, nevertheless enjoyed renewed and more vigorous commerce in this period. To the local commerce with Philadelphia and the revitalized trade with the Carribean it added commerce with Virginia and Maryland.[43]

Now, two decades into the eighteenth century, the New Jersey ports began to receive larger vessels (ships, brigs, brigantines, and snows), and the volume and diversity of trade increased. This increased activity and the presence of a few vessels owned by New Jersey merchants indicated that the latter might be hopeful of developing their facilities into major ports. Such an accomplishment might be hastened by establishing at this moment the major avenues of trade that would sustain growth throughout the colonial period. The success or failure of this venture at Perth Amboy, as well as the evolution of the port itself, are in large part revealed in the customs and naval officer records for this and subsequent decades.

Although less active than New York, Philadelphia, or Boston, the New Jersey ports engaged in sufficient shipping during the first third of the eighteenth century to merit consideration as potentially major commercial centers. But from about 1730 to 1780, while the port of Philadelphia tripled in size and both Boston and New York almost doubled the volume of their trade, the New Jersey ports of Burlington and Salem waned and Perth Amboy, after a brief period of expansion, began a general decline.[44] The high point of Perth Amboy shipping came during the 1720s. Its zenith was in 1726 when sixty-eight vessels called at the port.[45] (During the same decade, Philadelphia handled between ninety-six and 140 vessels per year.)[46] The future brought decline rather than growth, however; by 1763 a mere eighteen vessels passed through the port.[47]

The decline of both Perth Amboy and Burlington was reflected not only in the number of vessels using the port but also in the types of vessels entering and clearing the harbor. In 1726 almost 30 percent of the vessels entering and clearing the port at Perth Amboy were of the type most frequently used in transoceanic travel. Ships, the largest ocean-going vessels, comprised almost 18 percent of the trade.[48] By 1745, however, the number of vessels using the port had dropped to forty-seven entering and forty-one clearing,[49] while the total tonnage amounted to less than half that of 1726,[50] and the average size of the vessels in the port had decreased by thirteen tons. Sloops or schooners accounted for 88 percent of the vessels. They were used predominantly in the coastal and West Indies trade and averaged twenty tons or less. Ocean-going vessels now accounted for only 8 percent, and they were usually brigs, the smallest of the vessels most often used in transatlantic commerce. Larger vessels, such as pinks, snows, and ships, were absent.[51]

Perth Amboy's gradual decline during the 1740s might at first be attributed to the general problems encountered by all colonial maritime commerce during a decade of war with France. Hazards of war, such as privateers, kept many merchant vessels at home, and maritime commerce, when it was conducted, was usually done through a convoy system. Convoys under naval protection generally moved from one large port to another, working a further disadvantage to the small ports. After the war, however, Perth Amboy remained stagnant. Merchants operating without the hazards and restrictions imposed by almost a decade of conflict had in the immediate post-war period taken advantage of a market situation attributable to the scarcity of goods during the war. This commerce, as it affected New Jersey, seems to have reached its height in 1750,[52] when the average size of the vessels using the harbor was well over forty-six tons—larger than those recorded at any other time.[53] There was also a marked increase in tonnage passing through the port. The total of 4,152 tons was second only to the peak tonnage achieved in 1726.[54] In addition, the larger types of vessels (brigs, brigantines, snows, and ships) reappeared, and they now comprised over 38 percent of the commercial vessels.[55] But all this activity did not really constitute a regeneration or rejuvenation of the port, for the condition was artificial. Trading patterns of an ongoing nature do not appear to have been established. Rather, opportunistic trade involving large vessels dispatched for single ventures seems to have been the rule.

After 1750, New Jersey, with its sparse population, was probably saturated as a market; the records indicate a return to the pattern of decline that had been evident in the previous decades.[56] Even with the artificial stimulus of post-war trade in 1750, and even though Perth Amboy appeared to have stabilized for the moment, the port was comparatively worse off than in previous years: stabilization or minimal growth in a period of rapid expansion is as much a signal of decline as are more obvious indicators. For example, from January to September 1750, New York recorded a total of 518 vessels, while Boston recorded for two years earlier 970 arrivals and departures to foreign ports. Smaller ports such as Port Hampton in Virginia recorded, "Cleared 64 sloops, 46 schooners, 16 ships, 20 brigs, 10 snows. Entered 59 sloops, 40 schooners, 40 ships, 18 brigs, 12 snows."[57]

If there was any doubt that the increase in tonnage for the year 1750 was but an illusion of growth, such doubt was rapidly dispelled in the decade that followed. Throughout the 1750s, Perth Amboy experienced a downward trend in maritime traffic that foreshadowed its demise as an active port. Only twenty-two vessels entered the port in all of 1755; three years later there were only eleven.[58] During both 1755 and 1758 large vessels rarely used the port.[59] Customs returns for 1763 and partial returns for the following year showed no substantial change from this inactive stage.[60] The potential of New Jersey's eastern port, then, remained unrealized during the eighteenth century.

Philadelphia's rise portended difficulties for the ports in New Jersey's western division. By the 1730s, Salem, as earlier noted, had become a feeder for the growing metropolis downriver. But even as an appendage to Philadelphia, Salem's volume of trade was small, and on occasion there was no business at all that required customs clearance.[61] The rise of Philadelphia as a commercial center destroyed the port at Burlington, farther removed geographically from the burgeoning Quaker capital. In the 1730s, Burlington seldom saw more than six entries a year that required clearing through customs.[62] By the first half of the following decade this number had decreased by half, and the latter part of the 1740s saw a period of three years in which no ships officially entered the port.[63] To place the decline in perspective, one might recall that over fifteen years the total number of vessels calling at Burlington was less than one-fifth that handled by New York in 1750 alone.[64] During the 1750s and 1760s there were few vessels that were required to clear customs. Entries from March 25 to June 25, 1751, for example, showed only a single small river shallop belonging to Richard, Jonathan, James, and William Smith, of Burlington, clearing customs. It entered in ballast and cleared with flour.[65] The activity at Burlington in these latter two decades is best summarized by the notation on many of the quarterly customs listings. Here, time and again, in the fine hand of Charles Read, collector, was written, "For the period beginning [date] to the period ending [date] 'Nil'."[66]

Legislative Inaction

To many contemporaries, the cause of New Jersey's commercial stagnation and decline lay in the government's failure to enact significant legislation to aid commerce. Legislative inaction was a continual problem for the merchant-shipping community. Cogent arguments for increasing trade were publicized in 1718 by an anonymous pamphleteer. In a series of broadsides that was eventually published as a pamphlet, the author decried the lack of port commerce, "for all men know that no Country can flourish without Foreign Trade."[67] The lack of such trade, he declared, would make New Jersey and its people the "poor Slavish Dependents" of New York and Philadelphia.[68] The solution was simple:

> Let the Assembly lay a large Duty upon every [sic] the Produce of the Country that shall be carried to any Neighbouring Colonies, and we shall soon have Ships and Merchants come among us, I say a Duty upon Wheat, Flower, Bisket, Butter, Beef, Pork, Staves, Hoop Poles, Ship Timber, Plank, Masts, Yards, Pitch, Tar, Rosin, Whale Oyl and Bone, Fins, Blubber, Skins, Hides, Tallow, Live Hogs, and neat Cattle. . . . Let the Assembly [l]ay a custom . . . on all Rum and Wine Imported from and The Neighboring Colonies.[69]

The author, echoing the sentiments of many in the merchant community, chastised the assembly for bowing to pressures from New Jersey's farmers by repealing in a previous setting the Wheat Measure Act, "the only Act of benefit to the Country," and for compounding its sins by also removing the duties on hogshead staves. The assembly members could rectify their error, he suggested, by casting aside timidity and reinstating these as well as other important commercial laws, and thereby "Acquit themselves like Men, and free this Poor Enslaved Colony, that all Posterity may Acknowledge 'em the worthy Patriots of their County.' "[70]

The assembly's response to such prodding indicates some of the problems the merchants faced. The representatives failed to take corrective action, and a special committee constituted to investigate the merchants' complaints found them to be "scandalous libel," for in impugning the integrity of the members of the assembly the pamphlet endangered the entire province by "stirring up strife and Sedition amongst the Inhabitants thereof." The entire assembly concurred wholeheartedly in this conclusion. It further decreed that the offending work should be burned by the common hangman and that the governor should issue a proclamation announcing a reward for the discovery of its author.[71]

Nonetheless, in the years that followed, merchants and some public officials continued to voice alarm at the decline of maritime commerce.[72] Acting Governor John Reading, in an address to the assembly in 1758, aired complaints similar to those heard more than thirty years earlier. Again the decline of trade was emphasized and the dependence upon neighboring colonies decried. Legislative inaction, particularly the failure to enact duties on goods shipped to New York and Philadelphia, was underscored. But the legislative record shows that there was little response to Reading's remarks in behalf of the merchants.[73]

As the paucity of regulations dealing directly with the ports indicates, charges of legislative inaction were justified. In the seventeenth century, both East and West Jersey seemed content to do little more than establish ports, set commercial fees, and provide for the construction and tax-exempt status of wharves, bridges, and other public necessities.[74] Only in its early struggle with New York over the legitimacy of Perth Amboy as a free port had the legislature given direct support to the encouragement of trade by providing £150 country money to guarantee that the owner of any vessel entering and clearing at Perth Amboy, if seized and condemned by New York officials, would be reimbursed for losses.[75] Such actions proved mercurial, however, and the provision was withdrawn within the same year. The proprietors, through their agent, Governor Jeremiah Basse, were successful in their attempt to encourage trade at Perth Amboy by having a public road pass through it. But their requests for funds to pay off the debt incurred in the successful lawsuit to have Perth Amboy recognized as a legitimate port were ignored.[76]

In the eighteenth century only two laws that directly affected the ports were put into effect. Both were included in general laws to regulate fees levied by all public officials. According to a 1724 law, coastal vessels trading between West Jersey and New York or Philadelphia were specifically exempted from entering or clearing New Jersey customs.[77] The second law, passed in 1750, in an apparent attempt to stimulate commerce, reversed this procedure and required all such vessels to procure a transfer or certificate from the customs officials. The new law also changed the fee requirements from a tonnage assessment to an area duty, undoubtedly in the hope of attracting larger vessels to the port.[78] Apparently neither change was successful in stimulating trade, for the port continued to decline, and Governor William Franklin noted in 1774 that vessels were still carrying produce to New York and Philadelphia "without being entered at the Customs houses here."[79]

If the ports themselves were neglected by the assembly, there was little more success with proposals to stimulate commerce by legislative enactments regulating the cargo passing through the port. Agricultural laws dealing with commodities to be exported were of two kinds—those that regulated the amount, and those that assured the quality of goods. The former served a multitude of purposes. On the one hand, by placing duties on items to be exported, the legislature might encourage the development of a specific domestic market. The rather sporadic levying of duties on wheat exported from East Jersey, for example, seems to have been intended to aid the development of the flour industry.[80] On the other hand, the use of an appropriate export tariff could protect certain valuable resources needed for domestic uses. On one early occasion, for example, legislative fears were raised that there was a scarcity of cattle in the colony; to protect this resource the assembly instituted a total ban on the export of hides.[81] Similarly, the legislature imposed a duty intended to retard the export of timber and its by-products—staves, boards, masts, and naval stores—thereby preserving them for local needs. Such acts concerning lumber and timber appeared as early as 1678 and, with modifications, remained in effect throughout the colonial period. Their presence in the law books reflects a continuing concern about the eventual scarcity of this natural resource.[82]

The effect of these laws upon the course of commerce is difficult to ascertain. The law governing the export of hides, potentially the most severe, was of insufficient duration to have had any meaningful consequences. Restrictions on the export of wheat mattered little, for they could convert the wheat to flour or bread, and the volume of trade was seldom diminished. Duties on timber products, however, probably had an adverse effect on port growth. There does not appear to have been any attempt to collect duties on items such as pipe or barrel staves or in any way to enforce this law outside the port itself. This being the case, the law not only retarded exports, as it was intended to do, but also encouraged lumber producers, especially in the Egg Harbor region of South Jersey, to avoid the ports and to ship their products directly from the mill site to distant markets.[83]

The laws dealing with the quality of the product were more directly concerned with protecting and increasing the export trade. Items of an accepted standard of quality were more likely than those of an unknown variety to be purchased. New Jersey pork, for example, was preferred, especially in the West Indies, where a market for this product was always available.[84] Another important aspect of trade regulation was the standardization of weights and measures. Although not exclusively concerned with the export trade, such legislation helped to insure the value of the product; therefore, statutes concerning weight standards were often written in conjunction with those to maintain the quality of the product. Flour, beef, pork, and hides were the items of export most frequently regulated by the assembly. Pork export laws in particular were most stringently enforced. In the seventeenth century both East and West Jersey passed bills to halt "Inequality of Beef and Pork Barrels and ill ordering and management of Provisions exported [which] hath been highly injurious to Traders, and the Reputation of this Province, and consequently detrimental to the Increase of Trade therein."[85] East Jersey set the standard barrel size between thirty-one and thirty-two gallons,[86] while in 1693, West Jersey appointed for each town a packer who gave the assurance that he would "not authorize or put my Mark upon any Barrel of Meat, but such as shall contain Thirty one Gallons and half at least, and the Meat both as to the Savering and quality thereof to be Merchantable, and in good condition."[87]

In thirty years a more refined version of this law evolved, but the basic spirit and conditions remained the same. The packer was still responsible for seeing that beef and pork, according to a 1725 law,

> be wholesome and merchantable, no more than four half heads in one Barrel of pork, nor more than two shins in one Barrel of beef, each Barrel shall be twice trodden down at least in Packing and be Salted with a sufficient Quantity of Salt, no less than half a bushel, which Barrel to be re-packed, Shall be by the said packer branded with the letter N.J.[88]

Flour was likewise subject to careful inspection after 1751. Here the inspector representing the town or district from which the flour was to be shipped would use a special instrument to bore a hole in the head of the cask. After thus checking the flour in the barrel, the inspector would plug the opening and brand the name "New Jersey" on those barrels that passed inspection.[89] To prevent duplicity, the inspection officer's initials were also to appear directly below the colony's brand.[90] The quality of hides and leather goods was the concern of the town sealer, who carefully inspected them for aging and tanning process before certifying them as acceptable.[91]

The potential for growth represented by these laws was diminished by several factors. Although pork regulations remained constantly in effect, the need to enact stronger and more comprehensive laws was evident in the "many frauds and deceits" that occurred.[92] Legislative indecisiveness about the needs for controls on the export of flour left merchant-shippers uncertain about acceptable standards.[93] When controls were finally instituted, much of their effectiveness was negated because all flour shipped to either of the adjoining provinces was exempted from the regulations.[94] Finally, there were simply not enough laws. William A. Whitehead observed:

> losing sight of the fact that injurious consequences always result from an interference with the regular course of commercial operations of whatever charter, the proprietary Government first, and then the law makers under that which succeeded, in their attempts to make Amboy 'chief staple' and to dispense with 'intermediate agents,' so materially interfered with the trade of the province, throwing such obstacles in the way of a free intercourse with such places as the interests of the people prompted them to engage in—that they retarded, instead of advancing its prosperity.[95]

However, rather than attributing their difficulties in commerce to their failure to adopt a laissez-faire policy of government and economics, a more accurate contention would be that the limited number of items controlled, as well as the laxity with which most laws were enforced, produced the classic situation of too little control administered too late. What was needed was more government regulation, not less.[96]

Problems of Geographic Location

Legislation, or rather the lack of it, was one important aspect in the decline of New Jersey's ports. The geographical nature of the colony was another. It has been argued that Perth Amboy, despite its favorable location and deep harbor, was unable to compete with New York for commerce because of the lack of an extensive hinterland. New York's Hudson Valley, with its mighty network of streams and rivers, made accessible an area far larger and thus commercially more productive than that of New Jersey's Raritan River. This factor, it is suggested, assured New York's dominance in commercial trade from the very beginning.[97] Yet the lack of an interior river system like the Hudson, so important later for the growth of New York City, was not a significant factor in the seventeeth century and much of the eighteenth century. The reason, of course, was that in the early period the population density in the valley region was so sparse, and consequently this area's productivity and buying power were so limited, that the Hudson River system had little effect at this juncture either on New York City's growth or on Perth Amboy's decline. New Jersey's hinterland, its accessibility and productivity, were, however, extremely important factors in East Jersey's port growth.

Water transportation, as noted earlier, was a key factor in determining the nature of settlement as well as the nature of commerce. Accessibility to a navigable river, especially if enhanced by a landing or dock, added to the desirability and thus the value of land. Therefore, docks and landings proliferated along all of New Jersey's major and minor waterways. The proximity of a dwelling to river transportation was a major selling point in any land or business transaction, as evidenced by the numerous references in sale advertisements to "good Wharff at the Door for Vessels to Load and unload"; near the "common Landing"; "About half Mile above the Landing."[98] At some locations a combination of factors contributed to the development of public landings that in turn often became focal points for trade. Small towns such as Woodbridge, maintaining public landings over a period of years, developed a rather extensive local trade from those facilities.[99] This was also the case at New Brunswick and the Raritan Landing, where a series of geographical factors produced a major trading center that was to rival the official port at Perth Amboy and to contribute to that port's decline.

The early roads generally paralleled the water routes and required an extensive network of ferries to act as connectors for the rudimentary system.[100] One such link was provided by John Inians, who in 1697 procured a license for a ferry across the Raritan River.[101] As the hinterland became more settled, the ferry landing grew in significance, providing the intersection between intra-provincial road travel via the "Old Dutch Road" and river transportation from the hinterland.[102] Geographically, it was ideally located at the head of navigation on the Raritan River, making it the logical terminal for water traffic above and below that point.[103] Because the water depth at Inians Ferry, later called New Brunswick, was some ten to fifteen feet, vessels as large as brigs could use the docking facilities.[104] New Brunswick used its natural advantages to become an assembly area for flour, all types of grains, and occasionally other produce such as meat, which were brought in from the surrounding countryside.[105]

The hinterland, the largest and most productive area of New Jersey, was better served by New Brunswick than by Perth Amboy because of the influence of the natural channels of traffic created by the topography of the land. Farmers from Morris, Hunterdon, Sussex, Somerset, and Warren counties, and even from as far west as Bloomsbury in the Musconetcong Valley, sent their produce for export chiefly to New Brunswick instead of Perth Amboy, because it was cheaper and more convenient for shipping export commodities as well as all manner of items shipped into the Raritan Valley.[106] For example, if a farmer went by road, he had to pay a ferry fee to cross the Raritan River. If he went by water, he had to unload the vessel, transport the cargo by wagon to Perth Amboy, and then unload again and load another vessel, a complicated operation that cost him in time and distance as well as additional fees if extra labor was required. It was far better for merchandise to be brought up to the head of navigation in large vessels, the bulk broken down, and the cargos either transferred in smaller boats to various docks and landings in the interior or carried in wagons to areas not accessible by water.[107]

Because New Brunswick was becoming the center for much of the rural trade, entrepreneurs and merchants in the area began to build flour mills, warehouses, and retail stores to serve the needs of farmers. One such store was Janeway and Broughton. A brief perusal of its ledgers indicates that a large volume of trade was conducted, especially in merchandise sales, and that the clientele were almost all rural farmers who usually bought on credit and paid by barter.[108] In reinforcing the port's natural attractions, these businessmen helped make it the major grain depot for all of New Jersey.[109] Shippers were also attracted to the area, and some, such as the Low family, which might have settled in Perth Amboy, preferred to operate from New Brunswick, concentrating most of their trade between New Jersey's hinterland markets and New York.[110] The result of such merchant activities was to diminish the amount of trade for and with Perth Amboy.

The area at the navigable head of the Raritan River became so prosperous that it supported another rival commercial center, Raritan Landing. Although the landing was farther up river than New Brunswick, the latter had the advantage of deeper water, which could accommodate large vessels regardless of the tide; the landing required a flood tide to give the river sufficient depth to accommodate a sloop.[111] This was apparently a crucial factor, for rather than eclipse New Brunswick, as proponents of the landing had hoped, it became instead something of an annex to the larger development.

New Brunswick quickly became the mercantile hub of central New Jersey. In 1744, Dr. Alexander Hamilton described New Brunswick as a "neat small city in East Jersey Government built chiefly of brick."[112] By 1748 it had expanded sufficiently to impress Peter Kalm, the Swedish traveler, as a large commercial center whose "greatest part or rather all its trade is with New York." That trade consisted of "grain, flour in great quantities, bread, several other necessaries, a great quantity of linseed, boards, timber, wooden vessels, and all sorts of carpenters work."[113] Soon ships from New Brunswick had expanded their trade routes to include the West Indies and the New England states.[114] This continued a cycle of successful growth and led travelers at the end of the American Revolution to report that New Brunswick "carried on more business than Perth Amboy, lying 10 miles down at the mouth of the River."[115]

Although New Brunswick and Raritan Landing were not legally ports, they did become major local rivals to Perth Amboy, handling both intra- and inter-colonial commerce in ever-increasing volume. As trading centers, they served a large portion of rural New Jersey and removed this trade from the mainstream of commerce upon which Perth Amboy depended and without which that port suffered.

Geography also affected Perth Amboy by limiting the flow of agricultural produce from the area most naturally served by the port—that is, the area north of the terminal moraine. This area of glaciation suffers in many places from poor drainage; glaciated action has often buried the more fertile topsoil. As a result it is less productive than the fertile Piedmont and inner-coastal plain. Of course, agricultural pursuits are further limited here because it is colder than the Piedmont or inner-coastal plain to the south, and it has a correspondingly shorter growing period.[116]

Because it was less productive than other areas of New Jersey, the area north of the terminal moraine also tended to be more sparsely settled. Those who bought land in this area did so either because they arrived too late to acquire better land or, more often, because they were too poor to purchase more desirable property.[117] Poor people and poor land compounded the problems of importers and exporters in the port city. They were faced not only with a limited amount of marketable produce to export but with a limited market for imported merchandise among the rural inhabitants.

In West Jersey, geography was also important in Burlington's failure to develop as a port city. Here, however, it played more than a contributing role; it was a major factor in the decline of the port. Ideally located in the fertile inner-coastal plain in West Jersey, which parallels the Delaware River, Burlington afforded its earliest inhabitants a relatively safe port facility and extremely productive farmland. Neither advantage could be found along the Atlantic front. There the rugged coastline, devoid of good harbors, and the poor soil of the outer-coastal plain made both commerce and farming difficult.

As the inner-coastal plain's population density rose, settlement expanded north and south along the Delaware River from the center at Burlington. But as land became scarce, agricultural settlement moved into the infertile back-country area known as the Pine Barrens, where farm development slowed almost to a halt. This was an area of poor soil and correspondingly low agricultural productivity. Even modern agricultural technology has done little to increase the productivity of this area. The Reverend Carl Magnus Wrangel noted in 1764 that the country between Philadelphia and Egg Harbor "has been inhabited only during the last twenty years. Previously there had been only wild, barren ground [with] soil consist[ing] mainly of drift sand." Although some crops were now being cultivated, wheat, the most profitable crop, did not grow well. What few inhabitants

Evolution of the Ports 43

there were made their living "principally on the woods, which consist here of spruce, pine and cedar."[118]

This back-country area provided a natural boundary to expansion, limiting settlement to a strip along the river. When the rise of Philadelphia forced Burlington to depend almost exclusively on local resources, the latter found the population and the agricultural production of the area it serviced too limited by geographical conditions to compete with its rival on the Delaware.[119] Conversely, the geography and topography of Pennsylvania allowed for continual expansion of the population both west and south of Philadelphia. The fertility of the Piedmont region, with its accessibility to the coastal port, insured a steady flow of agricultural products to meet the increasing demand.[120] Thus, the geographical setting that enhanced Philadelphia's port proved a crucial factor in the demise of West Jersey's ports.

Adverse weather conditions, especially sub-freezing temperatures in the winter, also obstructed Burlington's development as a port. On numerous occasions, ice in the Delaware would halt navigation as early as December.[121] During most winters there were several days or even weeks during which the river was frozen hard enough to allow horses pulling carriages or sleds to travel on it. Although this situation was usually temporary, there were times when the river was frozen for a considerable period. For instance, the river was closed by ice from December 19 to March 13, 1740.[122] Icy river conditions made the winter months, never a period of highly active trade at any port, a time of almost total inactivity for West Jersey ports, while the seasonal nature of the operations not only hampered Burlington's growth but aided in the development of alternate ports of entry within West Jersey.[123]

No merchant wished to delay his vessel indefinitely while waiting for the ice in the Delaware River to abate. Ship captains were also cognizant of the hazards facing vessels held at anchorage along an unsheltered coast, especially in the winter when the storms were violent and somewhat unpredictable.[124] Alternate, if illegal, ports such as the landing at Egg Harbor provided relief for the captains and a means for merchants to conclude their business; a ship's cargo would be landed at Egg Harbor and then transshipped by wagon throughout West Jersey or to Philadelphia by way of Cooper's Ferry when river conditions allowed.[125]

Cargos that might well have been destined for New Jersey's official ports were thus denied to them. Although difficult to document, the apparently quasi-official status rendered the other ports during times of necessity generated the type of activity that attracted regular commerce. Much of this traffic was engendered by a desire to avoid customs duties. It was therefore conducted surreptitiously. Yet a large part of the traffic, especially when it involved the landing of non-enumerated goods that expedited service to the customers of West Jersey, was carried on openly and had the tacit approval of Jacob Spicer, deputy collector of the Cape May region. Pragmatism, combined with the semi-official status enjoyed by these landings, might also partly explain officials' reluctance to damage their popularity by attempting to enforce local export regulations, especially those on lumber products shipped directly to the other colonies or to the West Indies.[126] The presence of what constituted a rival port, the landing at Egg Harbor, although not nearly as significant to the disruption of trade at the legal ports as were those in East Jersey, nevertheless contributed to the decline of Burlington's trade.

Nowhere was the interlocking nature of the decline of maritime commerce more apparent than in the development of the network of roads that crossed New Jersey. Because the New Jersey ports had not yet proved adequate, New Jerseyans came more and more to rely on the major centers of New York and Philadelphia, giving an additional impetus to the development of a road system that would provide an alternate means of transportation to service the agrarian community. Extremely primitive at first, the road and ferry system had become superior to any in America by 1740.[127] Farmers in the hinterland, as well as those along the coast, were able to move their produce quickly to markets or urban centers outside the colony where prices and facilities for marketing were better developed. As its inland transportation system improved, New Jersey became an agricultural warehouse with a door at both ends, and this in turn helped decrease commerce at her own ports. As the ports subsequently declined there came a greater demand for a better road system linking New Jersey with the neighboring colonies, so that its ports were further deprived of much of the local commerce they needed to become viable.

While some factors stand out more noticeably than others—for example, the lack of legislation to aid commerce, or the geographical nature of New Jersey—no single factor wholly explains the failure of New Jersey's ports to realize their potential. But these combined elements—an unsympathetic legislature, the topographical nature of the colony, and the network of roads and ferries making other harbors more readily accessible—virtually assured that New Jersey would never sufficiently generate those socio-economic and political conditions that would enable its ports to prosper against the competition of rival ports in neighboring colonies.

3
Port Administration

OUR UNDERSTANDING of the manner in which port officials carried out their duties has often been based on our knowledge of the legal requirements and manner in which officials operated in such ports as Boston and Philadelphia. The motivation of those who served in such capacities has seldom been examined, except in relation to the coming of the Revolution. In fact, if New Jersey is any example, the manner in which these officials carried out their functions, as well as their reasons for seeking or accepting such appointments, varied greatly, especially in ports where shipping volume was small.

Although New Jersey had three official ports of entry, none was the scene of major activity. Two ports served West Jersey: Burlington, located in the approximate center of a district that extended for fifty miles on the Delaware, from the head of that river to the southern boundary of Gloucester County; and Salem, serving the counties of Cumberland, Cape May, and Salem (above Cohansey). Perth Amboy was the sole port for all of East Jersey.[1] Shipment through these ports was the only legal means by which commerce could be conducted by water through New Jersey, with the exception of shuttle trade between New Jersey and the adjoining colonies.

The Navigation Acts were part of an ambitious plan developed over almost a century by England to insure the mother country's increasing dominance as a military and commercial maritime power. Until the end of the seventeenth century this evolving system was only sporadically enforced and seldom obeyed.

Port Personnel and Procedures

With the consolidation of the Navigation Acts in 1696, major changes were begun, not in policy but in procedure.[2] One important change was the placing of personnel in the customs organization in America under the control of the customs commissioners in England to exact more stringent compliance with commercial regulations. With this change there evolved a more elaborate system of courts and governmental officials in the colonies to provide for the enforcement of the Navigation Acts.[3]

Ideally, a ship's captain entering a colonial port in the first quarter of the eighteenth century faced a formidable array of port officials intent on enforcing the Navigation Acts as well as preventing corruption within their own ranks by monitoring one another's performance of official duties. Upon arrival in the harbor, the shipmaster had to submit the necessary papers to the customs house for examination by both the collector of customs and the naval officer in order to obtain permission to unload. These officials opened the ship's cockets (documents certifying that goods have been duly entered and duties paid), which had been sealed by officials at the last port of call, and each in turn examined and recorded the number, type, and sometimes volume and weight of the cargo. The captain also presented the ship's registry, from which both officials ascertained that the vessel was British-built and -owned. This, along with other required information about the vessel, was entered in the official ledgers, along with the vessel's date of entry into the port, and "from Whence" it had come. After paying each officer the required fee, the captain returned to his ship, where two other officials, a tidewaiter and a surveyor, were listing the cargo on board and conducting a search for prohibited goods.

Only when they had finished could the captain begin to unload his cargo. At this point, he encountered another port official, the landwaiter, who recorded each item as it left the vessel. If the ship was late or for some reason was not completely unloaded, still another official was required: a watcher who stayed aboard the vessel to insure that nothing was put aboard or removed until the landwaiter returned. When the unloading was completed, each official checked to see that his list agreed with the others and the required duties were assessed. Any illicit goods were seized, and often the offending ship was condemned.

Even after a master had received official clearance, he still had to cancel his bonds and apply for new ones. Since bond applications were treated separately from the ship's entry and clearance procedures, the master had to appear again before the collector and the naval officer, and pay additional fees. Several weeks later, when clearing the port with a new cargo, he would undergo the same procedures in reverse.[4]

With some slight changes, such as the absence of a surveyor at the port, this was the accepted routine at Boston, Philadelphia, New York, and other large ports. At smaller ports such as Perth Amboy, however, which recorded only sixty-eight entries in 1726, a very active year, and twenty-five and thirty vessels respectively in more representative years such as 1724 and 1725, it would have been both expensive and superfluous to maintain a full complement of port officials.[5] Perth Amboy, perhaps because it was larger or on account of its potential as a more active port, had both a collector of customs and a naval officer. But the volume of trade throughout the eighteenth century did not justify the latter. At Burlington and Salem there was a collector of customs and on rare occasion a deputy appointed by them. These officials and their deputies also acted as naval officer, tidewaiter, landwaiter, and performed any other duties that might be required.[6]

The governor and the naval officer, along with the collectors at the three New Jersey ports, made up the entire machinery for regulating the maritime trade entering and clearing New Jersey. The degree of their activity was somewhat regulated by the seasonal nature of colonial shipping. The ports saw the greatest activity in the spring and summer, a decline in the fall with the onset of hurricane weather, and then an almost total cessation during the winter months. At Perth Amboy, for example, between 1722 and 1727, the entry lists record only nine vessels entering during the first two months of the year. From 1732 to 1748, Burlington had no vessels entering during those two months and only two vessels clearing. The spring and summer months witnessed a renewal of activity, and it was during this period that the port officials at Perth Amboy were most active and the collector at Burlington most expectant—that port in the 1730s and 1740s averaged only four vessels a year. Summer and fall were steady periods but not highly active. The approach of winter with its inclement weather and ice hazards made November and early December especially active months. Ship captains cleared New Jersey ports, bound for more hospitable climates. By the end of December the ports were once again barely operative. This, then, was the pattern of activity for shipping.⁷ Monthly activities for the ports varied little even over a twenty-five-year period.

The volume of trade was such that port officials had long periods of inactivity even during the most active months. In 1726, for example, April, which was always the most active month, saw customs officials at Perth Amboy handling a total of twenty-one vessels (eleven entering and ten clearing). This was probably the most active month of any in the years from 1722 to 1764. More representative of the collector's work load were the five vessels that entered and the four that cleared in April 1725.⁸ Vessels arriving in any given month were usually spaced over days or weeks. There were only a few instances when a collector had to deal with more than one arrival a day. Three vessels arriving at the same time was a rarity, and there is no record in the customs or naval office's listings of a New Jersey collector ever having to contend with more than that number.

The vessels themselves were small, usually between twenty and thirty-five tons with relatively limited cargo capacity. Many carried only four or five items, often the same commodity in different containers. For example, the thirty-five-ton sloop *John and Mary of Perth Amboy* arrived on May 20, 1723, from Barbados with fifteen hogsheads of rum, thirty-seven tierces of rum, eight barrels of rum, and some European goods. With so little volume, inspecting the cargo went rapidly; it probably took the port officials no more than two hours to perform all of the functions required of them. This factor, plus the infrequency of arrivals, meant that the collector or naval officer spent little actual time at the port itself. Under these circumstances it seems likely that the collectors as well as the naval officers operated from their residences. Here the port official recorded arrival or departure, issued such required permits as the license to load or unload, and collected his fees.

The payment of fees was regulated by the provincial assembly, and until 1750 the costs for official duties were graduated into three separate classes based on tonnage.⁹ That year a new law revised the system: fees were now determined by area of trade, not by vessel size. The law also expanded payments due the naval officer. Where prior legislation had decreed that "no Vessel or Vessels Trading with this Province, and to New York and Pennsylvania, shall pay," the law now decreed for the first time a fee of two shillings and six pence for "Transfers or Permits for Boats or Shallops to and from New York or Pennsylvania, for their whole load of Country products."¹⁰

Upon payment of the requisite fees, the captain, accompanied by the collector (and at Perth Amboy the naval officer as well), returned to the wharf, where he unloaded or loaded his vessel under official supervision. There were indications, however, that vessels were occasionally loaded without official supervision, either because no official could be located or simply because he did not wish to go to the dock. The paper work required for this as well as for both entries and clearings was often completed days or even weeks after they actually occurred.

Port Recordkeeping

Such procedures at Perth Amboy produced records that reflected this lack of immediate concern. Names of shipmasters were occasionally lined out and other names substituted (for example, entries after June 10 and June 18, 1725, in records of Naval Officer Alexander Mackdowall). Days, even months, were likewise changed or corrected. The recording of the arrival at Perth Amboy of *Dolphin of Rhode Island* on October 19, 1724, for instance, was apparently forgotten until November, and its entry rests conspicuously between entries for November 7 and November 9, 1724. Similar laxity was also reflected in the listing of the cargos. It was difficult to establish the amount of a given commodity after it was already unloaded and on its way to the consignee or consumer. Even when officials were present, they were sometimes hurried and would dispense with the normal careful counting of items. In either case the official papers would simply record goods such as axes, cheeses, gammon, hides, or saddles with the designation "some" or a "quantity."

Quite often, however, officials exercised great care to insure the accuracy of certain records. On August 7, 1723, for example, a vessel already loaded and cleared apparently placed seven more casks of flour on board, a fact that was duly noted by a dated inclusion in the official manifest. This was especially true of ships carrying enumerated goods. The sloop *Speedwell of New York* entered from Boston on June 28, 1725; with twelve pipes of Madeira wine, it had the annotation "Entered Here" listed across its manifest, indicating payment of duty at Perth Amboy. The sloop *John and Mary of Perth Amboy*, arriving from Rhode Island with three hundred pounds of tobacco, had a notation with its entry of April 12, 1725, indicating that the duty on that commodity had previously been paid at the last port of call.

Such notations as to place of entry and payment of duties on goods appeared throughout the records.

The shipment of enumerated goods required the vessel's owners or master to post bond. Bonds were issued at the port of origin and were usually canceled at the destination by the port officials. Bonds issued in England were apparently permanent and, although recorded, were not canceled. While New Jersey's collectors occasionally recorded and canceled temporary bonds issued at other local ports, the very nature of New Jersey's export trade, consisting mainly of non-enumerated agricultural products and other goods from the countryside that seldom required the posting of security. From 1722 to 1727 only ten bonds were issued at Perth Amboy. They involved naval stores that were possibly locally produced but probably being transshipped, as well as products of the West Indies being transshipped from New Jersey to other colonies.[11] At Burlington, from 1732 to 1748, bonds were so infrequently encountered—a total of five were issued—that Charles Read undoubtedly found himself unable to recall the complex legal format for their issuance and was forced to go through his seldom-used and often-outdated instruction and rate books to complete them. The handling of bonds, a time-consuming but integral part of the activities of the larger ports, was as sporadic and infrequent as other duties connected with the direct operation of New Jersey's harbors.

Aside from the infrequent contacts with vessel owners and masters at the harbor, port personnel were sometimes required to perform additional duties. They had to register vessels and administer the oath of registration. The oath was to be taken only by the owner, and the officer at Burlington was reprimanded for failing to differentiate between owner and master. He begged indulgence, as the case in point involved the first and apparently only vessel he ever registered.[12]

After 1729, collectors also exacted from the vessel's master or from the crew a six-penny monthly payment per man toward the maintenance of Greenwich Hospital, in England.[13] The collectors and naval officers also implemented the governor's instructions whether they came out of the Navigation Acts or additional directives conveyed through the governor, the Lords of Trade, or provincial legislative bodies.[14]

All port officials who kept official records were required to submit them quarterly to the governor, who, in turn, forwarded them to England. Once again, general laxity seems to have prevailed. A request from the Board of Trade to Governor Lewis Morris in July 1745 reveals that no "Quarterly Accounts of Ships entered and cleared in your Government" had been sent since 1727. The board asked that records going back at least seven years be immediately forwarded.[15] Four years later Morris's successor, Jonathan Belcher, found it necessary to apologize to the Board of Trade for his failure to send some of the accounts and for the general incompleteness of the records that were forwarded, noting, "I have so often ordered Mr. Frasier, the Collector for Port of Salem . . . to Send his Acct and can Obtain No Answer, that I am quite weary, and don't expect, to get his Account."[16] A year later William Fraser, spurred perhaps by a second complaint sent by Belcher to the Lords of Trade, made available the "return of the Imports and Exports for the Port of Salem . . . as far back as I can go." But the records he presented covered only the years from 1736 to 1740.[17] John Spicer, while acting as deputy for the district of Salem-Cohansey, seldom forwarded his quarterly reports to the governor. As he explained, not only was the volume of trade too slight—"Had the Entries been more Considerible, I should have Sent quarterly accounts"—but he found himself unable to collect duties because his books on the laws of trade had been burned in a house fire and no replacements or new set of laws had been sent him.[18] In 1764, Governor William Franklin wrote to the Lords of Trade what was probably a response quite familiar to them:

> The Custom House Accounts, indeed, have not been sent, owing to my not being able to get any Person to Act Naval Officer in the Western Division...as the Naval Officer in the Eastern Division don't make above Five Pounds a Year of his Office, he thinks it scarce the worth his while to be at the Trouble of making out the Account; he has, however, promised me to do it.[19]

Whether such accounts were eventually forwarded is not known, but it appears that throughout the period officials connected with the ports were notoriously careless in communicating those documents to England. Neither administrative functions nor port activities, even when not time consuming, were vigorously pursued.

While an active port such as Philadelphia maintained a full-time collector whose annual salary of £160 reflected the importance of his position, the collectors at New Jersey's ports seldom devoted full time to their official functions.[20] If the lives and activities of John Stevens (ca. 1682–1737), collector at Perth Amboy in 1717, and Charles Read, collector at Burlington from 1732 until the eve of the Revolution (when he left the colony), were typical, it would appear that the post was much sought after because it afforded many advantages with very little effort.[21] Aside from supplementing his income, the post gave an individual a degree of stature within the colony and afforded him political and social leverage. At Perth Amboy, for example, shippers preferred officials drawn from within their ranks for the obvious reason that enforcement of obscure statutes on a selective basis could destroy all but the most powerful merchants. Maintaining a relative or friend in the post of collector was a means of avoiding this hazard of maritime commerce.

John Stevens (ca. 1682–1737), of Perth Amboy

Perth Amboy's collector, John Stevens, was a man who knew how to make the most of his opportunities. Little was known about him prior to his arrival in the colonies in 1699, but once arrived he displayed all the qualities required for success. An aggressive youth, he began to amass wealth through land speculation and then further advanced himself by contracting an advantageous marriage to Anne Campbell in 1706. As the son-in-law of John Campbell, a leading social and political figure in New Jersey, and the direct representative of one of the East Jersey proprietors, Stevens acquired additional important political, social, and economic connections. Within two years he was involved in one of the largest land speculations in New York. While in New Jersey, he worked in conjunction with his brother-in-law to reap a small fortune from rising land prices. As his wealth increased, he began to diversify his economic interests and pursue official positions that would expand his political and economic base. He invested in diverse enterprises, among them the Redford Ferry to Perth Amboy. As a resident of Perth Amboy he participated in town affairs and helped establish an Anglican church there. More important, however, he was one of the prime movers in the local merchants' successful attempt to incorporate the town. When this was accomplished in 1718, Stevens became Perth Amboy's first treasurer.[22] In October 1716, prior to becoming town treasurer, he had begun to engage in the West Indies trade.[23] In order to protect and expand this enterprise, he successfully gained appointment as a deputy to John Barclay, collector at the port.[24]

One of Stevens's first official acts, on November 17, 1717, was to seize the sloop *Hanna* for violating an act of the assembly that had placed a duty on the export of wheat from East Jersey. The seizure was undoubtedly accomplished only with considerable difficulty and personal expense, for the small port lacked the necessary personnel and equipment for such an undertaking. John Stevens was forced to rent a small boat and hire three men to aid him in boarding the sloop to seize the 452½ bushels of wheat on which duty had not been paid. This accomplished, he placed a two-man watch aboard the ship while he procured a crew of seven laborers to help unload the condemned cargo into three large carts, which he had hired along with two extra men. Stevens had to provide not only rental fees for the carts and wages for the watchers and laborers, he also had to furnish meals, including the customary punch and stronger drink (over four quarts of rum) for the day's activity. Having unloaded, moved, and stored the wheat, Stevens had additional costs involved in the drawing up of various legal documents in connection with the seizure, and six months' storage fees on the wheat while the case awaited the court's pleasure. The total cost to Stevens was eleven pounds, thirteen shillings, and three pence.[25]

In May 1717, after considerable delay, adding to Stevens's expenses, the court finally ordered Elisha Parker and William Eier to appraise the wheat then in storage. They arrived at a figure of sixty-seven pounds, seventeen shillings, and six pence, and the wheat was undoubtedly sold for that price soon after. As Johannes Vanderhoven, master of the sloop *Hanna*, had been in violation of a provincial statute rather than the Navigation Acts, expenses incurred in the seizure, as well as the one-third due the deputy collector as informant, were to be paid by the assembly. It is apparent, however, that for a considerable time after the appraisal and probable sale of the wheat, Stevens went without payment of any kind, for he added an additional pound and three shillings to the eleven pounds, thirteen shillings, and three pence already spent ("To my Expenses to and from Burlington when sent for to the Assembly there in March 1720–21") when he submitted his account to the assembly.[26] Undoubtedly, John Stevens was eventually paid, but perhaps the time and expenses involved discouraged him and subsequent agents from such rapid enforcement.[27] Nevertheless, Stevens was aware of the real and potential power of the collector's office to alter a merchant's fortunes. His assessment of the position's value probably influenced his decision to accept the collector's post at Perth Amboy in 1717 after John Barclay was suspended for misdemeanors.[28]

The office of collector was restrictive, however. It required the posting of a £500 bond, and the official could not absent himself from his post except in an emergency. Nor could deputies serve in his place, even though he could appoint deputies to serve under him.[29]

Nevertheless, the advantages Stevens accrued as collector were considerable—the salary of £40 per year, as well as fees, was a tidy supplement to any income, for it was negotiable currency and, as such, was of more immediate value than the land or property usually used for posting the security bond required for the appointment.[30] As collector, Stevens was exempt from the most distasteful community services, such as serving on juries or with the militia. In addition, he was not subject to any local taxation.[31]

It is difficult to determine how long John Stevens held the position. But from the very beginning he ignored the prohibitions against collectors engaging in trade, serving as merchants or factors, or owning any part of a trading vessel. It was during his collectorship that he built and expanded his mercantile interests. After Stevens's death his son John (1715–92), later known as the Honorable John Stevens, continued both the mercantile tradition and the protection afforded that business by having the collector closely tied to the interests of the Stevens family. When in March 1770 the death of John Barberie, a close friend and collector for more than thirty years, seemed imminent, the Honorable John Stevens hurriedly wrote to the firm of Scott and Pringle, his agents in London. He requested their aid in procuring the collector's office for his brother Richard as soon as it became vacant and ended with a promise to pay all expenses that might be incurred in such an undertaking.[32] Ostensibly the post was to produce income to aid Richard, who was still recovering from "recent business difficulties." But equally important was the maintenance of an arrangement by which the enforcement arm of the Navigation Acts remained under the control of Perth Amboy's merchants.

Charles Read, of Burlington

Charles Read, collector at Burlington, also reaped many benefits from his humble post. He enjoyed a yearly salary of £40 for duties so undemanding that a year or more passed without his having to enter or clear a single vessel.[33] He had acquired the post in 1732 with the help of Sir Charles Wager and held the position until his death. Like John Stevens (ca. 1682–1737), Read's major interest and fortune was in land; for three decades after his appointment as collector he added almost yearly to his holdings.[34] Unlike Stevens, however, Read showed no real interest in mercantile pursuits. Instead, he used the appointment to provide the political leverage to begin his upward movement in New Jersey's political life. From the moment Read arrived in Burlington at the age of twenty-four, he had been politically active. He had purchased the office of town clerk, then secured that of collector of the port, and soon became clerk of the circuits, deputy secretary of the colony, surrogate of the prerogative court, and, upon the recommendation of Governor Belcher, a member of the common council.[35] By this time the customs office had become a minor holding in his political empire, but it had been an important stepping stone in his political career.

Although in reality the collector of customs was the most important figure in the operation of the port, in theory the governor was the key official, for among the instructions he received upon taking office was one that gave him the ultimate responsibility for enforcing parliamentary laws concerning commerce. The governor, of course, involved himself very little in the actual work of the port, collecting an occasional fee due him for some small service he performed in connection with shipping, and relaying to the port collectors the instructions he received concerning operations of the port or enforcement of Navigation Acts.[36]

He did, however, have an agent or representative in the naval officer, whose position was a patronage appointment of the governor. The naval officer acted in a sense as the eyes and ears of the executive and functioned as a check upon the customs collector, who was under the control of the surveyor general rather than the governor.[37] Since New Jersey's governors seldom appeared in the colony prior to 1738, the naval officer's post at Perth Amboy was more important than it would ordinarily have been. The duties of Alexander Mackdowall, naval officer throughout the 1720s, were almost identical to those of the collector: keeping the port records; and examining the papers and cargos of entering and clearing vessels. If the salaries of the naval officers in other ports were representative, Mackdowall received only minimal remuneration for his services, and the lack of trade at Perth Amboy meant that almost nothing was realized in the way of fees.[38] He and his successors most likely held their positions for the economic and political potential of the office rather than for truly gainful employment.

In later years, newly arrived officials appointed from outside the colony of New Jersey, and therefore lacking local social and political connections, found it difficult to realize any of the legal potential of their office. Some, such as John Hatton, collector at Salem in 1764, took advantage of the unofficial toleration of illicit practices to realize a profit by using his "good offices" to facilitate, on a large scale, the avoidance of customs duties. He did this by selectively allowing merchants, mostly Philadelphians, to enter through his port rather than their own, issuing them fraudulent entry papers or simply listing their vessels as entering in ballast.[39] Such collusion and the notoriety resulting from it added another and perhaps final dimension to the actions of the officials at the New Jersey ports.

The administration of these ports followed the practice used throughout the colonies to insure compliance with England's commercial statutes. It differed little with other customs districts, stretching from Falmouth, Maine, to Savannah, Georgia. At least in the colony of New Jersey, there was doubtless considerable laxity in the manner in which vessels were entered and cleared by customs officials; nor were the officials particularly conscientious in carrying out other official functions such as recordkeeping. There seems little question that, at least in the case of John Hatton, corruption in the customs service could and did exist at smaller ports, aided by the lack of an elaborate structure of checks and balances that might be found at the major ports. But it would be unwise to assume that New Jersey's customs officials were as dishonest and susceptible to bribery and graft as were those of Philadelphia or Boston.[40] Hatton was the exception rather than the rule. The collection of tariffs, regulation of trade, and desire to seek administrative posts for legal or illegal financial gain were secondary in New Jersey's ports. This was equally true in other small colonial ports where the volume of trade was slight and remuneration small. Most who served were like Charles Read, about whom a fellow colonist wrote, "No man knew so well as he how to riggle himself into office nor keep it so long nor make so much of it."[41] They valued the office less for its immediate monetary advantage than for what the position offered in terms of political and social advancement. It also offered the added advantage of furnishing them a means of keeping a finger on the pulse of colonial industry and commerce.

4
Patterns of Trade

THOUGH NEIGHBORING PORTS handled much of the trade for New Jersey, its own ports remained centers of activity in the colony. Perth Amboy and Burlington as dual capitals and Salem as the major town in the Cape May region remained the market and commercial centers for the agricultural populace. From the 1720s, seaborne trade from these ports had exhibited gradual but continual decline in total volume.[1] Yet several merchants continued to operate from the ports, especially from Perth Amboy, where they adjusted their trade patterns to accommodate the economic reality of being in immediate proximity to an emerging entrepôt.

Burlington and Perth Amboy partially resisted the tendency to become mere extensions of nearby ports and attempted to pursue their own independent course. Vessels at these two harbors arrived and departed from other colonies, as well as from Europe, Madeira, the Canary Islands, and the West Indies.[2] But the amount of trade within these areas was restricted because New Jersey's ports lacked merchant facilities or services for trading on a large or complex level; these services had to be obtained elsewhere.

New Jersey trade was more likely to be limited to a particular region when commercial services were removed from the colony, diverse cargos were handled, and relatively complex business transactions were involved. Transatlantic trade, which required the most sophisticated facilities, accounted for the smallest percentage of New

Jersey's trade; most of that commerce was conducted by using merchants' services available in the surrounding ports or by direct arrangements between individuals and overseas firms. West Indies trade accounted for a larger proportion of New Jersey's trade than did overseas trade, for it was more accessible, had more readily available markets in New Jersey, and required less complex merchant services. But here, as with transatlantic trade, direct trade between individuals or family groups or with mercantile firms in the West Indies was a limiting factor. Coastal trade accounted for the highest percentage of New Jersey trade. The coastal region was most accessible; the necessary merchant services for handling cargos were least complex and were widely available. This was especially true of trade with New England, which drew the greatest percentage of New Jersey's trade and was conducted via broader commercial centers rather than directly between individuals or firms.[3]

The availability of merchant services was, then, one of the key elements in determining the relative percentage of the total volume of trade from the New Jersey ports to various regions. As there was little possibility of developing such facilities in New Jersey, these percentages remained fairly constant. This was certainly true of Perth Amboy. Although subject to some change as the port declined, merchant involvement altered, and the colony matured, the pattern established in the formative years (1722–27) defined the broad outlines of the areas of maritime commerce in East Jersey for more than three-quarters of a century. Consequently, the relative percentage of total transatlantic trade, except for a brief period in the 1730s, stayed within a few points of the 11 percent established in the 1720s. Trade between Perth Amboy and overseas areas did, however, become more balanced between inbound and outbound traffic even though the port continually declined after 1740. The West Indies and Caribbean region took on added importance to the trade of East Jersey as the number of ships using the port declined. Nevertheless, the change was no more than 5 to 8 percent over the earlier base of 20 percent. Coastal trade involving Perth Amboy fluctuated most, varying as much as 20 percent but never accounting for less than 58 percent of the total amount of trade at that port.[4]

Much of this variation resulted from the decline of trade between Perth Amboy and the middle colonies after 1735 and the subsequent rise of trade with the southern region that eventually claimed between 15 and 20 percent of all trade. New England's trade remained fairly constant at between 40 and 50 percent.[5]

Perth Amboy Trade Routes

Perth Amboy in the 1720s entertained considerable overseas traffic, but the ships seldom entered Perth Amboy directly. They first unloaded in New York and then cleared, usually in ballast or with a minimal cargo, for the New Jersey port. At Perth Amboy these ships took on a full cargo, almost always departing for Madeira or the Canary Islands (especially Tenerife) where foodstuffs and timber were in great demand. The few (comprising less than 6 percent of the total port traffic) that arrived directly from overseas carried a minimum of goods. They picked up a general agricultural cargo and then were most likely bound to Madeira, the Canary Islands, Liverpool, London, or Lisbon. In all, clearings for overseas destinations during this period amounted to over 17 percent of the port traffic, with over 60 percent headed for Madeira or some other port off the African coast.[6]

By the 1740s, however, overseas shipping that involved Perth Amboy had undergone considerable change. The percentage of overseas trade remained basically the same, but the volume decreased markedly. New Jersey no longer functioned as a stopping point for vessels bound out of New York or other ports. Instead, trade was now conducted directly between Perth Amboy and overseas ports. Where previously ships of New Jersey registry had been involved in this trade only in a peripheral manner, now more than half was conducted by ships owned by New Jerseyans. Most of the overseas trade remained with the islands off the African coast, especially Madeira, from which New Jersey merchants such as the Honorable John Stevens imported wine while exporting local agricultural products.[7] A smaller amount of trade involving ships of New Jersey registry was conducted between Perth Amboy and Portugal (chiefly Lisbon) or England. By the 1750s the volume of trade declined further and amounted to six to ten trips annually.

The percentage in relationship to the total trade at Perth Amboy remained fairly constant, although New Jersey registries in the area dropped proportionately by two-thirds. The few New Jerseyans who continued to trade in this region produced a mixed pattern. Some operated in established areas such as Tenerife, while others began to explore newer regions such as Africa. By this time, the volume had reached the point where such trade involved no more than two to four New Jersey vessels annually. Non–New Jersey registries (four to eight ships annually) conducted most of the trade, originating now mostly in Europe rather than Madeira or Tenerife. By this time, however, the volume of trade to these regions indicated that they were no longer a significant part of Perth Amboy's trade.[8] In the 1720s, trade between the West Indies and the Caribbean on the one hand and Perth Amboy on the other was slightly under 20 percent. It was far more evenly balanced between entries and clearances than the overseas trade had been during the same period. Ships arrived from all areas of the Caribbean; the greatest concentration came from Antigua, Barbados, and Jamaica. Ships departing from Perth Amboy for the Caribbean were almost always bound for these three islands. Imports followed a regional pattern, consisting mostly of island goods such as rum, sugar, and molasses, with some cotton-wool and an occasional "negro servant." Exports to the islands graphically demonstrated that the West Indies economy could not support itself agriculturally and that the islands had little forested land. Of the vessels leaving Perth Amboy bound for the West Indies during the 1720s, 61 percent carried lumber and almost 70 percent carried grain, flour, or other breadstuffs. Dairy products were also in high demand, and about half the vessels bound from New Jersey to the islands carried butter.[9]

The exchange of island goods for agricultural products and timber varied little over the decades, but the participation of New Jersey registries in this trade changed consistently. While ships of New Jersey registry had amounted to 40 percent of the trade between East Jersey from 1722 to 1727, the number in that region rose dramatically as the overall percentage dropped in the following decades by approximately 8 percent. By 1740 eight of every ten vessels arriving at Perth Amboy from the Caribbean or departing from Perth Amboy to that region were of New Jersey registry. Shippers from New Jersey included in their trade a limited quantity of transshipped goods, supplying not only foodstuffs but manufactured goods, paint, and, increasingly, wines. Although less trade was being carried out in terms of volume, the areas of trade within the West Indies had become broader and now included occasional voyages to Saint Christopher and Curaçao. Fifteen years later the total volume of trade between East Jersey and the West Indies declined again, with five to eight vessels trading almost exclusively between Perth Amboy and Antigua or Saint Christopher. The relative percentage of that trade in relation to the total harbor traffic, however, was higher than it had been at any previous time. Yet there was almost a total absence of vessels of New Jersey registry. At one point in 1758 no vessel of New Jersey origin traded from East Jersey to the Caribbean.[10]

Patterns of Trade 61

One can only speculate as to the reasons for the withdrawal of New Jersey vessels from that trade. Possibly the pressure of war proved detrimental, for this trade had been in a fragile state due to lack of volume. Perhaps Perth Amboy's lack of a well-developed mercantile industry contributed by putting too much emphasis on direct and often long-standing relationships between individual merchants or firms. If terminated, these relationships left a void in the trade pattern that could not easily be filled. In the early 1760s a few New Jersey registries reappeared. But neither their percentage nor the overall percentage, remaining fairly constant over this period, had any real meaning in terms of a viable trade pattern.

Throughout the decades, trade between Perth Amboy and New England remained the largest in both percentage and volume. From 1722 to 1727 almost every other vessel at Perth Amboy arrived from or was departing to that region. The trading centers of Rhode Island and Boston were most active, with a trading ratio of more than two to one in favor of the former. These New England areas competed with New York as wholesale and retail suppliers for New Jersey. Exports from Rhode Island and Boston included, among many other items, earthenware, European as well as locally manufactured goods, kettles, pails, clothing, fabrics, farm implements, tools, axes, and barrels of nails. Rum and molasses, the latter accounting for 30 percent of all imports, were also shipped from New England in greater quantity than from the West Indies. (Perhaps to balance the spirit with the spiritual, one New England shipment included Bibles.)[11]

Exports from Perth Amboy to New England consisted of various New Jersey staples, flour, grains, beef, and pork. The New Englanders had a great demand for these commodities, some of which they assembled, along with a variety of goods from other colonies, for shipment to distant markets. Rhode Island merchants, in particular, built much of their fortune and trade by acting as clearing houses or entrepôts. They provided much of the overall market for New Jersey exports outside its neighboring colonies. From 1727 to 1764, though the volume of trade declined, the colony of New Jersey, through Perth Amboy, continued to act as a local food supplier for New England markets and as a limited market for various manufactured exports from New England.[12]

From the earliest period New Jersey merchants (those who had registered their vessels in New Jersey) had been active in the trade between Perth Amboy and New England. In the 1720s over 40 percent of the trade bound for New England was carried in the holds of New

Jersey–registered vessels. In the 1730s the overall percentage of trade to New England declined slightly, but then in the first part of the 1740s—even as the volume decreased in relation to that of the previous decades—it rose by 20 percentage points before dropping in the latter part of that decade to about half of all trade. From 1730 to 1750, New Jersey merchants, on a relative percentage basis, conducted over half of all New England's trade. Throughout the 1750s and into the early 1760s, though the volume of trade continued to decline (as to a slight degree did the relative percentage of trade with New England), the involvement of New Jersey registries continued to rise sharply. In 1758, of fifteen trips involved in the trade, all were carried out by ships registered in New Jersey. Even as late as 1763 more than six out of every ten trips involving New England were conducted by New Jerseyans. These activities made it appear that in this area, at least, a viable trade still existed. Actually, only two or three vessels were involved. A few local merchants operating what amounted to a shuttle trade mostly between Perth Amboy and Rhode Island made numerous short voyages that gave an illusion of a viable trade pattern.[13]

In the 1720s considerable trade requiring official clearance was conducted between East Jersey and the middle colonies, primarily New York. Of 185 vessels that arrived at East Jersey, thirty-six (almost 20 percent of all inbound traffic) came from this region, with thirty-one craft arriving from New York. Yet the actual trade between the middle colonies and Perth Amboy was small because it was usually an extension of an overseas pattern that originated from the other provinces. This accounted for the fact that over 40 percent of ships arriving from the middle colonies carried no cargo, while most of the remainder carried goods such as flour, timber, and breadstuffs that were intended not for New Jersey but as a part of the ships' general export cargo.

This pattern also produced an imbalance between entries and clearances, as slightly less than 7 percent of the traffic cleared for the middle colonies. Few of these vessels carried any exports; some cleared empty and others carried only a few special items, not of local origin, which were in the process of transshipment to a local merchant for his personal use or sale.[14] The situation remained much the same in the early 1730s. By the 1740s, however, as New Jerseyans began to engage in overseas ventures, trade from East Jersey to the middle colonies diminished, eventually becoming almost nonexistent.[15]

The middle-colony trade never used vessels of New Jersey registry to a great extent. Such vessels accounted for slightly over 16 percent in the 1720s and about 11 percent during the 1740s (mostly ships shuttling between East Jersey and Philadelphia or the Delaware River region). After that period no New Jersey bottoms were involved in this trade.[16] Trade with the middle colonies that required official clearances gave the appearance of great activity, especially in the earlier period, but had the least impact on the colony of New Jersey.

The smallest amount of trade during the earlier periods (5 to 7 percent) was conducted with the southern colonies, involving the colonies of Maryland, both Carolinas, and Virginia. The early patterns indicated that many of the vessels clearing for the southern colonies used the East Jersey port as a stopping point in a trade pattern that originated neither in East Jersey nor the South.[17]

Over the years a more direct pattern of trade emerged between Perth Amboy and the southern colonies. While the volume of trade to other regions declined, this area showed a slow but gradual increase, with a shifting emphasis on trade to North Carolina. By 1750 the overall percentage of trade between Perth Amboy and the South had risen to over 14 percent. Though the percentage remained fairly constant in the 1750s during the French and Indian War, the volume of trade dropped sharply as East Jersey's trade to almost all regions virtually ceased. In 1758, for example, only one vessel traded with the southern regions, going to Virginia.[18]

By 1763 trade between Perth Amboy and the South had resumed its previous volume. As the overall volume of East Jersey trade, especially non-coastal trade, declined still further, the relative percentage of southern trade to the total harbor traffic rose again to almost 20 percent, nearly all of which was with North Carolina.[19]

Imports from the southern colonies to East Jersey included foodstuffs such as rice and peas. Occasionally pork, beef, and Indian corn appeared as imports; they were apparently returned to New Jersey because of spoilage or lack of market. There was also a trickle of slaves (seventeen in three separate vessels), most of whom were probably retained to work the East Jersey farmlands.[20] In trade between Perth Amboy and the South there was considerable transshipment of goods. Imported hides and deerskins, for example, were obviously to be shipped elsewhere, most frequently to New England. Similarly, exports to the South consisted mostly of non-local items. Ships outbound to this region usually departed with some manufactured goods, both hardware and cloth, while a third of the exports included rum or molasses and occasionally a shipment of wine. The only New Jersey products exported with any regularity were pork in a variety of forms, dairy products (mostly cheese), and Jersey (apple) cider.[21]

Trade between East Jersey and the South came to be dominated by merchants with New Jersey registries. Starting in the 1720s with about a third of that trade, they eventually came to control over 70 percent. New Jersey craft carried 90 percent of the trade with North Carolina.[22] Although southern trade by 1760 involved only five to eight ships a year dealing on an individual basis rather than in general commerce, that trade had continued to grow in volume, percentage, and New Jersey registries. But by itself the southern trade could not revitalize the harbor at East Jersey.

Shipping from Burlington

The dream that Perth Amboy might become a port to rival any in the world rekindled briefly in the late 1720s but never flamed. The reality of the 1750s and 1760s was a small local port with a shuttle trade of limited coastal scope. While the nature of trade in East Jersey fluctuated over four decades, at Burlington it remained rather static over a period of more than thirty years. Already minimal by 1732, the volume of traffic continued to decline, and the trade patterns reflected that port's dependence on Philadelphia. For example, the inbound traffic from the Quaker capital amounted to over 35 percent of the total volume, accounting for much of the traffic that eventually cleared from Burlington for the West Indies or overseas. Half of those vessels arrived at Burlington empty. Moreover, the four vessels that constituted the 7.5 percent of the port traffic bound from Burlington to the Quaker city either had arrived earlier from some other area, unloaded, and proceeded down river for a new cargo, or had come from Philadelphia partially loaded and were returning there for additional cargo prior to their ultimate departure.[23] Almost all of the overseas trade followed this pattern. But about two-thirds of the West Indian traffic, which made up 30 percent of all of Burlington's trade, was conducted directly between this port and the islands, especially Barbados and Antigua.[24] That trade appears, however, to have been specific rather than general, in that only a handful of merchants participated, mostly the Smiths of Burlington and their relations. The volume of trade to the West Indies matched that to New England and, as with the former, most of it was direct.[25]

To an even greater extent than at Perth Amboy, Burlington's lack of a broad merchant class engaged in maritime commerce forced al-

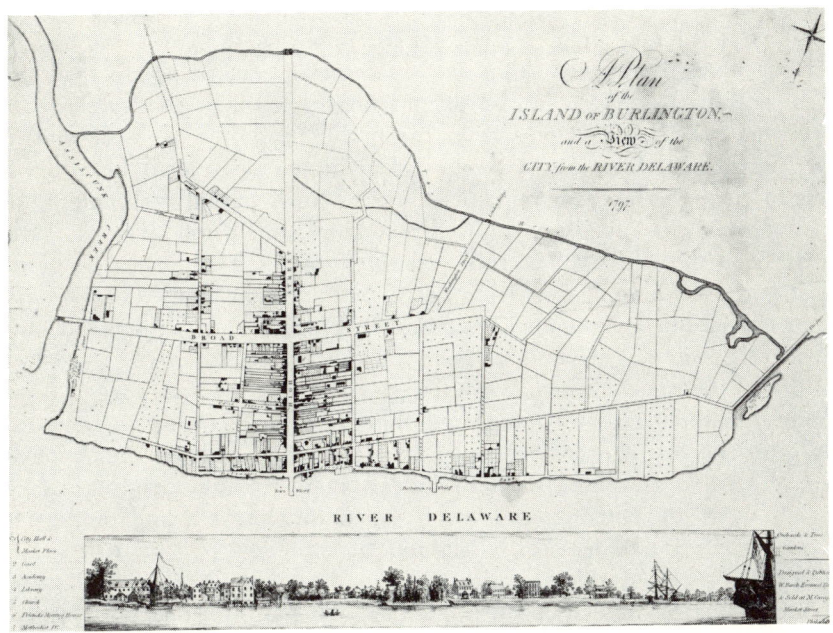

Commerce helped shape eighteenth-century Burlington. The area adjacent to the town's Delaware River wharves was heavily built up, as seen (above) *in "A Map of the Island of Burlington and a View of the City from the River Delaware," designed by William Birch, Philadelphia, 1797. Courtesy of the Library of Congress. The commercial decline of Burlington left it the sleepy port sketched* (below) *by Auguste Plée, 1821. Original in the Musée National d'Histoire Naturelle, Paris.*

most total reliance on Pennsylvania for business services, resulting in a trade pattern similar to that of New Jersey's eastern port, where the local populace engaged in almost no transshipment of goods. Shippers exported local farm staples from the middle colonies overseas and to the Caribbean. Like Perth Amboy, Burlington sent local farm products to New England for immediate use or for eventual reshipment.

Burlington received very few direct shipments from overseas. Imports from the West Indies followed the standard fare, although on at least two occasions vessels from there arrived in ballast. Most imports from the middle colonies were in transit. Flour, beef, timber, and other local products, which had been picked up in the area, were not unloaded because they constituted part of the export cargo, even though customs registries required that they be recorded as imports. Only on the rarest occasions were manufactured goods or rum, molasses, and sugar freighted from Philadephia. New England imports provided most of Burlington's stock of manufactured and non-local goods, as they had for Perth Amboy. In sum, Boston and Rhode Island acted as wholesale suppliers for the West Jersey region.[26]

Whatever the nature of Burlington's trade patterns, the port played only a relatively small role in the overall volume of colonial trade. Yet both Burlington and Perth Amboy provided a valid demonstration of the manner in which trade was conducted outside the major harbors of New York, Philadelphia, and Boston.

Regionalization of Trade

Standard generalizations about the nature of colonial trade patterns do not seem applicable to New Jersey's ports. Trade was assumed to flow in a triangular pattern from the colonies to the West Indies, on to Europe, and then back to the point of origin; or from the colonies to the Canary Islands, then to the Caribbean, and finally home. Such patterns evolved from the need to convert the produce of the forest, farm, and sea, unmarketable for the most part in England and Europe, to some acceptable commodity, such as sugar, wines, or bills of credit in order to pay European creditors and purchase manufactured goods.[27] Coastal trade supposedly followed a pattern of multiple exchanges as local merchants and entrepreneurs developed their own versions of a triangular pattern, either by using factors or simply en-

Patterns of Trade 67

gaging in "tramping" (seeking acceptable cargos on the basis of commercial instinct and immediate market conditions). With each transaction they hoped to improve the profit potential of the cargo, until finally they returned to the home port with some form of capital (paper or specie) or a cargo worth considerably more than the one with which they departed.[28] It is true that these patterns of overseas and coastal trade existed, but they may have been overemphasized. In New Jersey the greater number of voyage patterns, especially in the coastal trade, were singular in nature—that is to say, craft arriving from New England, the West Indies, or another region tended to return directly to that region—we call this a regional pattern.

Ideally, in order to illustrate this pattern of regionalization for trade, the individual vessels should be tracked, using a computer to record each clearing and entering vessel, with a time differentiation to insure that no additional areas were visited prior to the vessel's next appearance in the port.[29] As vessels seldom visited New Jersey ports more than once or twice, this system cannot be employed, but a high degree of accuracy is still possible by using an area analysis that makes a correlation between the region a vessel arrived from or departed to and the original point of arrival or departure.

Using this method, an analysis of all overseas and coastal traffic emanating from Perth Amboy from 1722 to 1727 is highly revealing. For Atlantic traffic, just under 28 percent of vessels clearing Perth Amboy for overseas voyages had originally arrived from the transatlantic region; the nearly 60 percent that entered the harbor from Madeira, Liverpool, or some similar region returned overseas. These figures are more impressive when one considers that during this period most overseas traffic at Perth Amboy was appendaged to New York —63 percent, or twenty-three vessels, clearing the port of Perth Amboy for a transatlantic crossing arrived from New York—so that the return of vessels directly to their region of origin may have been as high as 80 percent clearing and 70 percent entering.

This pattern of direct trade becomes even more apparent when an analysis of coastwise shipping is made. Trade with New England during this period accounted for half of all harbor traffic. Of all the vessels that arrived in New Jersey from New England, 90 percent returned there. Of the ships leaving New Jersey bound for New England, 80 percent had originated in New England. Within the New England region there was not much lateral movement, almost all vessels returning directly to the colony of origin.[30]

Such trade patterns provide insight into the nature of mercantile commerce and merchant activity, especially of the small entrepreneurs. Rather than taking high risks for high profits and for the sake of adventure, New Jersey traders appear to have been conservative in business actions, seeking to counterbalance market risks by means of a stable and somewhat controlled trade. Rather than calling at numerous ports, merchants usually made specific trips to a predetermined port to pick up or deliver cargo, then returned to the home port. The larger shippers behaved in an almost identical manner, except they used a number of vessels to pick up and deliver from a centralized point. The overall voyage patterns for New England and probably for most coastal trade follow not intinerant patterns involving many markets and ports, but rather trade routes between colonies seldom interrupted by other voyages. While the sample was relatively small, it includes a wide range of registries from all locales, so one can assume that the pattern was not unique to New Jersey's ports. Rather it is one that can be more widely applied to the colonial scheme.

Local ports appear, then, to have conducted two variations of this direct coastwise trade. The first involved patterns set by specific individuals and conducted on a one-to-one basis; the second was a general trade based on the ports' function as suppliers and receivers for major ports. Work recently done on patterns of trade at New York and Philadelphia lends additional credence to this contention.[31] Working with computers, several historians have concluded that there was little triangular trade in American colonial commerce. Rather a pattern of voyages emerged that resembled an H. Key areas such as Philadelphia and New York acted as entrepôts, collecting goods from a wide area for shipment overseas and serving as distribution points for incoming goods in much the same manner.[32] If New Jersey's trade patterns were reliable indices, then Boston and the ports of Rhode Island apparently served a similar function. Within the framework of this theory, New Jersey's voyage pattern also indicated that the entrepôts collected and distributed directly to a far-flung group of local ports, not haphazardly but in an orderly manner. This suggests that a rather sophisticated information network existed between these major commercial centers and even the smallest ports.

As New Jersey's inland transportation system improved and its citizens increasingly used the colony's convenient inland waterways, the ports of entry ceased to function as significant feeders even for New England. Local towns or staging areas along New Jersey's many rivers and estuaries, unencumbered by the official bureaucracy associated with port clearances, became feeders to New York and Philadelphia, circumventing the need for services previously provided by Perth Amboy and Burlington. But even though the official New Jersey ports finally ceased active trading, their transactions provide a means of understanding many of the aspects of the colony's maritime and agricultural economy, which eventually led to almost complete dependence on neighboring colonies. Most important, the results of the computer analysis of the voyage patterns involving New Jersey's ports suggest that the standard theories of merchants and trade routes need to be reappraised. This analysis also lends support and further clarification to newer theories of trade, which focus on centralized entrepôts and regionalization rather than on theories of triangular trade routes in colonial maritime commerce. If the trade patterns of the New Jersey ports afford us some insights into the nature of colonial trade, a comparison with another lesser port in terms of the evolution of trading patterns and the relative growth of shipping at a port may well provide some additional understanding of this aspect of colonial economic development.

Comparison with Piscataqua, New Hampshire

New Jersey was but one of several colonies with lesser ports. Some were more successful than others, but all were dominated by major commercial centers in their immediate proximity, and to some extent their development and their patterns of trade were shaped by that domination. New Hampshire's port of Piscataqua, which included several towns (among them Newbury, York, and Portsmouth where the customs officer resided), was in many ways similar to New Jersey's ports.[33] At the end of the seventeenth century this port region was struggling to develop its potential against the encroachment of its trade by Boston entrepreneurs and was battling the indifference of the local assembly where factions with other interests lent little support and even blocked attempts by the governor and his council to foster trade.[34] As in New Jersey, port growth competed with land speculation and development and suffered from the internal strife among four rival groups over the title to lands—a dispute that was not resolved until the American Revolution.

Under these circumstances, while the lumber trade flourished with over ninety sawmills operating in the region, New Hampshire's port grew slowly.[35] In the years 1694 and 1695, Piscataqua gave the appearance of a bustling and economically viable port, but most of its trade was of very limited scope. Exports to other ports in New England constituted 74.8 percent of all Piscataqua's trade and 85.1 percent of the total outbound traffic.[36] Almost all of this trade was carried in vessels classified as sloops. But the sloops were of such size—the largest appears to have been about fifteen tons—that the port officer seldom bothered to record their tonnage, registry, or place of construction, noting only their destination (usually Boston) and their cargo (usually processed lumber or, rarely, a West Indian product being transshipped).[37] In fact, the port's activity was similar to the "boat traffic" that plied its trade from the New Jersey shores to New York and Philadelphia, carrying similar cargos as well as agricultural goods. This trade, unlike Piscataqua's, was not recorded, but perhaps the activity at the New Hampshire port gives us some sense of the extent and volume of New Jersey's "hidden trade." At Piscataqua this trade, constituting 85.1 percent of the outbound trade for the entire port, involved a relatively limited number of vessels. For instance, the sloop *Speedwell* made seven or eight trips to Boston primarily from May through August, loaded with wood in all stages of processing.[38] The vessels often returned in ballast or occasionally brought back consumer goods purchased for sale or personal use. Judgments concerning imports, however, are mostly speculative, for as at Perth Amboy, the customs officers either were not required or did not bother to record the arrival of these small inbound vessels.

If we disregard the local trade of the port, then its activity toward the end of the seventeenth century closely parallels that of the New Jersey ports in the same era. The number of vessels engaged in trade was quite small. In a two-year period (1694–95), out of a total of 191 vessels clearing or entering the port, only six trips involved overseas trade. The most significant part involved shipping a few masts—the beginning of what was later to become an important part of the colonies' trade relations with England.[39] Transatlantic trade also involved importing small amounts of wine from Madeira, but such activity was less significant to the development of trading patterns in New Hampshire than in New Jersey. Instead, the major thrust of trade, even at this early date, seems to have been with the West Indies. That trade accounted for 56.8 percent of all trade and 56.6 percent of exports, excluding the New England shuttle.[40] Barbados was the favored port of call for the beginning of this small but promising trade route. Exports included such local products as timber, boards, and, interestingly, some small masts. In return, rum, molasses, sugar, and bags of cotton were imported.

Like New Jersey, Piscataqua at this time was primarily a port of call with few large vessels entering her waters. Sloops constituted 38.8 percent, while ships, brigantines, and similar-sized vessels made up 49.4 percent. Furthermore, the ownership of these vessels seems to have rested elsewhere. Three decades later the port of Piscataqua, like the ports in New Jersey, had grown considerably, although the opinion of the customs commissioners was that the original potential of the Piscataqua district was not likely to be realized. The pay of the customs officer for the region, which was based on the expected activity of trade, had been downgraded in 1725 from one hundred pounds to forty.[41] The small-vessel or shuttle trade to Boston and the surrounding region, while still active, was no longer considered an "official" trade and now went unrecorded. In fact, trade with Boston increasingly relied on a developing road system, tending to draw local produce from New Hampshire and Connecticut overland to Boston much to the detriment of the local ports. This form of "hinterland piracy" was also similar to that in New Jersey.[42] The maritime traffic that was recorded in 1727 amounted to a total of eighty-five trips, with thirty-three entries and fifty-two departures.[43] A preponderance of larger vessels filled the harbor and the average tonnage of all vessels in that year was over fifty-seven tons.[44] An overseas trade pattern had emerged, but as was true at other small ports, there were no significant imports. Salt and iron were carried for ballast, and sometimes the cargo included small amounts of textiles or European goods. As with other small ports engaged in overseas trade, the vessels, having discharged their cargos elsewhere, most likely Boston, then sailed on to pick up a specialized cargo of lumber, small masts, and other timbers for use in shipbuilding.

The West Indies trade began to dominate around 1725, though it had begun to evolve at the turn of the century; approximately one-third of this trade went to Barbados and Antigua.[45] Timber products and, surprisingly, ship masts were exchanged for sugar, molasses, rum, and occasionally slaves. This trade was the primary means by which local merchants acquired wealth from maritime commerce.[46] About 10 percent of vessels journeyed to the South, especially Maryland and North Carolina, in an attempt to open up new avenues of trade. One vessel in five engaged in trade with what are now the Maritime Provinces of Canada.[47]

The similarities in the development of the New Jersey ports and Piscataqua are readily apparent. Neither was involved in heavy shipping trade with England or the continent. Instead, they relied on converting local resources into a profit primarily through trade to the

West Indies. Perth Amboy would add direct trade with the Canary Islands for wines. This type of trade was the economic mainstay, although both New Jersey and New Hampshire also relied upon a specialization of coastal trade: the New England maritime region for Piscataqua and the New England region for the New Jersey ports, first to Boston and later primarily to Rhode Island. In both colonies such trade was supplemented by infrequent southern trips and other short voyages of adventure.[48]

There were, however, marked differences in the development of shipping in New Hampshire and New Jersey, not so much in the evolving trade patterns but in the composition of the fleets in terms of ownership, registry, and size. Though Perth Amboy's harbor received 40 percent more vessels in a comparable time (sixty-eight outbound vessels and a similar number inbound in 1726), New England's port region was economically stronger and more viable. At Piscataqua over 80 percent of the vessels inward or outward bound were registered in New Hampshire. In 1727 over 57.6 percent were substantial vessels of forty or more tons.[49] Ships over one hundred tons were a common sight in the port; several vessels larger than two hundred tons were locally owned, as was one ship of over four hundred tons. In addition, there were numerous brigantines. The presence of these types of vessels, locally registered, compared with the overwhelming presence of sloops and schooners at Perth Amboy, represented a far greater outlay of capital and is an important indicator of the commitment to develop maritime commerce in the region.

The merchants who operated from Piscataqua represented another major difference in port evolution, and here the contrast is most striking. While some New Jersey merchants, such as members of the Parker, Stevens, and Johnston families, did own vessels and use the local ports, relatively few of the vessels using New Jersey's ports were owned by local merchants. At Piscataqua, on the other hand, many locally owned vessels used the port. For example, among those who might be judged substantial merchants were George Jeffry, who had a sloop and a brigantine active at the port; his neighbor, Joshua Pierce, who had two sloops, a brigantine, and a ship; William Pepperell, on his way to becoming a merchant-prince, who watched his four sloops and two brigantines ply their trade from that port; a Mr. Wieberd, with a ship and a snow in port; and a Mr. Sherburne, with two ships, a brigantine, and a sloop were among those entrepreneurs whose vessels were recorded as using Piscataqua in this single year.[50]

This difference in terms of capital expended and personal commitment and involvement in the life of the port is the most significant

Patterns of Trade

factor in a comparison of Piscataqua and New Jersey's ports. In the 1720s New Jersey's ports held promise, and its merchants hoped for considerable growth. Their hopes, however, were without firm foundation. Piscataqua, in contrast, was economically strong and capable of expanding.

In the next three decades, while Perth Amboy became stagnant and then began a process of gradual decline, Piscataqua steadily expanded. By 1743 a total of 136 trips was recorded by the naval officer, and by 1759 the number had grown by more than 50 percent.[51] The trade pattern established prior to 1730 showed no significant change. The West Indies route continued to grow in importance, encompassing 36 percent of trade in 1743 and 53.7 percent by 1759.[52] The southern region now provided a considerable portion of the overall trade, while locally, trade to Halifax and Newfoundland continued at a high level. Equally important to the port's growth was the fact that local ownership remained at a very high level throughout these years and most vessels using the port facility had been built in the immediate region. Many of the vessels using the port were ships and brigantines, and the average size of all vessels using the port was seventy-eight tons and those locally registered were sixty-four tons.[53] Perth Amboy, by contrast, had in the same period seen a scant number of the larger vessels. The average size of the vessels at Perth Amboy were more than fifty tons less, while the home fleet was composed mainly of sloops and schooners.[54] Based upon these comparisons, the difference in the capital expenditure is significant and indicates a wide disparity in terms of local financial commitment to encourage port growth.

The level of commitment at the two ports is also demonstrated by the involvement of local merchants. At Piscataqua in the 1740s and 1750s, the more established merchants worked to build up the port. They replaced older vessels with newer ones and increased the total number of vessels in their personal fleet. New entrepreneurs, who themselves often owned several vessels, also contributed to this expansion.[55] In New Jersey waters the close proximity of New York and Philadelphia had drawn many merchants away from their native ports. The Smith family at Burlington and the Stevens and Parker families at Perth Amboy often plied their trade through the neighboring provinces. This was especially true at Burlington, where by the 1750s almost all overseas trade went through Philadelphia. By the same decade at least half of Perth Amboy's maritime trade was conducted through partnerships or other arrangements.[56] Such arrangements seem to have increased in the following years. Although on occasion one of these snows or brigs would find its way to the New Jersey shores, it came more for convenience than as part of an established trading pattern.

Merchants in both New Jersey and New Hampshire had begun the eighteenth century with expectations that their ports would become major commercial centers. Hopes were not realized in either colony. Each instead assumed a maritime role as a lesser port, defined as one doing no substantial overseas trade. Their development suggests that the lesser ports assumed multiple functions. Those which remained viable, which avoided being absorbed by larger ports, did so by carrying on very limited or no direct trade that required official clearings or enterings with the commercial entrepôts in their immediate region, choosing instead to develop their own coastwide commerce. This was the course of events at Perth Amboy and Piscataqua, and, based on a limited amount of data, one can surmise that it was also true for the southern port of Sunbury, Georgia.

It appears that for the lesser ports without significant overseas trade three other avenues of commerce generally evolved. The trade with the West Indies was one such avenue of special importance. In the absence of overseas imports (the foundation upon which had been built the fortunes of Hancock, Beekman, Lopez, and other merchant-princes), this market, though it might be volatile, provided the means to move from a marginal economy to one of expansion and growth. As this study has indicated and additional data for the port at Sunbury, Georgia, supports, West Indian trade was an integral part of port development, and there was a clear relationship between the volume of trade to this region and the relative prosperity of the port.[57] In general, this trade contributed very significantly to the local economy.

The second avenue of trade for the lesser ports involved regional specialization. For Piscataqua, regional routes were to Halifax and Newfoundland; for Sunbury, the route was to Charleston, South Carolina; for New Jersey, specialized trade was conducted first with Boston, then Rhode Island.[58] This trade was narrowly defined as primarily a shuttle involving mostly locally produced goods, but it provided economic stability and was the foundation upon which much of the on-going activity of the port depended. As long as this trade existed, a port could be said to have retained some degree of viability.

Finally, there were the speculative routes involving what might be termed trade of economic opportunity. Such routes usually took vessels overseas to the Canary Islands, as was the case with those merchants operating out of New Jersey and southward to Maryland, the Carolinas, and Virginia.[59] When warranted, these routes would often take on a degree of permanence, as happened with the southern trade routes from Piscataqua.[60] The key to success, however, lay not only in the development of routes, but in the level of commitment of personnel and capital to the home port. This commitment at Piscataqua was substantial and continual, as the high degree of ownership, the involvement of local merchants, and the large number of "costly vessels" (brigs, snows, ships) clearly demonstrated, and by 1760 Piscataqua had become one of the most active of the lesser ports.

By contrast, New Jersey's commitment, professed at great length in numerous written communiques, was never translated into capital expenditures or personnel commitment, perhaps because prominent merchant families such as Parker, Stevens, and Neilson relied on land sales and development rather than maritime commerce as their major means of acquiring capital.[61] Maritime commerce was simply one of many business enterprises in which they were engaged, and its success was important but not crucial to their economic survival. This lack of commitment and the presence of nearby port facilities, through which mercantile activities could be adequately conducted and which were increasingly used by New Jersey merchants, compounded the problem of New Jersey ports by retarding their development and leaving New Jersey harbors languishing for want of trade.

Among the most important types of eighteenth-century sailing vessels used in maritime trade were (clockwise from left): the ship *(three masts, square rigging, square mainsails, and a bowsprit);* the brigantine *(two masts and square rigging);* the sloop *(one mast and fore-and-aft rigging, sometimes carrying square topsails); and the* schooner *(two or more masts and fore-and-aft rigging). Drawings of vessels in Charles G. Davis's* Shipping & Craft in Silhouette, *Publications of the Marine Research Society, no. 20 (Salem, Mass., 1929), no. 8, 25, 28, 51.*

5
Vessels, Crews, and Cargos

COMPUTER ANALYSIS OF BRITISH CUSTOMS RECORDS reveals the variety and nature of sailing vessels, crews, and cargos passing through New Jersey's ports in the eighteenth century. Several important national trends in armament, crew size, and related costs may be examined as they relate to smaller ports. The sizes and types of vessels engaged in colonial maritime commerce provide an additional means of ascertaining not only the nature of the trade of a given port, but also the state of mercantile development of the general area.

Vessel Size and Cargo

One means of measuring the rate of commercial growth is the total number of ocean-going vessels and the dates when they appear both in the harbor and as part of the home port fleet. Larger vessels, for example, with their larger cargo capacity, required more sophisticated marketing facilities. When such vessels were present in large numbers, shippers were likely to be merchants as well, maintaining permanent marketing facilities in the form of warehouses and retail stores. The larger the volume of trade, the greater the need for a network of factors to report on market conditions, to handle sales abroad, and to collect items for eventual export. These undertakings in turn required voluminous correspondence and detailed accounting systems, which were further indications of a maturing economic system. Moreover, the type of vessel using the harbor and the economic sophistication of the merchant class reflect the activity of trade within a given region. Changes in the fleet or in the composition of the merchant class usually herald a corresponding shift in the emphasis of trade to a given area.

The availability of liquid capital and the proclivity to invest it are other measures of growth and maturity in any business enterprise. The size of locally built or registered vessels often indicated the amount of capital available for maritime enterprises. Vessel gradation and tonnage can provide an important measure of economic potential and growth, since size and degree of sophistication of equipment determine cost. The appearance in a port of newer and more technologically advanced vessels, such as schooners and brigantines, indicates a prosperous port and shipbuilding industry. By analyzing the number and percentage of the types of vessels using the port, as well as the types being built locally, we can more fully evaluate the degree to which both the shipping and shipbuilding industry have evolved in a given place.

Accurate reconstruction of local conditions depends on the extent to which vessel size and cargo capacity can be determined. For the colonial period these criteria are difficult to use because shipbuilders seldom worked from blueprints, and the ship registry recorded neither the length nor width of the vessel. Theoretically, size and capacity could be determined by the reported tonnage. Tonnage, a measure of a vessel's capacity based upon the ancient "tun" rather than on weight, was determined by multiplying the length of the keel by the ship's breadth, then multiplying the result by one half the breadth, and finally dividing that figure by ninety-four. These figures were often inaccurate, however, because many shipowners adjusted the tonnage recorded on the registry to meet a particular situation.[1] Where port fees were based on tonnage, for example, owners reported the smallest believable capacity. But if a ship were hired by a governmental agency that paid by the ton, owners reported the largest capacity. In many cases, tonnage listings might be inaccurate by as much as twenty or thirty tons.[2]

Because the reported sizes of vessels are not wholly dependable statistics, the type of vessel is perhaps as significant as tonnage in indicating size and cost. Therefore, it is a crucial element in any estimation of the nature of the local economy. Even here inaccuracy prevails. Since the recordkeepers (naval officers and customs officials) were far from precise in describing the vessels that entered or cleared their ports, caution must be taken in constructing definitive statements, based on their records, about the economic situation of the period. Nevertheless, the information they provide is helpful in understanding the general pattern of economic and maritime development within a colony.[3]

Colonial officials classified vessels according to the way they were rigged, the number of masts employed, and the design of the hull. But regardless of how it was rigged, a vessel pointed at its stern rather than square-ended was usually called a pink. There were two types of rigging: square, in which the sails hang from cruciform spars (mast and cross yardarm), set perpendicular to the length of the hull; and fore-and-aft, in which they hang along the axis of the length of the hull. Brigs and ships, the basic oceanic vessels, were so designated by their square rigging on the mast and by the fact that the brigs had two masts and ships three. In the eighteenth century a full-rigged ship design (a vessel with three square-rigged masts) was always constant in terms of the number of masts and the type of rigging, but modifications of the brig design were frequent. A brig could be converted into a snow by the addition of a small mast or spar attached to the mainmast, from which a spanker was hoisted. A brigantine, on the other hand, had a fore-and-aft rigged mainmast.[4] New Jersey port officials were rather careless about maintaining these distinctions, and they sometimes listed both snows and brigantines simply as brigs.[5]

Deep-water vessels employed square-rigging almost exclusively because its greater sail capacity was required to move large, heavily laden vessels rapidly and economically over long distances. Square-rigged vessels had limited maneuverability and were less effective in coastal trade. But they had a real advantage once at sea, where the square rig could be used most effectively. For these reasons full-rigged ships and brigs were most often found in the transatlantic trade or in direct trade between major ports and the West Indies.

Modified deep-water vessels were employed when maritime commerce required a large cargo capacity and maneuverability, such as when frequent port calls along a coast to load or unload cargo were necessary—in the West Indies, for example. Brigantines and snows were built specifically for use in that region. For coastal trade, fore-and-aft rigged vessels were most desirable. Able to tack close to the wind and to come about rapidly, their greater mobility allowed them access to the many small inlets and bays that dotted the coast and to the rivers and smaller estuaries along which community landings or individuals' docks were located. At a time when capital and manpower were scarce, the fore-and-aft rigged vessel had an additional advantage, for it was cheaper to construct than the square-rigged vessel and required fewer men to sail.

The single-masted sloop was the most widely used cargo carrier in colonial America. Of varying tonnage the smallest sloops were engaged almost universally in local trade, while the larger ones were able to extend their trade area to include the West Indies. Occasionally a vessel as large as a brig was rigged as a sloop, giving it a transoceanic capacity. The larger the sloop, however, the greater the sail requirements on the single mast. When the ratio of sail to hull became disproportionate, the advantages of the rig in terms of manpower were lost; the greater sail area made the vessel unstable, and it could easily capsize. To increase the sail area while retaining the handling advantages of the sloop, colonial shipbuilders added more masts, thus proportioning but not reducing the amount of sail while still retaining the fore-and-aft rigging. The result was the schooner, a vessel that had a larger capacity than a sloop but was still highly maneuverable and required minimal crew. Multimasted, fore-and-aft rigged, the schooner was a technological advancement in ship building. It began to appear with some regularity in the 1720s, and it demonstrated a natural tendency toward regional specialization because it was employed almost exclusively in coastal and Caribbean waters.[6]

The composition of the New Jersey merchant fleet illustrated the changing nature of the colony's maritime commerce.[7] Brigs, ships, and other deep-water craft were abundant in the 1720s, the heyday of New Jersey shipping.[8] They gave the harbor a bustling appearance and reflected the wide variety of trade being conducted with all parts of the world. The New Jersey fleet then constituted slightly less than a third of the harbor traffic,[9] and it consisted of sloops, some schooners, and an occasional boat.[10] Since the average size was slightly over thirteen tons,[11] most vessels were too small to be employed in the West Indies trade by any but the most adventurous or foolhardy trader. Although forced by limitations of size to operate mostly in coastal waters, the fleet carried on surprisingly few transactions with the neighboring province of New York. That trade accounted for less than 1 percent of the coastal activity. Instead, over 60 percent of the trade was with New England, especially Rhode Island and Boston; the former received 38.1 percent and the latter 19.5 percent.[12]

The situation presented might seem somewhat incongruous. The vessels using Perth Amboy constituted a broad cross-section of types with a multitude of capabilities, while the local merchant fleet, which logically should have reflected a similar variety, was made up of small coastal vessels engaged almost entirely in lesser trade. The explanation lay in the fact that even though New Jersey ports were most active at this time, Perth Amboy was undergoing a period of commercial evolution. A burgeoning New Jersey fleet engaged in shuttle trade, with the capital generated and trade patterns established by the principal merchants, would in time come to assume a large portion of the hoped-for international trade. Perth Amboy registries would have eventually reflected a fleet not only capable of but engaged in every avenue of trade. This was certainly the pattern that emerged at Philadelphia.[13] But Perth Amboy's trend was downward rather than upward, and the dream of worldwide commerce died. The merchants abandoned grander aspirations and concentrated on those areas of trade to which they were limited by conditions for the most part beyond their control.

Shipping at Perth Amboy generally decreased after 1730, as New York successfully wooed most of the deep-water traffic to its own facilities. The second phase of Perth Amboy's development, from the 1730s to the conclusion of the French and Indian War, saw a gradual increase in the percentage of vessels registered there and using the harbor.[14] From a low of 32.8 percent in the 1720s, the figure rose to slightly more than 58 percent in the 1740s. It then declined slightly in the mid-1750s and early 1760s, with the number of New Jersey vessels comprising no more than half of all port traffic.[15] During several periods the number of New Jersey vessels using the port varied a great deal. In the late 1740s, for example, the home registry rose for several years to over 70 percent, as merchants in particular and New Jerseyans in general became concerned about the hazards of war with France. They kept their vessels within the safer confines of home waters. Even with these oscillations, the available port records from 1733 to 1764 indicate that the New Jersey fleet accounted for an average of more than 56 percent of all harbor traffic. Clearly, Perth Amboy was in a state of gradual decline after the 1720s, but the port was never a mere stopping place for other vessels and continued to retain much of its own commerce through a substantial fleet of vessels owned and operated by New Jerseyans.

Equally important in analyzing Perth Amboy's commercial development were the subtle changes in the types of vessels and the increase in tonnage after 1730. Sloops continued to dominate and comprised slightly more than half of the fleet. Schooners comprised over one-quarter of the vessels. Some deep-water vessels, mostly brigs, were also integrated into the Perth Amboy contingent.[16] The average size of these craft had risen by more than ten tons since the 1720s; a considerable number of vessels were larger than forty tons.[17] The introduction of large sloops and the more advanced schooners, which accounted for almost 80 percent of the New Jersey fleet,[18] indicated the regional nature and specialization of a predominantly coastal and West Indies trade. It also allowed this segment of the fleet to operate more fully within New Jersey's sphere of trade. Deep-water vessels of New Jersey registry, which made up 10 percent of the fleet, operated differently than the coastal fleet. These brigs and snows contributed to the general West Indies trade, but on transatlantic ventures the same vessels returned to the same destinations again and again. New Jersey's transoceanic trade was far from being worldwide in scope or design. It was really an appendage to the coastal trade pattern. Small entrepreneurs probably used the offshore craft for limited ventures, not as part of major mercantile operations such as those of the Beekmans in New York or the Browns in Providence. Nevertheless, the vessels represented a considerable outlay of capital.

Age of Vessels

The outlay of capital for these and other vessels, which reflected the economic growth and prosperity of New Jersey's ports and lesser ports elsewhere, may be further evaluated through the development of a shipbuilding index. This index is established by recording the difference between the reported year in which the vessel was built and the date of entry or departure at the port. A vessel entering port in 1742 that had been built in 1737 would have an index number of five. The index indicates the number of years the vessel had been in service and is referred to in this context as *vessel age*. Using this system one finds that from 1720 to 1740 the mean or average age of all vessels using the port of Perth Amboy was relatively low (less than four and a half years in service based on over 450 observations.)[19] The average age of vessels (mostly sloops and schooners) registered in New Jersey was slightly over three and a half years.[20] The relative newness of the New Jersey vessels is a strong indicator of the availability of capital in the colony during this period. It suggests a willingness on the part of those engaged in maritime commerce to invest their money. Apparently the same held true for those others who used the New Jersey harbor.

Investment in shipbuilding and maritime commerce does not appear to have diminished over the next thirty years. In fact, vessels in New Jersey waters tended to be slightly newer than in previous decades.[21] If the age of vessels using the port is at all representative, the maritime economy remained strong. Though relatively few New Jerseyans engaged in commerce directly through their own ports, those who chose to do so continued to invest at a fairly high rate in new vessels. The New Jersey merchant-shippers showed a need or willingness to extend capital, which continued to be available for such ventures, as in earlier years. The shipbuilding index, when applied to vessels registered in New Jersey, strongly indicates the relative strength of the economy and the economic welfare of those engaged in seaborne commerce. The vessel age for all vessels at Burlington differed from that at Perth Amboy by less than half a year, with an average of three and a half years in service.[22]

Salem, with vessels averaging about five and a half years in service, was not significantly different.[23] But one might speculate that because Salem was from 1720 to 1740 primarily a feeder for Philadelphia and only occasionally a port of call, vessels used in this trade represented a less dynamic aspect of maritime commerce. As a result there was a less significant financial commitment as expressed in rapid reinvestment in vessels. This theory gains support from the regional trade patterns in which older vessels were most often used on less active routes, while newer vessels were to be found in the West Indies and other active trading regions. Far more significant, however, was the rapid replacement of vessels in all New Jersey ports and trading areas. Vessels plying New Jersey waters averaged no more than six years in service; those at Perth Amboy and Burlington averaged less than four years.[24]

Though few larger vessels (forty tons or more) entered Perth Amboy and even a smaller number of these vessels were registered at this port, there does not appear to have been a significant difference in vessel age between those of less than forty tons and those of greater tonnage. Replacement of vessels on the basis of a tonnage division at forty tons took place on the average less than a year apart, a factor to consider further in terms of capital expenditure and cost efficiency.[25]

In comparison, there were many vessels over forty tons in the New Hampshire port of Piscataqua. The average age of vessels employed in maritime commerce was similar to that of New Jersey's ports. Data available for 1727 is too limited to allow for any meaningful judgment beyond the suggestion that a number of relatively new vessels with less than three years service used the port. The average age of all vessels engaged in maritime activity at Piscataqua in 1743 was under four and a half years. Yet average size of the vessels was 92.5 tons, with locally registered vessels fractionally newer on the average.[26] Sixteen years later the average age of the vessels plying New Hampshire's waters was basically unchanged. The average vessel age from 1743 had increased slightly less than half a year for all vessels and slightly more than half a year for those vessels registered in New Hampshire.[27] From the data it would appear that, as had been the case in Perth Amboy, replacement capital over a significant period of time (more than thirty years) had been not only readily available but readily used. Replacement at Piscataqua as well as Perth Amboy does not appear to have been significantly influenced by tonnage costs. The aggregate difference in average ship age between vessels using these two ports was a matter of months (3.9 years for vessels at Perth Amboy compared to 4.6 years at Piscataqua).[28]

In the South, the ports of Savannah and Sunbury, Georgia, showed a slightly longer period of service for vessels in their waters than that in the ports we have previously examined. Though some of the information about the ports is a decade beyond that for New Jersey and New Hampshire, there is nothing to indicate that a comparison cannot be drawn. Vessels using Savannah averaged just under five years of age, while the smaller facility at Sunbury handled vessels that averaged slightly under six years of age. Regional patterns of trade in both instances showed only minor differences in vessel age. The exception was transatlantic trade, where the tendency was to keep the largest and most costly vessels in service longer.[29]

In comparing the length of service for vessels at New Jersey and New Hampshire ports with those at two ports in Georgia, one is again struck by the similarity of vessel age. The aggregate index shows vessels at Savannah were only a year older than those at Perth Amboy and those at Sunbury only two years older. The figures indicate vessel age was only slightly higher at Sunbury than at Salem, New Jersey, while it was lower at Savannah. New Hampshire's slightly older fleet was even closer in vessel age to Savannah-based vessels than to that of the Perth Amboy or Burlington fleets. Thus, while vessels in New Jersey and New Hampshire appear to have been in most instances slightly newer, the result perhaps of greater involvement with maritime commerce as a major means of livelihood, the differences at lesser ports between New England, the middle colonies, and the

South were apparently not very great.[30]

The study of vessel age in small or lesser ports shows that regardless of the frequency with which they might be visited or the extent of the trade the ports might generate, they were never so far out of the mainstream of maritime commerce that they became backwater areas serviced primarily by vessels that had outlived their usefulness and were no longer able to engage profitably in trade along major commercial routes. In short, they had not become colonial versions of the twentieth-century tramp steamer. All of the evidence presented so far indicates that few, if any, colonial vessels operating in coastwise and West Indies trade ever reached such age. The shipbuilding index also indicates that merchants operating out of the small ports, even when port activity was stagnant or in decline, seldom used older vessels that were less costly. Nor did these smaller entrepreneurs retain vessels for long periods in order to realize fully their investment. Instead, it appears that owners of vessels registered at small ports mirrored their counterparts in the larger entrepôts, at least in regard to the expenditure of capital to replace old vessels or build new ones. One must question the assumption that larger vessels were kept in service longer than smaller ones because the former were generally more costly to build and operate. This assumption may be valid for the largest ships, but it does not appear to have been true for vessels exceeding forty tons, such as brigs, brigantines, snows, and smaller ships. In fact, statistics on tonnage distribution and ship age for both Perth Amboy and Piscataqua show vessels over forty tons being replaced more rapidly than those under forty tons.[31] This may be something of an anomaly, but it appears that, based on vessel age, there was little to differentiate vessels under forty tons (primarily sloops and schooners) and those over forty tons, thus suggesting that the concept of using a cost-ratio relationship of tonnage and vessel longevity as a criterion for estimating shipping cost and productivity may warrant more careful scrutiny. By the same token, the limited lifespan of vessels suggests that total expenditures of capital for vessels may have been greater than has previously been estimated.

Finally, our examination of vessel age indicates several trends in the colonial maritime economy. It appears that despite American folklore of unparalleled craftsmanship and seamanship, the need to replace vessels because of failure in these two areas was exceedingly high. Considerable capital had to be expended regularly just to maintain a status quo in this area of economic endeavor. The low vessel age also reflects the continual introduction of growing numbers of newly built vessels into maritime commerce.

Shipbuilding

Although there remains considerable controversy over the extent and nature of economic growth during the colonial period, it would appear from our analysis of the shipbuilding index that the low age of vessels reflects not only the availability of capital but a surplus for use in the economic sector for continued expansion. This indicates not simply economic development but, for maritime commerce, substantial economic growth.

The composition of the New Jersey fleet and the shipbuilding index seems to indicate that although New Jersey's major port was declining, it was far from an impoverished colony. The number of shippers declined more because of lack of merchant commitment and support from the colony as a whole for maritime ventures than because of a lack of capital. There always remained a dogged few who, determined to operate from New Jersey ports, invested desire, knowledge, and capital to make a profit.

This hard core of optimists was present from the inception of the ports. They had capital for the purchase of vessels, a factor that undoubtedly encouraged the development of shipbuilding in the colony. Indeed, those shipping from Perth Amboy came to rely almost totally on local shipbuilders for their vessels. From 1722 to 1727, for example, 61 percent of New Jersey–registered vessels were built locally, while the figure fluctuated, reaching as high as 90 percent, between 1733 and 1764.[32] The composition of the local fleet generally kept pace with developments in the shipbuilding industry. Unlike the fleet, however, the shipbuilding industry continued to grow, supplying not only New Jersey but neighboring colonies as well with a wide variety of maritime carriers.

The increase in trade with the West Indies beginning in the 1640s and 1650s provided a major impetus for colonial shipbuilding. By 1700, New England had a firmly established shipbuilding industry; Pennsylvania, Virginia, and Maryland followed suit.[33] In the next few decades almost every colony had developed a shipbuilding industry to some extent. First the Dutch and then the English settlers saw in New Jersey's forests of cedar and oak trees a great potential for this trade.[34] Samuel Groome, a prominent figure in East Jersey's early development, had himself attempted to develop this potential for shipbuilding and commerce, but his death in 1683 left his shipbuilding endeavors incomplete, with the first vessel to be built in the colony still on its stocks.[35]

For the next two decades little was apparently done to extend Groome's initial venture, but by the turn of the century others had begun this craft on a moderate scale. Between 1702 and 1708 builders in East Jersey constructed four sloops and a large brigantine; at Burlington a single sloop and brigantine were built.[36] Boston in this period produced 143 vessels and Piscataqua twenty-six.[37] New Jersey's shipbuilding industry grew along with its port facilities.

In West Jersey, however, this growth was not as great as has generally been believed. Although Philadelphia was the primary market for West Jersey vessels, recent work on shipbuilding in the Delaware River region shows that just 3.7 percent of Philadelphia's vessels were built across the Delaware.[38] In the ten-year period from 1730 to 1740, shipbuilding records for the Delaware valley show 285 vessels built in Pennsylvania and twenty-seven in West Jersey. In the next decade sixteen vessels were registered as being built in West Jersey, compared with 261 in Pennsylvania.[39] Vessels built in West Jersey remained comparatively small. A study of output over time for shipbuilding in the Delaware region shows that mean size increased for all vessels, but a close examination reveals that though there was great variation in size among those vessels built in New Jersey, the average size of vessels built from 1722 to 1775 remained unchanged, averaging thirty or more tons smaller than those built in the Quaker colony.[40]

New Jersey merchants did help to stimulate the industry by purchasing locally built vessels. In the 1720s over 30 percent of sailing vessels at Perth Amboy were built locally.[41] But the volume at New Jersey ports was relatively small. New Jersey timbers may well have produced the vessels without which the expansion of trade at New York and Philadelphia would not have been so rapidly accomplished, but it appears that New Jersey did not contribute in any other major way to the building of those vessels.

The English government's concern over naval self-sufficiency also contributed to the industry's growth. Prodded by the Lords of Trade, colonial officials in New Jersey and other colonies began a concerted effort after 1714 to involve the populace in the production of naval stores in order to insure English self-sufficiency in this crucial area. New Jersey contributed to the scheme in the area of manufacturing. The production of pitch and tar was, however, fraught with difficulties, and these commodities were not produced regularly.[42] Hemp, on the other hand, was grown quite successfully and in sufficient quantities to be exported occasionally.[43] Contributing to the development of the industry was the publicity created by colonial officials concerning ship-related industry, the eventual production of these commodities, and the availability of timber for masts and planking. There seems to have been considerable local interest and support for such an enterprise, but such support was not directed toward maritime commerce per se. Local legislation from 1714 to 1775 reflected the concern that the export of timber would be injurious, especially to shipbuilding; one of the avowed purposes of acts limiting the export of lumber or timber was to protect the shipbuilding industry.[44]

The nature of the industry was such that it could, to some extent, exist apart from maritime commercial centers. Vessels were constructed not only in the immediate areas of the major ports but also throughout the colony, at Shrewsbury, Newbridge,[45] Little Egg Harbor,[46] or wherever there were rivers or estuaries capable of floating such craft. That shipbuilding activities were dispersed throughout the colony is easily documented, because areas of concentrated population such as Perth Amboy and Woodbridge were often designated by name in the official registry as the place of construction.

Building large vessels such as ships, brigs, or snows required a more permanent facility that used a skilled work force of ship's carpenters, caulkers, sailmakers, and others. But smaller vessels, including large sloops, could be and often were built by farmers who began working on them after the fall harvest had been completed. In the colonial period it was not unusual to see these part-time builders dragging vessels, sometimes literally built in their backyards, over the snow with horse or oxen and down to the water's edge.[47] This cottage industry produced vessels rapidly. Farmers and others such as small builders could not afford to tie up capital by allowing vessels or even timber to season, nor were they likely to have on hand the large amounts of timber that allowed for careful selection and matching of woods. The result was poorer-quality vessels, but such low overhead that the price was greatly reduced.[48] Vessels built in New Jersey were attractive to prospective buyers in neighboring provinces because vessels built in the countryside used relatively inexpensive labor and readily available timber and thus were less expensive. From 1722 to 1727, for example, evidence for Perth Amboy shows that almost a third of vessels built in New Jersey were registered in New York.[49]

But even if vessels built in New Jersey were sold in neighboring colonies, shipbuilding was never a major source of economic development in the colony. The construction and repair work of New Jersey's ships' carpenters was limited to some extent by the financial resources that local merchants were willing to commit, as well as by the level of commerce through the three legal ports.[50] Some such carpenters developed not a flourishing local industry but rather a catch-as-catch-can operation that used shipbuilding as a capital supplement to other enterprises in which they were involved. This was especially true for the agrarian population. By such enterprises the New Jersey farmer could supplement his farm income without changing his lifestyle. Since the intercolonial demand for sailing craft almost always exceeded the supply, it was not necessary to engage in or even support maritime commerce in order to reap the economic benefits of a shipbuilding industry. But New Jersey's shipbuilding industry would have been better served by a more developed local shipping establishment.

The relationship between vessel size, the number of crew employed, and armament compared over time may be used to estimate changes in maritime productivity. These changes in turn allow for a better understanding of economic growth. Numerous works have indicated that favorable changes in the ratio of tons, guns, and men occurred by the beginning of the eighteenth century and are attributable in part to the suppression of pirates and privateering.[51] This accomplishment greatly reduced the hazards associated with maritime trade and was reflected immediately in lower insurance costs for vessels. There also occurred a major change in vessel configuration. Large, heavily manned and multi-gunned vessels that had been needed to prevent seizure on the high seas were now replaced by smaller lightly armed or unarmed vessels with fewer men. The result was a further decrease in operating costs.[52]

Crew Size

Studies of maritime commerce focusing on entrepôts such as New York and Boston throughout the eighteenth century show that while the size of colonial vessels remained fairly constant, the number of tons per man increased over time (i.e., fewer men were required to operate the vessel) and armament, especially after 1763, declined significantly. The decrease in guns and men per vessel was the principal indication of continuing economic productivity and growth at the major ports, for wages were constant, shipbuilding costs increased only slightly, and vessel speed remained virtually unchanged.[53] Cost reduction was also evident at the lesser ports. At Piscataqua the ratio of change of tons to men closely paralleled that at New York and Boston; at Perth Amboy changes were similar but less dramatic.

Throughout the 1720s and the 1730s the tons-to-men ratio at Perth Amboy was 5.3; in the next three decades this ratio improved little more than 0.2 percent. More significant was the reduction by almost half in armament carried by vessels in Perth Amboy's waters.[54] Yet such aggregate data, especially regarding tonnage and men, is misleading and belies important changes in productivity as reflected in a regional analysis.

In its formative years regional specialization had not yet evolved in terms of the type or size of vessel to be most economically employed. Vessel utilization had not been matched to market, thus the tons-to-men ratio in the New England region was relatively high. There was one sailor for every 3.7 tons, and vessels averaged under eleven and a half tons. Small cargos and relatively high manpower drove up the cost per mile. The overall cost for trade in the New England region was high as well. Similarly, the West Indies trade to and from Perth Amboy used more men per vessel than would have been expected.[55]

Vessels registered in New Jersey showed a more pronounced tendency in this direction, with an average of more than three men employed aboard a vessel of less than ten tons on runs to Boston, Rhode Island, and other New England ports and slightly more than six men to a vessel of approximately twenty-two tons operating in the Caribbean.[56] These two areas, New England and the West Indies, were important in the earlier stages of Perth Amboy's development and would continue to be active trading regions for that port in the future. As such these trading patterns tended to evolve more rapidly in terms of economic efficiency than other less popular trade routes. In the 1740s, for example, vessels trading to New England showed an improved tons-to-men ratio. The ratio increased by more than two tons per man, and the vessel size more than doubled. West Indian trade gained one and a half tons per man, and vessel size increased by more than ten tons.[57] Thus, in both these crucial trade areas there was significant improvement in shipping productivity, lowering the cost in trade in these regions, a factor not readily apparent in the total aggregate for the port. Similarly, at Piscataqua the total improvement in the tons-to-men ratio from 1727 to 1743 showed no appreciable difference from that recorded in New Jersey for the West Indies. From 1743 to 1759, however, the difference was almost one ton per man. As at Perth Amboy, this condition, an indication of rapid improvement in this area of trade, is not readily revealed in the total activity of the port.[58]

Cost efficiency as measured by a decline in armament and men did occur in varying degrees at the lesser and smaller ports as it had at the entrepôts. It might initially appear that a port such as Perth Amboy, less active and less viable than Piscataqua, was also not as cost effective in terms of the number of men required to operate vessels engaged in various regions of trade.[59] But other factors tended to make vessel and cost effectiveness in New Jersey competitive with other ports.

Vessels operating out of Perth Amboy to the West Indies in the 1740s and 1750s averaged over forty-two tons; those out of Piscataqua in 1759 averaged just under ninety tons. The larger vessels made far more efficient use of manpower, requiring approximately one man per eleven tons, compared with the small vessels' need for approximately one man for every six tons. In Savannah, Georgia, there were vessels engaging in trade to and from New England that were in excess of fifty-five tons with a respectable ratio of nine tons per man; vessels operating from Perth Amboy to New England averaged thirty tons less and required proportionally a third more crew to operate.[60]

Economic advantage clearly rested with the larger vessels, yet several factors made them less than cost effective. A major problem for these vessels was underutilization.[61] In an era when the acquisition and sale of cargo was conducted on a very small scale, the larger vessels often found it necessary to assemble cargos from several sources. Even then vessels often sailed with unused space. The use of middlemen to help assemble a cargo and the failure to fill all available space raised any venture's total cost. In contrast, those shipping out of Perth Amboy with smaller vessels were usually able to acquire their cargo at a single location. Even when this was not possible they could still be filled to capacity more rapidly than vessels double or triple their size. One problem smaller vessels encountered was that sometimes cargo had to be stacked in tiers on deck and secured with ropes and boards, making the vessel unstable and thus dangerous to operate at sea. Nevertheless, smaller vessels seldom sailed without full cargo.

Similar conditions prevailed in the West Indies trade. In a region where one or two vessels could flood the market, the smaller vessels had an advantage in being able to dispose of their cargo more easily. Shippers operating from such small ports as Perth Amboy had an advantage, for those vessels of twenty to forty tons that made up so much of their trade volume were often better suited to the regional market than were the vessels from the larger ports. There is strong evidence that vessels from the smallest ports, especially in the New England area, operated almost exclusively in the West Indies.[62] Although they lacked the flexibility of larger vessels sailing to many different trading zones, the average Perth Amboy vessel seems to have been more cost effective in space utilization.

Vessel cost in terms of capital construction was another factor in equalizing operating costs between larger and smaller vessels, for the relative advantage in cost of crew was more than compensated for by the higher cost of building larger vessels. Brigs, snows, and other vessels over forty tons, in order to be more cost effective than smaller vessels, had to be maintained in service for an appreciably longer time. But as our shipbuilding index has indicated, there was only a minimal difference between building and replacing vessels under forty tons and those over forty tons.[63]

The vessels operating at Perth Amboy, although lacking the larger vessels' flexibility for trade and unable to generate the volume of trade necessary to expand the port, were able to operate on a competitive basis with larger and seemingly more cost-efficient vessels from more active ports by employing a pattern of limited regional trade with vessels adapted to the market.

The eighteenth century saw improved conditions at lesser ports. Reduced vessel cost and increased vessel efficiency worked to reduce operating costs. Most striking was the reduction in vessel armament, which made both building (iron was extremely expensive) and operating (six men were required to operate a single cannon) vessels cheaper, a condition paralleled in the shipping industry throughout colonial America.

The reduction in crew costs and the vessel efficiency that resulted at the lesser ports in the eighteenth century is an important indication of economic growth. But variations from port to port show that a study of cost effectiveness in tonnage must include an examination of regional patterns, lest we give a distorted view of the nature of economic growth in maritime commerce during this period. Even the most cursory analysis of selected regions for vessels operating out of Perth Amboy and Piscataqua displays sufficient differences to suggest that similar analyses of larger ports are necessary if we are to evaluate not only economic growth but the nature of that growth.

Construction, Design, and Costs

Like other colonial shipbuilders, New Jerseyans constructed several types of vessels, but the most popular was the sloop. Simple in design and construction, it was also the least expensive to build. In the 1720s the problems associated with the early stages in the development of shipbuilding—not so much a lack of capital in New Jersey as a lack of facilities, aged or seasoned timber, and skilled craftsmen for the construction of large vessels—made the sloop more practical from the builder's point of view. Sloops accounted for almost 90 percent of the vessels built in New Jersey and registered in the colony during that period. As the industry became more sophisticated and as shipyards began to appear with greater frequency in populous areas, this figure decreased dramatically. But throughout the colonial period sloops accounted for over 50 percent of locally built vessels.[64]

Many schooners were also built in New Jersey. Generally larger than sloops, they were cheaper to build than corresponding deep-water craft. The schooner increased in popularity during the eighteenth century; as the pattern of trade became more regional, the demand for schooners became greater, and shipbuilders in New Jersey eventually came to devote slightly more than a quarter of their efforts to producing this type of craft.[65] One reason for this was that sloops and schooners might be built for general sale (a completely outfitted sloop might run approximately £600), but deep-water craft required a far greater outlay of capital.

Although New Jersey shipbuilding costs were undoubtedly less, the cost of building a ship in Philadelphia gives us an idea of cost. In 1740 the hundred-ton ship *Mary* fetched a price of £1,123 for building, ironwork, and outfitting. Six years earlier the eight-ton ship *John and Anna* had cost its owners £1,256, while a completely outfitted ship had cost Elias Bland and Company over £3,500.[66] Such high cost often led New Jerseyans to build only by contract with individuals or groups. Much of the capital for such ventures came from outside New Jersey.[67] It was fairly common to have snows, brigs, and brigantines built in New Jersey on the registries of neighboring colonies. The forty-five-ton snow *Mercury* is typical. It was built in New Jersey in 1737 and occasionally used New Jersey ports, but it was financed by Philadelphia merchants who registered her in that city.[68]

The records indicate that after 1732 approximately 14 percent of the harbor traffic identified as locally built were deep-water craft.[69] These figures provide a rough gauge to the relative percentage of large craft fashioned in New Jersey. Although most of the vessels averaged only slightly over twenty-five tons, the New Jersey shipbuilders were capable of producing vessels comparable to any in the colonies. Building a 120-ton vessel was unusual, but not beyond the ability of those at Perth Amboy.[70] Burlington also had the capacity to build large vessels. In 1744 the shipyard at Barbarroux wharf, located at the foot of Talbot Street, turned out the privateer *Marlborough*, which could carry a crew of 150 men.[71] Indeed, as commercial shipping declined at Burlington, shipbuilding probably compensated somewhat for the economic slack, for this industry had been economically important since the early part of the century.[72]

Non-trading vessels also constituted a portion of the industry. Fishermen, like farmers, had long periods of idleness, and during these lulls fishermen and their families built many of the small fishing craft required in the trade. New Jerseyans also built special craft for transportation along New Jersey waterways. The most famous of these were the Durham boats, bargelike vessels sixty feet long, eight feet wide, and almost four feet deep. Durham boats carried grain, ore, flour, and other materials down the Delaware River to Philadelphia.[73] Such vessels, because they were not involved in inter-colonial trade, went unregistered and thus are largely undocumented. But the overwhelming evidence is that shipbuilding in New Jersey was an active economic enterprise, not a developing industry.

There were many opportunities for building vessels, since maritime shipping during this period was a hazardous business with frequent loss of vessels and human lives. Ships were not built for the crew's safety. Rather, they were designed to provide maximum capacity for the cargo. The most flexible design was a barrel shape, which relied primarily on ballast for stability and therefore was notoriously unstable.[74] Colonial newspapers abound with reports of sailing vessels lost through capsizing. New Jersey ships were apparently no exception, as the following news items indicate: "A Boat going from Amboy for Middletown was overset, and two Men in her Drowned"; "a small Sloop coming in suppos'd to be an Egg harbour Man, was seen from that Island [Staten Island] to overset near the East Bank, and no Relief being possible, in all probability they were all lost."[75]

Aside from the hazards engendered by design, many colonial ships were built with inappropriate timber that was quick to rot or with unseasoned timber that shrank.[76] In either case, vessels so built were likely to spring sudden and massive leaks. This was apparently what happened to a boat headed to New York from New Jersey. Having sprung a leak off Middletown, it sank upright in about ten feet of water, the top of its mast providing a refuge for the survivors, who clung to it for twelve hours before being rescued. William Branford, master of the sloop *Albany*, was likewise a victim of this unhappy fate. Bound from New Brunswick for the West Indies, the *Albany* sprang a leak at sea. The sloop sank, but Branford and his crew were fortunate in being rescued by a passing vessel.[77]

The basic problems of material and design were intensified by the severity of the weather, which in itself accounted for heavy ship losses; storms, sudden squalls, or ice conditions caused many vessels to be "driven ashore" and "stoved to pieces." Added to these natural hazards was an apparently high degree of poor seamanship illustrated, for example, when, through lack of judgment on the part of the captain, vessels ran aground and were usually lost.[78] Finally, there was the continual hazard of wartime privateers and peacetime pirates whose raids took a toll of New Jersey's as well as all colonial shipping.[79] The hazards of construction, of nature, and of man combined to make commerce risky for merchants. Ship losses accounted for sufficient turnover virtually to insure the success of the shipbuilding industry.[80]

Shipmasters and Sailors

The men who operated the vessels (the master, the supercargo, and the sailors) played an integral part in the shipping industry. The crews of New Jersey ships, as well as the crews of ships using the colony's ports, provided a good cross-section of shipping life, though there were some local variations. In all cases there was a shipmaster or captain who had ultimate responsibility for the craft's destination and safety. The captain's business relationship with the shipowners reflected the nature of the trade. In some cases he was simply an employee of the vessel's owner or owners, this was most often the case when the vessel on which he served was large and costly, when the vessel was part of a small fleet owned by an individual or family, or when the vessel was primarily an investment of owners whose main concern was not maritime trade.[81] In other instances, the shipmaster might be an employee of the owner but also a relative; such an arrangement might be preferred because it was assumed that the bonds of kinship would insure greater care and responsibility for the vessel and cargo. Finally, there were many instances in which the master was either full or part owner of the vessel he commanded. This occurred most often among small entrepreneurs whose livelihood depended almost exclusively on maritime pursuits. When the master was essentially an employee of the owner, he was not always responsible for a vessel's cargo, although he was responsible for the craft itself. If the vessel were a large one, or if it carried a valuable cargo, the owners would add to the crew a trusted business associate to act as supercargo, with responsibility for selling or procuring cargo. For the most part, however, the shipmasters operated in this capacity.

Masters, as well as supercargos, were part of the maritime life in the New Jersey ports. At any one time one might encounter captains from such vessels as the schooner *Anne and Judith* in Perth Amboy harbor. Her captain, Samuel Vincent, newly arrived from the French West Indies, might be found with his partner, Caleb Stelle, discussing this rare voyage or how best to dispose of the cargo of Muscovado sugar, molasses, indigo, and four black servants. At another time one might find at the dock the snow *Joseph and Betty*, its cargo of bushels of wheat and pipe staves recently stored below. Joseph Manesly, captain and sole owner of this British-built vessel, might have taken the opportunity to dine for a reasonable price at the residence of one of the local widows. No doubt he relished every morsel, knowing it would be his last good meal until arriving in Madeira. As for Samuel Bradshaw, captain of the ninety-ton ship *Anne and Sarah*, at anchor in the harbor, there would be little time for camaraderie. He was employed by Joseph Cressoenor, Samuel Stairts, and Thomas Davis and Company (London), and most likely served for wages and privileges. He was also the ship's supercargo and would be expected to spend his time diligently scouring Perth Amboy, New Brunswick, or even New York for a suitable cargo (wheat, Indian corn, lumber at a reasonable price) to be shipped to the Canary Islands.[82]

Although all categories of personnel were represented at Perth Amboy, the limited activity of the harbor, as well as the fact that most vessels using that facility were under twenty-eight tons, seems to indicate that masters who owned their own vessels dominated the port. These individuals, due to their limited resources, were most likely to own the smaller craft and to work the smaller ports. An analysis of the master-owner relationship at Perth Amboy after the 1720s indicates that such entrepreneurs did not completely control the trade, but the small shippers, captaining craft of slightly over eighteen tons, accounted for 41.9 percent of the harbor traffic and thus played a significant role in the commercial life of the port.[83]

The more than 57 percent of shipmasters employed by others at Perth Amboy usually commanded small vessels that were restricted to coastal trade.[84] The majority of masters who were not owners were employed by larger merchant-shippers using several small vessels in a shuttle service to pick up cargos and deliver them to New Jersey ports, as well as to a host of large and small ports along the coast. At

Burlington small entrepreneurs did not dominate trade, even though 60 percent of shipmasters were also owners.[85] This group probably had less influence on trade at Burlington than it did at Perth Amboy, because the majority of these masters were probably not small shippers; the average size of their vessels was larger than those at Perth Amboy, with most capable of transatlantic travel.[86] These masters were more likely to be substantial merchants or investors who preferred to protect their investments by overseeing the trading operations themselves. This contention seems to be borne out by the fact that many Burlington shipmaster-owners were in partnership with several other investors.

Although these masters sailed vessels with a great deal of trade flexibility, the pattern at Burlington was again similar to that of Perth Amboy in that it was mostly shuttle trade. As earlier noted, Philadelphia, not Burlington, was the focal point for trade in the Delaware River region. Although captains might clear from Burlington to an ultimate destination in Europe or the West Indies, Burlington was a secondary port of call within the sphere of the larger Philadelphia trade.

During the second half of the eighteenth century, the dual pattern of trade as revealed in the master-owner relationships persisted. By the end of the 1750s, however, we do begin to see a shift at Perth Amboy, which perhaps indicates that the smaller entrepreneurs, many of whom were from New Jersey, had abandoned their enterprises and left the field to a few larger shippers.[87]

Masters, whether owners or employees, constituted only a part of the vessel's operating personnel. There were also, of course, the sailors. Few of the men who made up the crews of the New Jersey fleet were born to the trade or consistently followed it.[88] The majority were fishermen, farmers, or sons of farmers, who periodically took to the maritime trade for adventure or profit and then returned to their original occupations. Unlike Boston, Philadelphia, or other large port cities, the New Jersey ports had relatively few professional sailors among their inhabitants. There were even cases when ship departures at Perth Amboy were delayed for want of qualified or willing crew members.[89]

In most ways, however, the lifestyle of New Jersey's sailors seems remarkably similar to that of others throughout the colonies. Like their counterparts at Boston or Rhode Island, they were beset with the general problems of the profession. Drownings were quite frequent, for sailors were notorious for their inability to swim. John Tom, a New Jersey mariner, drowned when he fell over the gunnel of his boat, and two sailors on a trip from Perth Amboy to Middletown suffered a similar fate when their craft capsized. From all reports such accidents were quite frequent. Pirates proved another hazard, but few sailors suffered the double jeopardy of John Wilson, a crewman on William Fraser's *William of Perth Amboy*, who was taken off that sloop by pirates and forced to assist them. He subsequently faced death by hanging when the pirate ship on which he was sailing was captured by an English man-of-war. Wilson was saved only by the depositions of his fellow mariners, who described his seizure and maintained that his presence was involuntary. Always present was the danger of loss of life or freedom through such actions or through legal but equally odious impressment into the English Navy. Sometimes the dangers a sailor faced were of his own making. A friendly, if somewhat drunken brawl between two shipmates outside a tavern at Perth Amboy, for example, resulted in the eventual death of one of the participants. More often, however, the mariner's fate was likely to be that of the vessel on which he served. If it were caught in the ice and broke up, as did a sloop from Shrewsbury, he would be lucky to escape with his life. Or he might be among the less fortunate, such as the eight or nine men who "Perished in the Sea" when a New Jersey sloop bound for Rhode Island could not lower its ice-encrusted sails and therefore overturned in a gale.[90]

Even with all these hazards, the opportunity to make money at a maritime trade attracted many. The wages themselves were not high, and often sailors were paid in kind rather than in specie, but the augmentation of wages by "privilege" cargo space on outward and homeward voyages allowed crew members to become small-scale entrepreneurs. Those who were either lucky or adroit at marketing could reap a handsome profit.[91]

For the merchant-shipper in New Jersey, operating costs in terms of wages were not great, and they remained fairly stable throughout most of the eighteenth century.[92] Sometimes a disgruntled employee might raise the overhead by jumping ship with a month's advance in wages. This occurred in Perth Amboy, much to the consternation of Captain George Fraser, who sought to recover the money through a legal suit if the sailor could be found. On another occasion, Abel Smith, a mariner from the Salem-based shallop *Molly*, absconded with the ship's money.[93] But this was an unusual occurrence. Most of the New Jersey shippers were able to minimize the personnel component of operating costs by using the minimum number of crew.[94] Throughout the eighteenth century, owners of larger vessels increasingly employed minimum crews.[95] Cost, then, as much as efficiency or ease of handling, helped to keep crews small on colonial ships.

By examining the relationship of a given port to its sailing vessels, their place of registry, place of construction, and makeup of crews, we are afforded a vantage point from which to ascertain the nature of maritime development and change within a colony. In New Jersey the predominance of sloops and other small craft at the ports indicated a largely coastal trade. Over four decades the gradual proportional increase of these types of vessels suggests a shift toward an almost exclusive reliance on coastal trade patterns. As the ports declined, more New Jersey registries appeared, suggesting that the port rapidly changed from a potentially international harbor to a basically local port. At the same time, however, the shipbuilding industry flourished, as the ratio of New Jersey registries to vessels built in the colony increased and more vessels built in New Jersey but registered elsewhere appeared. More broadly, the relationship of shipmasters to owners suggests that the trade of small ports depended equally on the small entrepreneur and the large merchant-shipper, who also employed small vessels as part of his business enterprise.

The Navigation Acts

Like all aspects of colonial commerce, trading routes and patterns were developed amidst a complex structure of statutes known collectively as the Navigation Acts. Evolving throughout the seventeenth century, these acts defined the manner in which maritime trade was to be conducted. All goods were to be shipped in British or colonial vessels commanded by English masters with crews that were at least three-quarters English. Certain enumerated goods could be shipped only to England, though they might be and often were exported from there to areas outside the empire. Similarly, goods imported from outside the empire were to pass through England prior to shipment to the colonies. Finally, certain exports and manufacturing practices were prohibited to the colonies, while others were encouraged, in an effort to implement mercantile theory, assure regular exchange of manufactured goods for raw materials, and encourage some degree of economic self-sufficiency in the context of the orderly development of trade and commerce.[96]

The nature of commercial restrictions controlling such items as tobacco, rice, and indigo had a greater effect on the economy of the southern colonies than it did on the middle colonies. The latter region produced primarily non-enumerated agricultural commodities (grains, flour, and livestock) and thus was seldom affected by these regulations. As the port cities of Philadelphia and New York grew in size and volume to become entrepôts, they were perhaps to a limited degree affected by adherence to British mercantile theory.

In New Jersey, however, the Navigation Acts might encourage a fledgling hemp industry or lead some of the bolder merchants to seek additional profit through a bit of illicit trade, but these were relatively minor activities. New Jersey's imports and exports, on the whole, were virtually unaffected in any direct way by the Navigation Acts, largely because the ports enjoyed a relatively modest volume of trade, with limited imports and predominately agrarian exports.

The Navigation Acts, however, have been the subject of such historical controversy regarding their effect on the colonial economy, and thus their role in the coming of the American Revolution, that further discussion is warranted. Those inclined to believe that economic forces provided the underpinning for the American Revolution have tried to assess the role of the Navigation Acts and British mercantile theory in the development of the colonial economy.

Lawrence Harper was the first to offer actual estimates of some of the gross burdens and benefits of the Navigation Acts rather than the standard qualitative judgments. He concluded that the British mercantile system was detrimental to America's growth and placed a considerable economic burden on the colonies. Unlike Louis M. Hacker, who envisaged the ensuing struggle as a conflict between two competing systems, the older mercantile system of Britain and an emerging American capitalism, Harper suggested that the economic burden was not a major cause of the American Revolution. Rather, continual changes in regulations following the Peace of Paris (1763) acted as the catalyst for revolt. Harper did demonstrate that the degree of exploitation in terms of cost of colonial goods was quite high because cost depended not so much on tax assessed as on hidden costs resulting from transshipping enumerated goods outside the empire.[97]

The view that the acts of trade worked against colonial interests has been challenged by several scholars, most notably Oliver M. Dickerson, whose detailed study of the economic consequences of the Navigation Acts suggested that little economic constraint or disruption resulted from these acts and that in many ways they were economically beneficial. The cause of the American Revolution, he contended, must therefore be found elsewhere.[98]

These earlier interpretations did not explore in depth the economic data available. Recent historians, using improved techniques of measurement and often equipped with some formal training in economics, have reexamined this material in an attempt to provide new insights into the role of the Navigation Acts in America's development.[99]

The most ambitious work of the new economic history on this issue is that of Robert P. Thomas, who, using the pioneering work of Robert Fogel on economic growth and the national railroads, constructed a counterfactual model to test the effects of the Navigation Acts on the colonial economy. A counterfactual model is simply a means to measure the significance of what actually happened, forming hypotheses to suggest what would have happened to the colonial economy in the absence of the acts of trade. Using post-Revolutionary cost figures as a basis for estimating the costs of goods traded through Britain from the European continent, as if they were traded directly to America, he has reassessed both cost and the increase in volume of trade that might have been forthcoming. Taking into account the benefits, most notably military protection, of being a part of the empire, he has concluded, as Dickerson had earlier, that the acts of trade had little effect on colonial commerce.[100]

A controversy over this interpretation has since raged among those styled new economic historians. Much of the criticism has centered on the way in which both Harper and Thomas arrived at statistical measurements. Peter McClelland and Gary Walton have been among their most vociferous critics and supporters respectively. McClelland maintained that the conceptual framework of both these writers was so badly flawed as to render their judgments speculative at best, and he offered his own estimate of the economic cost of Navigation Acts to the American colonies. Walton, criticizing this analysis, argued, "It seems doubtful that McClelland's measure of the costs of British regulation will be widely accepted amongst interested scholars." Walton, through his analysis of Harper and Thomas's methodology, concludes that although flawed in many places, their ideas are still valid.[101] The controversy that has followed has concerned itself very little with the causes of the Revolutionary War and instead has become increasingly technical.[102]

As a result, certain economic historians have suggested that this line of inquiry needs a rest, for at present neither the new history nor the old has given a definitive analysis of the economic burdens of the Navigation Acts. Perhaps the contentions of Stuart Bruchey are most telling. He says that a counterfactual argument, while developing a rational view of an event, does not produce an end in itself. Action is the result of human judgment, which does not always respond solely to economic facts but also to fears and desires that are often sociopolitical. This type of emotional upheaval in turn may produce the misperceptions that, in the case of the American colonies, did much to produce the Revolution.[103]

Much of the response of New Jerseyans to the British mercantile system seems to fit this latter category. New Jerseyans, as we have seen, were little affected by commercial policy. In resisting British "tyranny," they seemed to lag behind the surrounding major urban areas. In the end it was largely political and social pressure from its neighbors that led New Jersey to an emotional response that reflected not economic conditions but the judgment of contemporaries about such events.

Cargo Trends

By the first quarter of the eighteenth century the volume of trade through New Jersey's ports primarily involved Perth Amboy. New Jerseyans had increasingly found avenues besides the official ports by which to carry out commerce, usually by way of New York and Philadelphia. Perth Amboy's official trade, although only a fraction of the total commerce conducted by the colony, is nonetheless sufficient to provide a general understanding of the nature and extent of change in this basically agrarian colony. It also gives some indication of the extent to which rural New Jersey, like the surrounding colonies, experienced a rise in the standard of living, and it reveals the growing economic dependence on neighboring colonies that forecast further social and political dependence.

Cargo manifests from 1726 to 1764 show that this colony experienced only a modicum of change from its agricultural and rural nature. New Jersey's need to import both foreign and colonial manufactures demonstrates the degree to which agriculture dominated the colony. Although some items, such as bricks, glass, and cloth, were manufactured in New Jersey, manufacturing activities in the first half of the eighteenth century were localized and limited.[104] As a result, a great diversity of manufactured goods was imported; these goods indicate, if only peripherally, something of the local life and economy.

Goods associated with a growing rural economy predominated. A small but steady quantity of hardware (axes, hatchets, pails, sieves, handsaws, and the like) passed through Perth Amboy every year, as did finished leather goods such as saddles and bridles. Small quantities of iron were imported in the form of barrels, tons, or ingots, depending on whether it was scrap iron or newly processed; the imported iron would be converted into more finished products, such as building nails, or other items for home, farm, or manufacturing use.[105] Metal, including iron, was also imported in the form of iron pots, iron or brass kettles, frying pans, all primarily for use in the home, along with more refined articles such as pewter and cutlery. Like hardware items, they appeared rather consistently in the cargo manifests over the years, but in small number and volume. Items for the home also included general household goods, earthenware, and straw ware. None of these items ever constituted more than 5 percent of the imports in any year, but they too were imported regularly.[106]

Such items indicated a developing agricultural community, but not necessarily economic growth. Growth is suggested by the more frequent appearance of more sophisticated or luxury items. This type of purchase indicates a rise in per capita income and a small capital surplus to be spent raising the standard of living. Such an increase in capital is generally viewed as an example of economic growth. Cloth, for example, found its way through the New Jersey ports in pieces, parcels, and reams. The most popular fabrics (osnaburg, duck, calico, and muslin) were well suited to agrarian life because they were relatively cheap and durable and made excellent farm and work clothing. Surprisingly, a nearly equal quantity of the better fabrics (linen and wool) found their way into the wardrobes of New Jerseyans, along with hats and other types of haberdashery.[107]

Although some of the more refined items destined to become apparel were intended for New Jersey's more well-to-do merchant class and landowners, it is likely that some was purchased by the rural element, which, as it became more affluent, began to want and appreciate these fineries. But change was slow; import records reveal that there was at first little call for the fineries associated with a more sophisticated and urban environment—an infrequent box of wigs, a looking glass, an assortment of books, a feather bed, or a writing table was overshadowed by more essential items.[108] More sophisticated or luxury items became more frequent in cargo manifests during the eighteenth century. Linens, sugars, wines, books, and other such items appeared regularly in the 1750s and 1760s. Imports through New York and Philadelphia, moreover, contained large quantities of dry goods and hardware for New Jersey customers.[109] New Jersey, then, may have been more dominated by agricultural concerns than were neighboring colonies, but it did not have a static economy. Like the American colonies as a whole, New Jersey was experiencing both expansion and growth.[110]

The two items imported most frequently were rum and molasses, and they too give us the flavor of the local life and economy. These two items were extremely popular throughout colonial America. Spirits, along with molasses, were sometimes prescribed for medicinal purposes. For the most part, spirits were drunk and molasses was used as a sweetener. Rum and molasses were especially marketable in the countryside, where people could not afford the more expensive wines and sugars. These two commodities comprised more than 40 percent of East Jersey imports in the 1720s, while wines and sugar constituted no more than 11 and 5 percent, respectively, of all East Jersey imports. Most of these wines and sugars were then transshipped to regions outside New Jersey.[111] The percentage of imports of rum, molasses, wines, and sugars fluctuated only slightly over the years.[112]

Exports also indicate the overwhelmingly agrarian nature of the colony and reveal the wide variety of agricultural and related goods that were produced for export. Among the items exported from Perth Amboy were small quantities of apples, onions, garden seeds, beeswax, bayberry wax, candles, tallow, and lard. But New Jersey's main exports were both natural and refined grains, prepared meats, and dairy and timber products.[113] The Perth Amboy export list for the 1720s illustrates why New Jersey was considered one of the "bread colonies." Perth Amboy's export trade during this period was dominated by grains, especially wheat, which alone accounted for almost a third of all exports, and also rye, oats, and Indian corn. These "bread goods" were supplemented by prepared meats. One departing vessel in every ten carried pork and beef products; one in five carried lumber or finished forest products such as shingles and staves.[114]

Throughout the period, these items remained the major export from East Jersey. But the raw products were increasingly being converted to a more processed form prior to shipment. Although manufacturing was very limited in New Jersey, there was considerable industry and industrial expansion in areas associated with agriculture. Wheat exports from Perth Amboy, for example, began to decline proportionately after the 1720s, as the grist mills became more numerous and could convert almost all available wheat into flour, which was more profitable and more convenient to carry. By 1741 wheat was exported only half as often as it had been in the 1720s; by 1758, less than a quarter as often. Conversely, flour exports rose almost 10 percent by the 1740s; cargo lists no longer cited "flour and bread," but said merely "flour." By 1758 flour cleared the port four times more often than it had three decades earlier, and bread exports, another flour-related product, also significantly increased, doubling between the 1720s and 1740s, quadrupling by 1758, and then doubling again within the next five years. Grains, of course, continued to be exported frequently. But the type of grain exported was an indication of industrial growth, for wheat was replaced by corn and other grains less profitable to process.[115]

Timber products underwent a similar change to more refined goods. Lumber was less frequently exported from Perth Amboy in the 1750s. It had accounted for 20 percent of the total volume of exports in the 1720s, but it declined to 10 percent by the end of the 1750s. Exports of staves and other more refined wood products rose more than threefold in the same period.[116] Some additional agricultural exports also appeared, with beer and cider sporadically listed and accounting at times for as much as 10 percent of outbound goods. Some agricultural products, most notably hemp, were produced specifically for export; despite constant government support and encouragement, however, hemp accounted for only a very small part of those goods intended for export.[117]

East Jersey's imports and exports illustrate the changing character of agricultural life in the colony. Burlington's port records, except for the importation of slaves, closely paralleled those of Perth Amboy. The records are not of sufficient volume to allow comparisons over extended periods, but they do indicate several similarities. Real imports were minimal and consisted more of necessities than luxuries. Rum amounted to about 40 percent of the total imports. Beef comprised 10 percent of the total exports and rye and wheat amounted to less than 10 percent. Bread came to nearly 50 percent and flour to nearly 60 percent of all Burlington's exports.[118]

The products passing through New Jersey's ports give some measure of its economic development and suggest that from 1720 to 1760 the colony did mature economically, especially in agricultural development. Because New Jersey failed to mature in some more economically diversified way, it provided those working out of its ports with the possibility of an additional cost advantage not enjoyed by the more sophisticated regional ports, for the limited volume of trade and the limited commodities being exported, especially to the New England region, further reduced the need to find markets. A few paradoxically gained from this condition. Yet the ports and the colony were to suffer as the neighboring colonies came to dominate New Jerseyans economically, then politically, culturally, and socially.

The extent of the colony's economic dependence was evident in various reports of New Jersey's officials. As early as 1721, Governor

William Burnet noted, "They [New Jerseyans] are Supply'd from New York and Philadelphia with English Manufactures, having none of their own." Governor Lewis Morris reported in 1732 that "the product it [New Jersey] yields is chiefly sent to New York and Pennsylvania in return for goods they are supply'd with from those places." Governor Jonathan Belcher rendered a similar judgment in 1754.[119] They attributed New Jersey's dependent status to a lack of maritime trade, reporting that New Jersey had very little foreign trade and that its commerce had remained static.[120]

An analysis of the port records supports these two contentions. While the colony's population had risen 46 percent between 1726 and 1738, when it reached a little over 47,000, and then in the next seven years rose another 34 percent,[121] Burlington's trade had virtually ceased and Perth Amboy's continued to decline. After 1740, imports, drawn almost exclusively from Rhode Island, greatly decreased in proportion to the increasing population. Slave imports also reflect the failure of New Jersey's eastern port to meet the needs of the citizenry. By 1745 the black population in New Jersey more than doubled from the 2,581 recorded in 1726, but only a fraction of that number appeared in the official import records.[122]

The increasing dependence of New Jersey's growing population on commodities imported through neighboring colonies was nowhere more graphically demonstrated than on the shelves of New Jersey stores. Country stores, such as Andrew W. Leake's shop on the forks of the Raritan and Lamington rivers, boasted a greater variety and quantity of products than ever passed customs at the New Jersey ports: hardware such as shoe buckles, gun flints, teapots, horsewhips, spectacles with a case, and snuff boxes; dry goods such as necklaces, silk handkerchiefs, stockings, and hats of almost every type (felt, fine wool, castor, beaver); and other commodities such as stationery, spelling books, primers, almanacs, and Bibles, both large and small.[123] The contrast between the items offered for sale in Leake's store from 1756 to 1766 and the imported goods listed by New Jersey's customs officer in that period shows the almost total reliance on New York and Philadelphia. Exports from the late 1750s on, although reflecting the changing nature of agriculture, included only the smallest volume of the better-known New Jersey agricultural and timber products and almost none of the newer exports generated by rock and bog iron and copper mining.[124]

6
Merchant–Shippers

THE TERM *MERCHANT* was loosely defined in colonial America and was often applied to anyone who handled imported or exported merchandise.[1] Because the term is vague and the relationships of individual merchants to the shipping industry were complex and changeable, it is difficult to define *merchant* specifically. Nevertheless, there are several general categories of merchants who were part of New Jersey's maritime industry.

Many New Jersey merchants had little or no connection with maritime ventures. Others paid for shipping a cargo but neither owned nor invested in a vessel. In addition, many dealers conducted little or no business through their own ports, instead using those of the neighboring colonies. Of the prominent Perth Amboy merchants who had petitioned for their own charter in 1718,[2] none officially owned vessels that passed through New Jersey's ports in the following decade.[3] Nor was this situation unique. Of the fourteen "Chief and Most Substantial Merchants" of Perth Amboy whose involvement in intercolonial trade led them to complain officially in 1726 about New York's discounting of "New Jersey Money," only four (Andrew Johnston, William Williamson, Michael Kearney, and Ebenezer Lyon) owned vessels using Perth Amboy in that decade.[4]

New Jersey's fragmented mercantile community can best be studied through sketches of individual merchants as representatives of several types of merchants. Cornelius Low, whose dry-goods business was situated at Raritan Landing near New Brunswick, was a typical New Jersey merchant. While he occasionally purchased goods locally, he obtained most of his merchandise from New York, where his son and partner, Isaac Low, had a similar business. Small sloops or boats apparently brought these transshipped goods from New York directly to Raritan Landing, since there is no record of the Lows ever owning a ship that entered or cleared through New Jersey's ports of entry.[5] Henry and James Shotwell, Quaker merchants at Woodbridge and Rahway, are further examples of businessmen who had no direct maritime connections with New Jersey ports. They, too, operated a store in New York that was apparently, as was the case with Low, a distribution point for their New Jersey concerns.[6] These individuals were important in terms of the general commerce and economy of the colony. In terms of the development of New Jersey's ports, however, their influence was negligible.

The term *merchant* also designated individuals such as Daniel Hendrickson, who owned a small country store and at least one vessel.[7] His primary interest lay not in commerce but in his Monmouth County farms and in real estate. For him, maritime commerce was primarily a means of acquiring more capital, which he could use to expand his non-maritime pursuits. He was principally a cargo carrier rather than a merchant-shipper, although he himself often invested in a cargo for sale to some third party. Hendrickson began his career with an inheritance. His father had been a wealthy landholder and bequeathed considerable property to Daniel and his three other sons.[8] The entire family seems to have prospered from their inheritance. Although Daniel was a minor when his father's will was written in 1727, by 1750 he became a wealthy landowner in his own right and began to look for ways to diversify his capital. Eventually he decided to venture into the West Indies trade. For this purpose he made a considerable investment in the thirty-ton sloop *Catharine*. The hull work, which included the cost of iron and the labor of a blacksmith, joiner, and carpenters, came to nearly £400, with the carpentry work accounting for just under 70 percent of the total cost of building the hull; fitting the new vessel required another £300 or so, most of which went for sail cloth and rigging.[9]

Patrick Boyle, as captain, assumed the operations of the sloop *Catharine*, conducting trade in accordance with such instructions and guidance as Hendrickson felt was necessary to carry out these enterprises profitably. In 1752 he ordered Boyle to "proceed from Sandy Hook to Kingston in Jamaica," where he was to deliver his cargo to the firm of West and Cook, Hendrickson's agents in the West Indies. Upon his arrival Boyle was to attempt to sell the spars on board himself, but if he could not get above £25 he was to leave them with the agents. Hendrickson urged that he return "immediately, as soon as possible" but hoped that he would be able to collect whatever possible in terms of freight and cargo that "will be of Advantage," again reminding Boyle "that dispatch in trade is the life of business."[10]

Hendrickson's Jamaican venture and another with his three brothers, carrying cargo and freight for his own family and others, seem to indicate that the business was profitable.[11] West and Cook at Spanishtown kept Hendrickson well informed of conditions in Jamaica and the surrounding islands, and they had little trouble selling the flour, shingles, gammon, and other agricultural commodities, especially Jersey cider, that he sent them.[12]

Even with these successes there were some setbacks. Six hundred bundles of onions shipped in 1752 on the account of Peter Remsen and John Bergen paid a mere £6:13:3. The voyage apparently took so long that the onions arrived at Monserrat "very much rotten spoyled."[13] The following year a voyage to Curaçao required ten weeks because the weather was rough. The vessel arrived with her sails almost spent and her captain in poor health. Because no cargo or freight was available at Curaçao, the *Catharine* was preparing to sail to Jamaica where, perhaps through the offices of West and Cook, Boyle would be able to procure a cargo. The captain noted, "This voyage has prove'd But Very Indefrent."[14]

There was, then, considerable risk associated with such ventures, as well as considerable expense. In 1763 and 1764 the cost of operating a sloop in the West Indies trade was £1,238:4:6 for the year. Operating expenses came to £172:19:7, including insurance at £21:6:2, repairs for worn cables, and maintenance to the boom and new blocks for £20:8:8, in addition to £149:13:2 for the crew's wages. The remainder was used to obtain cargo, mostly agricultural produce and various timber products, the greatest outlay being £670:18:8 for 282 barrels of flour.[15]

Eventually a profit on such enterprises would probably be realized, but both sales and payments, especially from the West Indies, were often slow. Ventures of this kind might temporarily extend the investor's own credit, as well as tie up much of his capital. Perhaps with this in mind, or perhaps because he required immediate capital for some other enterprise, Hendrickson, in July 1753, four months after the Curaçao voyage, sold a quarter share of the sloop *Catharine* to

James Van Brankle, a mariner also of Middletown, for "the sum of One Hundred and Fifteen Pound Currant Money of the Province."[16] Hendrickson did not abandon shipping, however, for among the papers relating to his activities in the next several decades are various bills of lading and a page from an account dated 1778 showing he owned shares in the privateer sloop *Maria*.[17]

Although Hendrickson continued throughout his life to invest in maritime ventures, it is not likely that he and other merchant investors like him had any appreciable effect on the development of small ports such as those in New Jersey. Hendrickson had no real home base and for the most part freighted cargo for others. As a result, his vessels (and, we may suppose, those of merchants like him) went where such trade was available, infrequently returning to the same harbor. It seems reasonable to assume that such men were primarily speculators, not maritime merchants. Thus, they were concerned more with profit than with the development of the port or of a distinctive merchant class.

But another kind of small entrepreneur, the owner-merchant, was deeply involved in commerce and had most of his capital tied up in the vessel he owned and the merchandise he carried. Although investments varied—some owned a small sloop while others owned a brig—they often commanded their own vessels and acted as their own supercargos. These men were often in a state of transition, hoping eventually to become large merchant-shippers. Most started small; the sloop *Charming Betty*, for instance, was owned by three small merchants, Mr. Rawson, William Acton, and William Burroughs. Burroughs acted as captain and was assisted occasionally by Acton. With a crew of four to five, including the captain, the sloop carried freight, cargo, and passengers between Salem, New Jersey, and the surrounding area, sailing mainly to Philadelphia and the Cape Fear region of the Carolinas, with an occasional speculative trip to Boston or Jamaica.[18]

Maritime Bookkeeping

A ledger kept for the *Charming Betty* is quite revealing, because it illustrates the nature of trade and the working relationship of one group of entrepreneurs. It was a typical account book of the colonial period in that it was tailored to immediate needs and individual situations and therefore did not necessarily follow a consistent recording system. As a result, the relatively simple single-entry accounting system is rendered more complex, since accounts are often combined or are kept within other accounts.

The general account was kept on the vessel itself, as if it were a company, and reflected expenditures and income during each voyage. There were individual partners involved in their own transactions or in those of the sloop that they handled personally; they accrued a credit or debit on their own behalf as designated by their initials in the left margin opposite the transaction. When the sloop's ledger was settled at the end of the voyage, these individual accounts were cleared by payment from or into the sloop's account. Then the profits or the losses as indicated by the ledger were divided among the trio according to the percentage of the vessel that each owned.[19] Thus, when William Burroughs paid himself six months' wages as captain of the vessel, that £30 was credited to his personal account as an individual outlay and was charged against the ship as an operating expense.[20] This particular system seems unique, but the use of initials in ledgers to identify both individual transactions and ownership of cargo was quite common in this period. The initials usually correspond to initials marked on items as a means of differentiating cargo placed aboard the vessel.[21]

The *Charming Betty* ledger also contains accounts for individuals with whom the company—that is to say, the sloop—did business. It appears that most of the transactions involved merchandise on request. Aside from agricultural produce from the middle colonies, the ship carried and sold such items as men's and women's shoes, boots, pocket knives, books, spring locks, small bowls, and knitting needles. At times the sloop must have resembled a floating store.[22]

Almost all sales were transacted on the basis of credit, a necessity in an era of scarce specie. Some income was also derived from freight. The vessel was likely to carry almost anything, from twenty-four barrels of flour to two tubs of apple trees; a surprising number of persons booked passage at £3 one way, a graphic reminder of the difficulties of overland journeys in or between colonies.[23]

Expenses were mostly for wages, but considerable expenditures were required for the upkeep of the vessel.[24] The Hendrickson account, for example, contains numerous entries for cables, ropes, anchors, work done on the sloop, oars, repairs to the sails, and so on. These expenses, combined with the cost of dealing with administrative officials—the naval officer and customs officers collected between £2 and £3 to enter and clear the sloop—indicate that maritime ventures were costly enterprises; not everyone was willing to undertake the risks. After a few voyages, Mr. Rawson apparently decided to abandon the enterprise, selling his half-share of the *Charming Betty* to Acton and Burroughs, who had actually been operating the sloop.[25]

Entries in the ledger of the *Charming Betty* may also cast some light on the development of trading patterns. Owners of a sloop lacking extensive merchant connections and having relatively limited capital apparently did not attempt to search out markets over a wide area. Although more ambitious ventures yielded greater profits, we may assume that the risk was also greater, and with so much of their money tied up in the vessel, the two remaining entrepreneurs tended to be relatively conservative; they generally stayed within a narrow trading area where they personally knew the market and the individuals with whom they dealt. Only rarely did they venture to Boston or Jamaica. This pattern was probably typical of the small owner-merchant operating from New Jersey, or in its waters, and probably applied to most entrepreneurs in this category.

Owner-merchants such as those of the *Charming Betty* were likely to assume an active role in the life of their ports. Their imports and exports, when carried out with some degree of regularity, established an important flow of trade for the port. But that alone was not sufficient to insure a port's success. Growth and expansion also required political involvement at the highest levels, for the improvement of harbor facilities, the encouragement of trade through tarriffs and duties, and the support of a maritime merchant class were often an integral part of the activities of the local assembly. The small owner-merchant, often lacking the necessary social and economic standing, was not likely to be a politician or to have political influence. He probably did not have much capital. He was thus a contributor to the general development of the port but was not really the essential element for its growth.

The names of Burroughs, Acton, and Hendrickson are seldom recorded in the annals of maritime history. These men were, in maritime commerce, the middling sort whose role has seldom drawn even minimal attention, for they were often transient in their enterprises and had small capital investments. Yet such men undoubtedly represented a significant segment of maritime life. Their trade contributed to the colonial economy and provided local merchants with an opportunity to acquire or expand the capital by which they might achieve further upward social and economic mobility.

Versatility of Merchant-Shippers

At Perth Amboy, growth and development depended not upon small owner-merchants but upon the continual involvement of a number of merchant-shippers. They combined wholesale and retail merchandising with the ownership of several small vessels, a few large ones, or a combination. Though a merchant-shipper might occasionally ship his goods with others or rent a vessel, he preferred, for a variety of reasons, to own vessels. Most important, ownership assured him available vessels and helped to control shipping cost. He also was able to choose the market he believed would be most profitable and order his vessel there. In addition, by freighting his own goods he could eliminate the expense of the middleman. Since freighting and marketing were often thought of as inseparable, most viewed ownership of vessels as a means of increasing the profit margin.[26] The merchant-shipper usually carried his own cargo, often supplemented by freighting for others. His merchandising operations were likely to be dispersed over several locations or colonies, administered by family members or trusted firms.

Though his principle interest and involvement was in shipping, he also engaged in a number of other activities, not all of them related to maritime commerce. The merchant-shipper served as a commission agent and broker for others; he was a banker of sorts, exchanging foreign currency as well as bills of exchange, and acting as a moneylender. Sometimes he also acted as an agent for others, usually on commission. He engaged in a number of diversified activities as well, for only through diversification was it possible to achieve real wealth.[27] Land speculation was often one of his chief interests, but manufacturing, mining, candlemaking, whaling, and other activities also drew upon his time and capital.[28] These outside activities were often integrated with his shipping and trade activities. The merchant-shipper also played an important role in the local economy and in the political, social, and religious life of the province in which he resided.

The functions of the merchant-shipper often produced partnerships that, considering the risks connected with maritime commerce, were an integral part of the business life of the colonial merchant. Throughout the American colonies family relationships provided the nucleus for such associations. The manner in which they evolved and the activities of a merchant and entrepreneur are well illustrated by the commercial life of Perth Amboy's John Parker. Plying a lively

The Parker Castle (above) and the Long Ferry Tavern (below) were closely associated with the merchant class of eighteenth-century Perth Amboy. John Parker (1693–1732) built this fieldstone house on Water Street, not far from the Arthur Kill Sound; his son James (1725–97), the merchant-shipper, added the frame structure in front of it before the Revolution. Perth Amboy's first tavern was established close to the Long Ferry pier on the Raritan River and served as a meeting place for the town's business and political elite. Engravings in William A. Whitehead's Contributions to the Early History of Perth Amboy . . . (New York, 1856), pp. 137, 262.

trade from that port with numerous vessels, Parker rose in the early 1720s to a position of prominence both as a merchant and as a political figure. His success was due in part to the firm economic and social base established by his father, Elisha Parker. The elder Parker had begun his career as a yeoman farmer in Woodbridge, but by 1694, a year after the birth of his son John, he had risen to become a high sheriff and was on his way to being an important political figure, a substantial landholder, a gristmill owner, and a merchant at Perth Amboy.[29]

To this heritage John Parker added his own abilities and ambition. He was a captain of the local militia by the age of twenty-two and eventually held the rank of colonel. By the age of twenty-six he had become a member of the governor's council in New Jersey and was carrying on an active career as a merchant both there and in New York. At his death in 1732, he had extensive landholdings in Woodbridge and on the Passaic River, a magnificent residence, the Parker Castle, at Perth Amboy, and a second dwelling located on the Woodbridge-Amboy road. He also owned a part-interest in a sawmill at Pine Brook, and two merchant establishments, one at Perth Amboy and the other at New Brunswick.[30] It is a testimonial to the man's ambition and to the socio-economic mobility of the burgeoning province that all this was accomplished in less than twenty years— John Parker died at the age of thirty-nine.

Parker's meteoric rise was undoubtedly aided by a fortuitous marriage to Jennette Johnston, daughter of Dr. John Johnston, one of the most prominent political, social, and economic figures in the colony. This marriage and that of Jennette's brother, James, to John's sister, Elizabeth Parker, fused these two families in all aspects of life. James Johnston was involved in several business ventures with his brother-in-law; Andrew Johnston, Jennette's eldest brother, was not only a trusted friend and confidante of her husband—he was named as an executor of John Parker's estate and co-guardian of the Parker children[31]—he was also John Parker's partner in almost every shipping venture the latter undertook at Perth Amboy.[32]

Andrew Johnston, like John Parker, could be called a merchant-shipper. His career, if less rapid in development, followed in a similar pattern. He was an active merchant in both Perth Amboy and New York and had extensive landholdings. A high-ranking military officer, Johnston was politically active at the highest levels of colonial government, being a member of the assembly and at one time the president of East Jersey proprietors.[33] Like John Parker, he brought influence and considerable economic resources to any venture he undertook.

These two merchants owned (at various times jointly or in concert with others such as John Heard, George Fraser, and James Johnston) four sloops that used the port. A few times annually one or more of these vessels (the *John and Mary of Perth Amboy*, the *Woodbridge*, the *Lark*, and the *Eagle*) appeared in the harbor. Their trade was divided between the coastal and West Indian regions, with an occasional vessel from Madeira. From this latter area wines were imported; to it, grains mostly wheat, were exported; within the coastal waters Parker and Johnston imported rum, wines, molasses, and some manufactured goods from Boston and the Rhode Island ports, and they carried out a two-way trade with Philadelphia and the Carolinas. With Philadelphia they exchanged imported manufactured goods and foodstuffs; from the South they received shipments of pitch, tar, and peas and sent in return rum, wine, apple cider, some local farm produce (most notably cheese), and some European goods. They sent substantial quantities of foodstuffs and some naval stores to Antigua and Barbados, the major areas of operation in the West Indies, and they imported molasses, rum, and sugar.[34] In exporting goods, the Parkers and later some other merchant-shippers had an additional advantage when they were able to ship wheat and other commodities acquired directly from their own farms and estates, or from tenant farmers who often paid land rental fees in produce.[35] By freighting their own commodities to markets of their own choosing at the most opportune moment, they had a considerable cost advantage over small-port merchants.

Of the wide variety of imports they handled, Parker and Johnston retained some for personal use or for local consumption. But they transshipped or exported a great deal, especially cargo imported from New England and the middle colonies, either because of market advantages locally, as seems to have been the case with the Philadelphia trade, or to complete an order for a customer, as was more likely in the South or the West Indies. Transshipment was as important an aspect of their trade as the wholesale or retail business they conducted locally.

A good deal of bookkeeping was required in this trade. John Parker and other Perth Amboy merchants kept careful accounts. Many of the ledgers employed a simple credit-debit system that allowed a reasonably accurate appraisal of losses and gains. Detail was quite important, as an examination of the surviving records on the Parker vessels indicates.[36] Occasionally, a transaction might be embellished with the inclusion of such things as tracing ownership on a bill of exchange that had been received in payment. On the basis of the Parker family accounts one would agree with Stuart Bruchey's assessment that the casual or haphazard accounting attributed to colonial merchants by W. T. Baxter does not seem true of most of New Jersey's most prominent shippers after about 1730.[37] Still, there were occasional lapses in an otherwise careful system of bookkeeping, as when the younger John Parker noted, "When I went out with Lewis I. Parker, I took about £16 with me and when I returned I had but £7 so that I spent with him £9.0.0".[38]

Bookkeeping, merchant sales, and shipping were all part of the merchant-shipper's life and livelihood. Other merchants, such as Cornelius Van Horn, operated in a similar fashion. Van Horn, like Johnston and Parker, was a merchant of influence and capital who also used the local facility. Like others of his station, Van Horn invested much of his wealth in land. He held a substantial tract in central New Jersey and enjoyed an influential position in government; in 1727 he was appointed to the governor's council. But unlike Johnston and Parker, his merchant business and New Jersey residence were not at Perth Amboy. Instead, in partnership with his son-in-law Joseph Reed, he established a mercantile operation consisting of a wharf and several warehouses on the Raritan River, two miles west of Middle Brook.[39]

For the trade conducted by Van Horn and Reed, New Jersey served as a stopping point within a larger pattern of commerce, a place where selected cargos, probably assembled at their wharf on the Raritan River, could be loaded. Their rather substantial fleet of two snows, *Eagle of Amboy* and *Burnet of New York*, and a brigantine, *Mary and Catherine*, would arrive in ballast from New York, bound for Lisbon or Glasgow. The vessels might take on a cargo of lumber and lumber products (staves, oak planks, and red cedar) and some agricultural products before such an overseas departure.

Other shippers, apparently from New York, continued to view New Jersey as a market of opportunity, a port of convenience in a larger scheme of trade. The log of the 120-ton ship *Catherine* reveals something of this relationship.[40] Under orders issued by its New York owners in spring 1733, the *Catherine's* Captain Farmar had taken the vessel to the African coast, where he had assembled his human cargo of slaves. This completed, and with the loss of some of this "perishable commodity," he returned directly to New York.[41] Despite the description in the log, as he worked his way up the Hudson in early July with some 130 Angolan slaves, 300 "redwood sticks," and an elephant tusk, Captain Farmar stopped briefly at Perth Amboy, seizing the opportunity either to sell or directly deliver twenty-seven of his reluctant passengers before continuing to his reported destination.[42]

While the arrival of a slaver and the depositing of a portion of its cargo were atypical of Perth Amboy's commerce, the inclusion of Perth Amboy in a New York vessel's journey was not. Later that year, the ship *Catherine* again touched New Jersey shores, this time to engage in a more typical pattern of trade, one that often linked the commerce of New York and New Jersey. Now Captain Farmar was bound for Madeira to pick up a cargo of wine. Departing New York in ballast, the captain arrived at Perth Amboy on October 21, 1733. For the next month he waited while his rigging was repaired and a cargo assembled. His cargo consisted primarily of wheat and pipe staves, along with an odd cask or two of beeswax, forty-eight kegs of oysters, and three African slaves. The vessel cleared customs on December 3, 1733, picked up a pilot, and proceeded downriver to Sandy Hook, where the pilot was dropped.[43]

Captain Farmar then began what was in many ways a typical Atlantic crossing. December is not a good month for an Atlantic crossing, and the ship *Catherine* encountered heavy weather that damaged her sails and rigging, fortunately not to the extent that the crew could not repair it on board. After a journey of four weeks, Madeira was sighted, and the vessel came to rest safely at anchor. Two weeks later, loaded with wine, the ship cleared port. Running in light winds, the vessel averaged 125 miles a day, with one exceptional period in which she covered 149 miles. The good weather during the day allowed the crew to do maintenance work on the vessel, airing out the spare sails and reworking the spare cable. But in mid-February the voyagers encountered the heavy weather so typical of the Atlantic in winter, making sixteen miles in one day and only nineteen on another. Despite several days' loss as the vessel was required to do some tacking, the *Catherine* dropped anchor in New York harbor on the fourth of March, approximately six weeks from the day she departed Madeira.[44] The entire trip from Perth Amboy to Madeira and then to New York, a winter voyage in mixed weather, took about three months.

This type of trade pattern encouraged the local economy by providing an occasional export market for native materials, and it stimulated some local merchant activity. The harbor also benefited by the arrival of a number of vessels apparently owned by New York merchants who were related to Reed or Van Horn.[45] It seems that the partners either ordered or handled the goods directly or acted for their relations as factors, providing them with marketing information and arranging for disposition or collection of their cargos.

Competition from across the Rivers

Although none of the New Jersey merchants during this period used Perth Amboy with any great regularity, their involvement and that of other merchant-shippers in the harbor led some to believe in its potential development as a mercantile center. Its future vitality and growth, however, depended upon an ever-increasing involvement of such men. It was apparent that Perth Amboy could attract interest and some investment but required a commercial complex with all the critical middleman functions in order to maintain such interest.

Since Perth Amboy lacked such a commercial complex in the 1720s, many of the merchant-shippers residing in New Jersey and using its ports were forced either by economic necessity or preference to conduct business through New York, where these functions were already well established. Cornelius Van Horn, for instance, although he resided in New Jersey, was always referred to as a New York merchant.[46] In fact, both he and Joseph Reed had registered in New York, the major center for their commercial activity, the snows and brigantines used in New Jersey waters.

In business affairs, the elder John Parker and Andrew Johnston tended to gravitate toward New York, where their connections with the Alexander and Van Cortland families provided the contacts, influence, and prestige needed for successful business undertakings in that colony.[47] John Parker had, for example, in addition to his New Jersey business, a mercantile firm in New York that he operated from 1726 to 1728,[48] and he registered at least one New Jersey–operated vessel there.[49] While one can only speculate about how much emphasis he put on his New York operation, it was perhaps significant that his son James studied law with James Alexander in New York after Parker's death and then went on to pursue the mercantile aspect of the family business, concentrating most of his efforts in New York, where he was a highly successful merchant.[50]

The nature and extent of trade through New York is difficult to ascertain. New Jersey's merchant community was small and extant business records are meager. The proximity of New York and the ease of travel doubtless reduced the need for lengthy or formal correspondence, and written communications in this period were always scant, mostly because of the tempo of trade rather than because of any shortcoming on the part of New Jersey merchants. Even the largest merchant firms had relatively little correspondence. John Watts sent only 112 letters in a year; Thomas Hancock sent only sixty-two a year in the 1730s and averaged slightly more than one letter a month in return. A less active merchant sent two to three letters a month. The office time of the average merchant was around three hours a day.[51]

For Perth Amboy the available correspondence and sources give a sense of its growing dependence upon the neighboring province in the conduct of maritime commerce. A careful scrutiny of the records involving owners of vessels entering and departing the harbor at Perth Amboy shows that from 1750 on there was a growing mixture of New York and New Jersey merchants in various partnerships.[52] Such partnerships, often with merchants who were participants or partners in large New York mercantile concerns, reflect a growing reliance on New York and its commercial services, for it seems most likely that such arrangements used New York firms to conduct trade. Once such relationships were established, they were undoubtedly continued by New Jerseyans beyond the limited activities of the partnership and expanded into areas of commerce and shipping that did not involve the New Jersey port.

The sloop *Little David*, registered in New York, suggests one such commercial relationship. This vessel, operating in several periods in and out of Perth Amboy, had at one time as partners in its ventures both David Johnston and James Parker (1725–97) of New Jersey and Waddell Cunningham of New York.[53] Cunningham was an invaluable New York connection, for he was the managing partner of Greg, Cunningham and Company, a firm that owned as many as thirteen vessels at one time and had extensive connections in England and Ireland.[54] That same sloop also provided the vehicle for a commercial venture with Beverly Robinson.[55] A partner of Oliver De Lancey and brother-in-law of Fredrick Philipse (he had married Susannah Philipse), Robinson was well placed to provide commercial assistance to his New Jersey partners in this or other ventures in which they might engage together or separately.[56]

A frequent visitor to the Perth Amboy port was the New Jersey–registered brig *Salley*, jointly owned by Thomas Chapman, William Bethell, and Anthony Van Dam.[57] The latter was a powerful and active New York merchant who also ran a New York insurance office adjacent to the Merchant Coffee House.[58] Van Dam's trading interests found their way to New Jersey, and he undoubtedly was willing to assist any merchant of that province who wished to reciprocate.

Other merchants, who were not necessarily in direct partnership with New Yorkers, conducted their commerce through New York. On several occasions James Neilson dealt with the New York merchant John Watts, sending lumber and heading for him to ship.[59] Watts in turn acted as a banker for Neilson at times. In an age when overseas credit was essential for any merchant wishing to deal in European imports, John Watts, whose firm and reputation were well known in England, could be an invaluable contact. In May 1763 Watts wrote to Henry Cruger, Jr., in Bristol, England, a merchant he had dealt with before, to arrange a credit exchange with James Neilson through Cruger, saying, "I do not deal in dry goods myself." At the same time he suggested, perhaps at the urging of James Neilson, that he would make a valuable client. "Mr. Nielson I have always found a Very honest punctual Man, is very industrious & in good Circumstances. I mention this that you may not be a stranger to the Character of the Man, if he sho'd Continue his intercourse with you, which I have begun in hopes of doing you a Service."[60] In this way a New Jersey merchant was aided in his commercial ventures by his dealings and friendships with a New York merchant.

Correspondence in the papers of both the Parker and Stevens families concerning maritime activities shows that the vessels they owned or leased sometimes operated elsewhere, often in New York or occasionally Philadelphia, and that they relied heavily upon the services of fellow merchants and friends in the neighboring colonies in conducting much of their business. James Parker, as we have already noted, had shares in the *Little David*, which occasionally visited New Jersey. Most of its activities, however, centered in New York, and this relatively small sloop made several trips to Madeira. On one voyage in 1753 it carried flour and fish for sale on that island, the goods being carried on the account of James Parker but handled through the New York firm of Beverly Robinson and Company.[61] In the West Indies in the 1750s, James Parker and David Johnston, working in partnership, shipped on their account some 170 barrels of flour and one pipe of wine aboard a sloop bound for New York. This was also the destination of the brig *Katy* and the sloop *Swan*, both out of Jamaica and carrying on account goods for Parker and Johnston. Bound also for New York in 1752 was the sloop *Delight*, which carried rum and sugar on the account of Parker and Johnston. In trading at Jamaica, James Parker often dealt with Henry Livingston, frequently arranging for sale and payment through his brother John Livingston, a New York merchant. An overseas shipment handled by the firm of De Lancey, Robinson and Company in 1763 contained for the account of James and John Parker linen, cotton stocking, and other goods.[62]

In much the same way the Stevens family depended on New York and also operated occasionally out of Philadelphia. This is most vividly demonstrated by the voyages of the Stevens brig *Catherine*, which was registered in Perth Amboy and could sometimes be found in that port. In one instance, however, returning from Belfast, Ireland, in 1743, the brig was ordered directly to New York, and on a proposed voyage to Madeira for wines the brig was to depart from Philadelphia and "when finished in Madeira return here [Philadelphia] with the vessel then with whatever freight you can get to New York or Perth Amboy."[63] The brig *Molly*, another family-owned vessel, was registered not at Perth Amboy but at Philadelphia, with Richard Stevens acting as master.[64] In fact, Richard Stevens eventually set himself up as a merchant in Philadelphia, providing the family with a valuable contact there, although in 1742 he was plying the waters of the West Indies, headed for Antigua.[65] The brig *Molly* occasionally docked at Perth Amboy, as did the Honorable John Stevens's ship *Elizabeth*, the Stevens family brig *Two Friends*, or Stevens's brig *Funchal*. But New Jersey was not a regular port of call for them, and all the evidence suggests that New York and Philadelphia were as much their home as was New Jersey.[66]

When not using their own vessels, members of the Stevens family often conducted business through New York or Philadelphia. In 1742, as a result of an earlier voyage to Madeira by the *Catherine* that had left unsold freighted cargo, John Stevens, acting as an agent, wrote Scott, Pringle, and Scott, his factors at Madeira, that a "cask Capt. Smith left with you of wax marked J N belongs to Mr. James Neilson of New Brunswick send proceeds to NY in care of Samuel Farmar merchant."[67] In the 1750s, John Stevens shipped goods on his account in a number of vessels, among them the New York–based *Seahorse*. There is no evidence that any of these vessels entered New Jersey waters. Other opportunities also presented themselves, again, often in other colonies. In 1739 Moses Rolfe of Philadelphia proposed that Richard Stevens invest in a wartime venture to trade goods in enemy-held territory under a government-sanctioned flag of truce costing £150. The vessel, a new ship built in Boston, would try its fortune in Curaçao.[68] Whether Richard engaged in this venture is not known, but a little more than twenty years later John and Richard Stevens did undertake a flag ship, taking a quarter share in the venture.[69] Also in 1739 John Stevens shipped goods out of Philadelphia in the snow *Betty and Salley*, taking care to insure his cargo for the substantial sum of £2,000, probably warranted by the risk of war-related hazards.[70] From 1740, John Stevens's correspondence with Madeira for wine constantly refers to "wine for the New York market," leaving little doubt about where the principal sales and transactions would take place.

From the evidence available it is apparent that New Jersey merchants conducted considerable maritime commerce that did not directly involve the New Jersey ports, and that this activity increased greatly after 1750. The amount of trade that was handled through New York or Philadelphia cannot be quantified, but a qualitative estimate from the Stevens and Parker family papers suggests that at least 50 percent of the major transactions involving commerce were carried out through neighboring provinces by the 1750s, and after 1763 probably three out of every four.

During the 1740s and 1750s, however, some merchants were able to integrate New Jersey commerce into a more direct pattern of West Indies overseas trade, though they still relied on New York for business services and often operated from that port. The Honorable John Stevens was one such merchant. In 1739, two years after his father's death, he was well on his way to becoming a successful merchant.[71] He gained experience by personally captaining trading vessels to the West Indies and Madeira. By the time he was twenty-seven he had become one of the dominant merchants in New Jersey. He had several partners and was so engrossed in trade that he could no longer go to sea himself. Instead, he employed others, among them his brother and sometime partner Richard, to captain his growing fleet.[72]

Already a financial success, Stevens expanded many of his business connections and partnerships. He married Elizabeth Alexander shortly before his thirtieth birthday. With increasing regularity thereafter the names James Alexander (Elizabeth's father) and James Parker (1725–97) appeared along with various Johnstons in John Stevens's business dealings.[73]

The Business of Agents

In conducting trade, the Honorable John Stevens encountered a problem that many of his contemporaries also faced. Some merchants, such as the Beekmans and Livingstons in New York, conducted trade using an extensive family network in which brothers, uncles, cousins, and other relatives were engaged in trade in England, Europe, and the West Indies. Most merchants, however, were without the advantage of immediate family in far-flung places. To solve this problem, merchants such as John Stevens turned to factors, or agents—firms or individuals located in a given region of trade who would act as their agents and protect and promote their interests. The agent was crucial to the success of business, for he provided information on local economic conditions, suggested what commodities to ship, helped arrange for cargos to be exported, and often held goods consigned by the merchant until, in the factor's best judgment, the highest price could be obtained. Often merchants developed a relationship with the factor that reached beyond a strictly business association to friendship and trust, and agents were occasionally called upon for help and assistance, as if they were indeed members of the immediate family.

James Parker (1725–97) asked the assistance of Henry Livingston, who often acted as his agent in Jamaica, calling upon him as a businessman and friend to help in his brother John's adjustment to his new role as supercargo. Apparently despondent over the recent death of his brother Elisha Parker, John, seeking a change of scene, had journeyed to Jamaica. His brother James wrote:

> I shall finish this letter with introducing you to my Brother John who goes to Jamaica in the character of a Super Cargo the method of life he has been used to being quite disagreeable, It would be very unreasonable in me to expect from any person the assistance I fear he'll stand in need of tho' at the same time think youre so much my friend that you'd not be offended at my begging your advise to him in anything that does not Interfer with your own business which I'm well assured he'll always acknowledge with gratitude.[74]

A similar relationship, though perhaps not as intimate, existed between John Stevens, of Perth Amboy, and the firm of Scott, Pringle, and Scott, which acted as his agent in Madeira. Unable to journey to the island himself in 1742, he had his brother Richard deliver a special present, probably to "Mr. Pringle" with whom he was best acquainted. The present, a mockingbird, was intended to entertain and amuse, and John Stevens suggested it could be best displayed on a balcony and would most likely remain healthy if fed "Indian Corn, finely cut apple, and occasionally a hard boiled egg."[75] This feeling of friendship extended into business, and Stevens appears to have been quite understanding when the Madeira firm sent him eight pipes and one hogshead of inferior wine, "being new not Extra." Although it could not easily be sold in the New York market, he wrote that he realized they had sent the best they could.[76] It was expected that such gestures of trust and understanding would be reciprocated. If Stevens, in his dealings with other agents in Madeira, found himself short of cash, he expected that "Mr. Scott, Pringle and Scott will make good." On other occasions shippers were instructed to see John's agents for any sum under £100 sterling, and at least once he instructed his London agent Richard Jeneway to arrange for £1,200 insurance on a vessel and to seek payment from Walter and Robert Scott. It seems obvious that more than simple business relationships existed when such credit was given so readily and under such conditions.[77]

Things did not always run smoothly between merchant and agent, however. Scott, Pringle, and Scott on several occasions chided John Stevens for poor judgment in business. "You know what a miserable article Gammon are here," they wrote. By sending so many on both his and other accounts they feared the result would be "both of us will lose on such ventures."[78] But harmony seemed to prevail generally, with Scott, Pringle, and Scott requesting that John Stevens recommend the firm to his friends in Philadelphia who were apparently unhappy with their Madeira agent; they expressed genuine concern for Stevens's well-being during the period in which he undertook to be inoculated for smallpox.[79]

Elsewhere, John Stevens had other agents. In London there was Richard Jeneway, to whom he once sent a number of bills of exchange, asking the agent to make good on any that could not be cashed and to inform him of those protested so that he could repay him.[80] In effect, he asked for an unsecured loan. Stevens also insured the brig *Catherine* several times through Jeneway. Overseas insurance for vessels like the brig *Funchal* was provided by others with whom he had dealings, such as Willing and Caldwall in London. Stevens's brother-in-law William Alexander (Lord Stirling) also acted on occasion on his behalf.[81] Henry Steers and later the firm of Brome and Baron were his primary agents in Lisbon, but Scott, Pringle, and Scott were undoubtedly most important to Stevens because of his involvement in the wine trade. Much of that early trade was conducted by the brig *Catherine*, on which Stevens had first acted as master for the owners, Andrew and Lewis Johnston, then himself bought a quarter share of, and finally became the principal owner. By 1742 he no longer traveled to Madeira himself, but employed John Smith or his own brother Richard as master, with the latter sometimes acting as supercargo.[82]

John Stevens traded many commodities to Madeira, principally for wine. His cargo might include gammon, pipe staves, a box of iron, but the main cargos were flour and wheat. The money he received from such shipments often went into buying "New York wines," usually shipped in pipes securely bound by iron hoops. (The number of iron hoops used to bind each pipe was apparently important, and numerous references are made to them.)[83] Additional wines were purchased on credit.

The voyage of the brig *Catherine* in spring 1741, when John Stevens was captain but had not yet acquired a share in the vessel—he had leased it on occasion—is typical of the transactions and costs associated with the wine trade. William Oake had consigned to Stevens's care a large shipment of wheat, which Stevens sold on the Madeira market in May at prices varying from thirty-two to thirty-five Portuguese milreis. (A reis would be the equivalent of one-ninth of an American cent, and a milreis, or a thousand reis, would be worth about $1.11.) Some of the wheat had been damaged, perhaps by water or exposure during the voyage; this damaged commodity Stevens was fortunate to be able to sell at nine milreis a unit. All told, William Oake's cargo netted him a little over 383 milreis. From this total were deducted slightly over 100 milreis for expenses, the greater part of which, 80 milreis and 600 reis, was for freighting. In this instance, the price of depending on another shipper ran to over 20 percent of the total sales. The remaining costs were taken up by customs payment, measuring the wheat prior to sale, and Stevens's commission for disposing of the cargo. With the remainder, Stevens purchased for Oake a quarter cask of wine and seven pipes, for a total expenditure of 256 milreis. When the cost of customs duties, fees for placing iron hoops on the pipes, Stevens's 3½ percent commissions and incidentals were included, the total expenditure neatly balanced the profit from the sale of wheat at 283 milreis and 534 reis.[84] When the wine was sold in New York at £32 New York currency, or in Philadelphia or even the West Indies, William Oake could expect to make a substantial profit.

In the next few years John Stevens found himself an owner in the vessel he had once captained, a shipper of wheat and flour, and a substantial purchaser of wine. In this role he often procured insurance for both vessel and cargo. A typical policy provided coverage from Perth Amboy to Madeira and remained in effect on the cargo until twenty-four hours after safe anchor. The insurance apparently remained in effect on the vessel but was reinstated on the cargo only after loading at Madeira, remaining in effect until twenty-four hours after safe anchor at Perth Amboy.[85] Sometimes, when the risks were considered greater (for example, on a voyage of the brig *Catherine* in 1744 from Belfast to Madeira, via Lisbon and then New York), Stevens employed the common practice of setting an arrival date and requesting additional insurance on the vessel if it had not arrived by that date. Thus, he asked for £150 sterling on the *Catherine* and its cargo, provided his brother Richard had not brought her to Lisbon by December 10.[86]

The same concern for his investment that led him to insure his vessel and cargo probably led him to employ another common practice in order to insure that the pipes of wine shipped from Madeira were not short in measure. Whenever possible, the captain personally saw that each pipe he was to carry was "filled up to the Bung."[87] For such duties and for the responsibility of assisting in the sale and purchase of the cargo and obtaining insurance on the cargo and the vessel, the shipmaster received not only wages but "privilege." On one voyage, for example, Richard Stevens carried twenty-one hogsheads, paying the freight cost on thirteen, while the remaining eight were carried without cost as his privilege.[88] In this way he gained a tidy supplement to his wages as master.

John Stevens generally did well in his business enterprises in Madeira. But as was the case with all merchants involved in a high-risk venture, he sometimes encountered some adversity in trade. Unforeseen events and marketing errors made by both Stevens and his factors could cut deeply into profits or force him to operate at a loss. On one voyage Indian corn sent to Madeira spoiled en route, and he lamented, "I shall loose considerable."[89] On the same unfortunate voyage, his cargo of wheat turned out to be short on measure. Although Scott, Pringle, and Scott were willing to credit him for the full amount of five hundred bushels, he felt obligated to share in the loss. At the same time he asked his agents' assistance in procuring some wines to be shipped on his account, for a shipment of good wines could help "Ease me in the badness of the voyage."[90] In marketing, aside from the gammon fiasco alluded to earlier, Scott, Pringle, and Scott had held wheat Stevens shipped to them in the spring of 1746 in anticipation of a better price. However, as the summer began and the price stayed low, they became apprehensive that they might suffer a loss if they continued to hold it; the subsequent sale gained only a meager profit for the Perth Amboy merchant. Shortly after the sale, no additional wheat or flour arrived at Madeira and the market price rose. Of little consolation to Stevens was his factors' candid admission that in gauging price and the time to sell "we were deceived."[91]

Richard Stevens also proved a problem. Scott, Pringle, and Scott were apparently apprehensive about dealing directly with him, expressing concern to John because he himself was not more involved in the process.[92] That Richard was doing well in arranging the Madeira accounts in 1746 must have been small comfort in view of the news that his departure had been delayed because he had stoved in the brig *Catherine* and repairs to the vessel were proving difficult.[93] A year later, despite direct orders to the contrary, Richard sold the brig to Edmond Field, Fowkes, and Company, while with the *Catherine* in Lisbon. "No doubt," wrote Richard to his brother, "the sale comes as a surprise." He promised to explain the circumstances that led him to act "against your orders" upon his arrival home. He was traveling now as a passenger from Lisbon to Philadelphia.[94] Richard's business acumen (or lack of it) eventually brought him to bankruptcy, and John must have felt a degree of trepidation in his dealings with Richard, both as his employer and as his partner.

Despite an occasional setback, trade with Madeira was profitable. Not only was there money to be made in the wine trade, but for the enterpreneur who owned his own vessel additional income came from freighting for others. For example, one might charge forty shillings, New Jersey proclamation money, to ship a pipe of wine from the island to Perth Amboy. As an agent for other merchants, Stevens received a commission of anywhere from 3 to 5 percent, arranging for the purchase of wines to be charged to their account and often providing for its delivery to a third party. He also obtained insurance at times for those whose cargo he carried. For example, he procured insurance of £150 sterling for Peter Kemble to cover his effects being shipped from Madeira aboard the *Catherine*.[95]

These activities required, on occasion, the skill of a banker, for Stevens had to deal in reis, pounds, New York currency, pistoles, New Jersey proclamation money, moidores, and bills of exchange, as well as commodity equivalents, to name the most frequent media of transactions. Like most merchants, he frequently found himself mixing several of these media of exchange in a single enterprise. Stevens often availed himself of similar services on the part of other merchant-shippers in an attempt to take advantage of immediate market situations when none of his own vessels was available.[96]

Above all, John Stevens recognized that reduced marketing risks meant improved chances of profit; he seized every opportunity to improve his circumstances. Once he learned that a vessel then in Madeira was planning to carry wines to the West Indies for sale; the vessel's captain intended to ship "New York wines," so that if the market in Jamaica or Barbados proved to be less than expected, the vessel could simply proceed to New York, thereby providing an alternate source of profit. Stevens hurriedly wrote to his Madeira factors, for he felt that this scheme might well provide a competitive edge. He instructed them that he wished to adopt a similar plan, "That I may lay under no disadvantage."[97] It was by such attention to business that Stevens achieved his success in the wine trade to Madeira. John Stevens was also active in the West Indies trade, operating in much the same way he did in Madeira. Agents, however, were not as frequently employed in the Caribbean as in Madeira. While Madeira represented a single market, the West Indies had many potential markets; the need for imports and availability of exports varied from island to island almost with every trip. Under such conditions, the ship's captain most often did the buying and selling of cargo.[98] This had been John Stevens's own experience when in 1739 he had taken the sloop *Martha* to Jamaica. Andrew and Lewis Johnston, its principal owners, had given him much latitude in marketing, sales, and routes. By their instructions he was to sell to the best advantage, sending in return cash, bills of exchange, or island produce. He was to use his judgment as to which would provide the greatest advantage and to return home directly or go elsewhere as the market warranted. Finally, the owners instructed him that if, in his judgment, he could obtain a good price for the vessel, it, too, might be sold.[99] Few captains were given that much freedom of action, but most were allowed to exercise some judgment about market and price so that flexibility might be maintained in this elusive marketplace.

Though the shipmaster often acted as supercargo, there were many times when merchants used agents to assist in the West Indies trade. Stevens most often used William Byam as his agent in Antigua, and the firm of Reade and Livingston performed the same function for him in Jamaica.[100] These agents sent him merchandise on account and kept him apprised of market conditions in the islands, on one occasion suggesting that the situation was such that a small vessel with foodstuffs and candles should be sent immediately to Jamaica.[101]

The trade system Stevens employed was varied. He operated his own ships from several colonial ports, one time sailing a ship like the *Elizabeth* from New York, the next time using the same vessel to clear from Perth Amboy. He shipped out of the New Jersey ports usually when he had a complete cargo for a specific destination. This was most often Madeira and occasionally the West Indies. Imports were arranged in much the same manner. Stevens also handled goods consigned to him, but carried by craft other than his own, as well as cargos for other merchants. In these transactions he again shipped from Perth Amboy when a specific cargo was called for or a market readily available.[102] When goods were carried on his account as part of a larger general cargo of another merchant, or when he planned to send the *Elizabeth, Funchal,* or another vessel to a number of possible locations seeking markets, he transacted business from New York.[103] For these ventures he was likely to assemble a variety of cargos at New York, including items sent over from New Jersey.[104]

Although John Stevens was fairly active at Perth Amboy in the early 1750s, he used the port infrequently in the late 1750s and early 1760s, apparently lured as others had been to a greater use of the facilities at New York. His brother Richard, now himself a prominent merchant, continued to use the port and in all probability freighted an occasional cargo for John, thus indirectly continuing the latter's involvement with Perth Amboy.[105]

Financial Difficulties

Richard Stevens's apparent success was illusory, for in 1767 he was on the verge of bankruptcy, deeply indebted to a number of Philadelphia merchants, among them Adam Hope, Nathan Hyde, and Robert Morris. In an attempt to extricate himself from this situation, he met with these three men and two others, John Macie and John Startin—the five were his major creditors—and negotiated a settlement involving the surrender of his entire estate, real and personal. This satisfaction of debt agreed to, some of his creditors then refused to accept the settlement, forcing him to flee Pennsylvania for New Jersey, lest he be arrested and prosecuted for debt. Being unable to return to Philadelphia made it extremely difficult, he exclaimed, to support his family.[106]

Five years after this unfortunate incident, Richard Stevens had an attorney prepare a petition to the legislature asking relief from all demands and debts contracted before February 1767.[107] In his endeavor to reestablish himself in trade and commerce, Richard Stevens had the support of his more prosperous brother John, whose appraisal of Richard's situation was doubtless tempered by the knowledge that any merchant could fall upon hard times.

The Stevenses were not the only local merchants to experience serious financial difficulties. In 1764 James Johnston found himself in debt for what appears to have been the modest sum of £30.[108] Plagued by several of his creditors, he pleaded with James Parker for a cash advance: "for the whole about Thirty pounds, if could be gott would put me out of danger of being sued before a magistrate, and make me much easier in my mind as I actually now am afraid to see any person coming near the house least it be a dunn or constable."[109] Business failure, temporary or more lasting, seems to have been common among the merchant class, and at Perth Amboy the Parkers were often called upon to help resolve the difficulties of fellow merchants.

If the continually changing nature of commerce proved disastrous for some Perth Amboy merchants, the changing nature of traffic in the harbor in the late 1750s and 1760s portended still another stage in the port's decline. The small merchant owning his own vessel abandoned the port, perhaps due to pressures imposed by war and certainly because New Jersey still lacked a well-developed merchant class. Most East Jersey trade fell into the hands of one or two individuals, who operated out of New Brunswick and cleared customs at Perth Amboy.

New Brunswick Merchants

New Brunswick, located on the banks of the Raritan, was well suited for shipping and quite early attracted a number of merchants. Jacob Hude was one of the town's early merchants. By 1724 he was shipping the produce of the countryside aboard the sloop *Brunswick* in partnership with William Cox and Jacob Oake.[110] New Brunswick's commercial potential was recognized early by these men. In 1730, along with James Neilson and others, they secured a charter for their town and then served in various civic capacities.[111] They also continued in a small way to engage in shipping; aside from the *Brunswick*, Hude was a partner in the late 1740s in two vessels that cleared through Perth Amboy, a small sloop and the 120-ton snow *Belfast*. Jacob Oake in the same period owned a sloop and a boat, which occasionally could be seen at Perth Amboy, and William Cox seems to have joined in several maritime partnerships.[112]

The most prominent figure, however, was James Neilson. For more than half a century he conducted a mercantile business out of New Brunswick. He owned a number of warehouses that served as collecting points for some of the produce from the surrounding countryside, having on hand at any one time two thousand bushels of wheat and one thousand of corn.[113] In addition, he owned several mills in the area, and several stores. He imported textiles, hardware, spices, paints, and books from London, mostly via New York, shuttling cargo

The possibility of loading and unloading cargo at countless inlets, landings, and harbors across the colony contributed to the failure of New Jersey's three ports. This sort of localized trade is illustrated (below) in a water color of Hillyer's Store, New Brunswick, 1802, by Archibald Robertson (1765–1835). The sloop unloading in New Brunswick might just as well have docked in the countryside, as we see (left) is a detail from an idealized British view of an American farm, "A Design to Represent the Beginning and Completion of an American Settlement or Farm," engraved by James Peake, London, [1768]. NJHS.

across the Hudson.[114] To pay for these imports and to acquire other goods for his store he joined in a partnership with other local merchants in the snow *Belfast*, to trade with the West Indies.[115] But he was quick to realize that cities such as Boston and Providence could provide much the same advantage as West Indies trade in the exchange of agricultural and timber products for items that could eventually be credited against British imports.

The schooners and sloops used to conduct such a coastwise trade were particularly well suited for the New England venture. They could easily navigate the winding and shallow Raritan River to New Brunswick, where such vessels as the *Brunswick Swallow*, the *New Brunswick*, or the *Hanna* would be loaded, probably under the watchful eye of their co-owner Richard Gibb, who served as captain and supercargo on almost all these ventures.[116] Fully loaded they would then sail downriver into the Hudson and up to Perth Amboy to clear customs. From there it was a quick run to Boston or Rhode Island and back. Employing two or three vessels in a shuttle trade Neilson and Gibb were fully committed, with six to eight clearings a year, to the use of the harbor and its facilities, bringing in goods for New Jersey consumption (manufactured items and various West Indian products) and exporting local farm products.[117]

James Neilson, Richard Gibb, and a handful of others at this late period in the port's development were able to use it to their advantage and to conduct their business on a cost-effective basis, because New Jersey's maritime life had diminished to the point where a few individuals, operating within a very narrow sphere, could provide all the services required by maritime trade and desired by the community. Such a commitment, then, marked not the rebirth but rather the demise of New Jersey's shipping industry, reducing Perth Amboy to little more than a local port with limited coastal trade.

West Jersey Merchants

While several merchant-shippers were involved over an extended period of time with New Jersey's eastern port, the Smiths at Burlington were the only family of means and commercial connections who used the latter port in the period under consideration. Daniel and Samuel, two brothers among the first generation of Burlington's Smith family, although interested primarily in land and the legal profession, engaged in some commercial ventures, beginning at the turn of the century. From this early beginning, the next generation built a substantial commercial empire, primarily through trade with the West Indies. Daniel Smith's sons (Daniel, Jr., Robert, and John) and Samuel Smith's son (Richard, Jr.) were very active in all aspects of maritime trade.[118]

The Smith family was very closely knit, and in varying degrees its members combined their efforts in almost every commercial venture they undertook.[119] Richard Smith, Jr., who built a fine house on what is today High Street and had wharfs at Burlington on what are called the Green Banks, was the leading merchant in the family and apparently provided the leadership for most of the family's commercial ventures.[120] West Indian enterprise, the area of the Smiths' greatest commercial activity, was made easier when John Smith took up residence in the West Indies in 1726. Additional ties with that area were provided when Katharine Smith, Richard's cousin, married William Callender, an important merchant in Barbados. Although after the marriage Callender moved his operations to Philadelphia, other members of that family remained in the islands, providing a network of contacts.[121] On occasion, either William Callender or Joseph Callender, who still resided on Barbados, joined the Smiths in their shipping ventures.[122]

The Smith family used its local port at Burlington as an extension of commercial ventures generated from Philadelphia, much as their counterparts had done at Perth Amboy in the 1720s. Similarly, their business and social life was interwoven with that of the neighboring colony. As a family, the Smiths were on excellent terms with many of their Pennsylvania brethren, and they moved among that colony's Quaker elite, which included among their intimate friends the Pemberton and Logan families. Richard Smith's second son, John, married James Logan's daughter Hannah in 1748.[123]

In the Quaker capital, where religion and social position were so closely intertwined with business, the Smiths had every advantage for continued commercial success, and this was where they made their major efforts.[124] Then, too, Philadelphia, like New York, provided the commercial services that Burlington could not. Burlington was no longer an active port by 1730 but was, rather, a stopping place for ventures originating or destined for completion elsewhere. Within this pattern of trade, vessels such as the *Elizabeth*, the *Mary and Elizabeth*, and the *Seaflower*, a sixty-ton ship built in Burlington in 1733 and registered in New York, carried the banner of the Smith family and the Smiths' friends.[125] These vessels were in Burlington a few times in a year. They arrived primarily from Barbados or came up almost empty from Philadelphia, carrying rum, sugar, and molasses. Then they departed with foodstuffs and lumber, almost always bound to the West Indies, usually going to Barbados and occasionally to Antigua.[126] Often they were only partially loaded, then sailed down to Philadelphia, staying as long as a week while additional goods were loaded, before they continued to the West Indies.[127]

Farther down the coast, a few merchants such as Jacob Spicer engaged in maritime trade. Spicer was one of the leading merchants in the Cape May region. Entering politics at the age of twenty-eight, he devoted more than twenty-one years of service as a member of the assembly. During those years he acquired a considerable amount of land and engaged in an active mercantile business.

Spicer did not have a large fleet. He owned one or two small vessels and traded in a variety of commodities. Corn, wheat, and timber products were shipped to New York and Philadelphia; there was an occasional voyage to New England, mostly Rhode Island, and sometimes in the winter a trip south to North Carolina.[128] Spicer carried his own goods on such voyages, as well as freighting goods for others. He charged six shillings per barrel to North Carolina and slightly more on the return trip, and he shipped shingles to New York at five shillings per thousand.[129] On many occasions he shipped wheat for others, sometimes storing some of it at his own home prior to shipment.[130] One of his vessels, the twenty-ton sloop *Dove*, worked directly out of Salem.[131] But much of the traffic Spicer carried was local, from Egg Harbor, Townsend's Inlet, and other places in Cape May. He used several vessels, one a shallop that he refurbished in 1760 and another that was built for him in Philadelphia in 1761 at a cost of £70.[132] Most of his business was conducted through Philadelphia, and Spicer's diary is replete with entries such as "in Philadelphia compleating my business there." From Philadelphia he imported dry and wet goods, principally cloth and wine.[133] In return he exported large quantities of shingles from his own landholdings, and some foodstuffs and dry goods, including furs that he had taken in barter transactions with Cape May residents.[134]

Jacob Spicer was a careful and methodical man, qualities perhaps reflecting the years he spent as a lawyer and as a compiler (with Aaron Leaming) of the laws of New Jersey. He was constantly estimating the market available to him, determining the potential imports and exports for his region: how much each family made; how much "ready cash" his competitors, who had introduced rum sales into the region, could be expected to make per month or per year; what damage such sales would do to the local business.[135] In the same vein he developed rules of trade for himself. Credit, which was the lifeblood of trade in rural regions, was to be given for dry goods, initially for six months and extended if necessary for a longer period. But Spicer required "cash when received" for consumable luxuries, principally "Wine, rum, sugar, molasses, tea, coffee and chocolate." Always the lawyer as well as the businessman, he determined that barter goods were to be received at a fixed price, but if the price proved higher in Philadelphia, where Spicer exchanged such goods, then the difference was to go to the original seller.[136]

Part of Spicer's success as a merchant was undoubtedly due to the manner in which he involved himself in trade. He was helped by his political connections, developed through his long service in the legislature, as well as those of his father. In 1745, for example, he worked in conjunction with William Mott to send supplies worth £1,000 aboard the sloop *Dolphine* to the governor of Massachusetts, William Shirley, for the use of the military at Cape Breton.[137] In 1755 he purchased military supplies for the New Jersey government, taking that occasion to cement further connections with the Philadelphia merchants with whom he dealt. He wrote Abel James, of Philadelphia, "Gratitude inclines me to give you a preference, provided I can do it consistant with the Trust reposed in me."[138]

He was an astute observer and kept careful account of agricultural conditions in the region. He knew who had planted what and how much yield could be expected, and he knew what would be available for marketing, and when.[139] To keep his finger ever on the pulse of trade he occasionally carried out trade himself: he planned in July 1761 to carry a load of clapboards for Joseph Savage to Rhode Island or some other market in return for one-third the value, but last-minute judicial and legislative commitments required him to dispatch "some good hands" to undertake the voyage.[140]

He eventually found the pace of mercantile life too hectic and time consuming. Perhaps due in part to the demands of his constant travel to Philadelphia, he finally withdrew from the business. He noted in his diary, "July 2, 1765, Have left off trade." But a Spicer continued in trade, for his son and namesake was apprenticed to a Philadelphia mercantile establishment and later became a successful merchant.[141]

By the 1730s, Burlington had been eclipsed by Philadelphia as a commercial center. The decline of its harbor was inevitable and was doubtless hastened by the fact that most of the trade conducted by the Smiths neither originated nor terminated at Burlington. At Salem the almost total dependence of local merchants on Philadelphia for imported goods had relegated that port to feeder status. Yet the occasional use of the port by local merchants' ships and a few other craft at least maintained a pretext for operating the harbor as a port of entry, and that in itself gave limited focus to the general commercial life of West Jersey.

Maritime Partnerships

Those engaged in maritime commerce were fully cognizant of the cost of such enterprises, both in terms of the initial investment and in terms of the risk that the entire vessel might be lost through some hazard, natural or otherwise. It was quite common for large vessels (ships, brigs, and snows of over eighty tons) to be owned by four, six, ten, or more persons; in the case of a privateer, twelve, twenty, or perhaps an entire village might own shares.

A study of the New Jersey ports indicates that multiple ownership was not limited by the size of the craft or by the amount of capital invested. In waters where the majority of the vessels were sloops and schooners of thirty tons or less, almost 50 percent of the owners, composed of all merchant categories, employed partnerships.[142] This was especially true of small entrepreneurs,[143] because multi-ownership of vessels was often the only means by which such merchants could gain sufficient capital to engage in trade.

Merchant-owners took a far greater relative risk—the loss of a single sloop (probably their only one) could destroy them completely—than did investors or the merchant-shippers. Men in the latter category—such as John Parker, Andrew Johnston, John Stevens, and others—were apparently reluctant to consolidate their funds in any single enterprise, preferring to disperse their capital among several vessels, as well as among such diverse investments as transportation, land, and mining. They were, of course, exercising a native caution, but they were also often acting through necessity borne of a lack of real capital.

The nature of partnerships varied in New Jersey, as it did throughout the colonies. Over a period of years a vessel was likely to be owned by several different combinations of individuals, with one or two men providing the base and others joining, often on a voyage-to-voyage basis. At Perth Amboy it was quite common for sloops to be owned jointly one year, to be owned singly the following year, and then within that same year to be owned jointly again by the same individuals who had formed the first partnership.[144] John Hanse, owner of the sloop *Dove*, had a different partner every year he used the port.[145] At Burlington, the *Seaflower* began its existence in 1733 with a partnership of three members of the Smith family and Oswall Peel. In the same year, William Callender was added to the owners' list, but after several voyages he withdrew and was replaced by Robert Callender.[146] Both these men were related to the Smith family through marriage, and indeed most partnership arrangements in New Jersey appear to have involved family members and relations.[147]

The amount of capital required often determined the size of the partnership. As indicated earlier, large vessels were usually owned by four or more persons. Quite often the partnership was large enough to be referred to as a company ownership and was so listed on the registry. Between 10 and 20 percent of the craft entering Perth Amboy prior to 1750 were designated as company-owned, although that number eventually decreased as larger vessels ceased to frequent the port.[148] The most popular arrangement, however, seems to have been a partnership of two or three individuals, probably because of the limited size of the craft using the harbor.[149] But the problem of available capital and the high degree of risk encouraged larger partnerships even in relatively small sloops like the *Eagle of Amboy*, owned by James Johnston, John Parker, Isaac Stelle, and George Frasor, or the *Brunswick of East Jersey* and the *Charles*, both of which were company-owned. Partnerships, then, allowed the various merchants to conduct the widest possible business at the least risk; furthermore, many merchants operated in partnerships, not only in shipping but in their other business endeavors.

In many ways, New Jersey's merchants, in their diversity of investments, in the nature of vessel ownership, and in their varying functions within specific categories, were similar to merchants throughout colonial America.[150] But the relationship of the port users to the development of the harbors was unique. All the merchants wished for viable ports in New Jersey, but they were caught between desire and economic necessity. Their dilemma was self-perpetuating, for the merchant-shippers had to gain their livelihood by relying on the neighboring colonies at the expense of the very ports they had hoped to develop. This in turn discouraged the development of a large class of merchant-owners. Consequently, the New Jersey ports were deprived of the strong merchant class and thriving trade needed for economic development of the ports.

7

Dark and Dismal Days

BY THE 1760s PERTH AMBOY was but a shadow of the *"portus optimus"* proclaimed by the town elders in 1718. It was a convenient port of call for the occasional vessel needing an additional cargo, and on rare occasions it was visited by a sloop, schooner, or brig owned by a local merchant. Burlington and Salem gave the appearance of bustling ports, but the vessels that used their waters were engaged almost exclusively in shuttle trade with Philadelphia, other parts of New Jersey, and, infrequently, New York. Vessels engaged in this shuttle trade were issued permits that allowed them to operate without officially clearing and entering customs. Overseas and coastwise trade that required official clearance was limited, although a few vessels carrying cargos of local produce and timber still sailed for Jamaica or Barbados.

A similar situation existed at Cape May, Little Egg Harbor, and other small harbors along the coast. Although these were not official ports of entry, Jacob Spicer, deputy collector for Salem-Cohansey, had taken a pragmatic approach in dealing with the needs of shipowners operating them. He realized that in some cases clearing ports required shipowners to make a journey of fifty, sixty, or seventy miles, a situation that produced "a hardship almost unsurmountable." To circumvent the law, Spicer left blank clearances at centrally located areas along the coast. He entrusted them to people of integrity who would act as his representatives and could fill them out as the need arose.[1]

This solution, which undoubtedly violated official policy, ended abruptly late in 1764 when Spicer was informed by his immediate supervisor, John Hatton, the newly appointed collector of customs at Salem-Cohansey, that the surveyor general now required all entries and clearances to be signed by the customs officer under his seal. Spicer found the requirement foolish. He noted the inconvenience of sending down signed and sealed blanks and suggested that under the new rules, "might not Inconveniences ensue to collectors in particular, as well as the Trade in General?"[2] Emphasizing the inappropriateness of this new edict, Spicer pointed out, "The permits I have received are not in the usual form appearing rather to Grant permission to Load for the port than to Depart thither and conclude with a Direction to the waiters, none of which we have." He further queried Hatton as to whether small craft were now required to take permits to load and unload, as Hatton's instructions seemed to suggest. Here both the pragmatist and lawyer in the man are apparent, as he reminded the collector,

> the Laws of the province to the best of my memory Grants no fees for permits to load and unload any other than foreign Vessels. . . . [P]lease to inform me how the fees for the same are to be received which if provided for in Clearest Terms and Insisted on, with the Bonds Directed to be taken on the Exportation of Lumber I apprehend will Occasion great muttering.[3]

Spicer was sensitive to the public mood. That he perceived a growing resentment directed toward what were believed to be the unwise policies of a distant government is indicated in his insistence,

> Before even I attempt to Carry it [these new regulations] into execution I[t] must be you'll Send Advertisements to Cape May to Notify the public that you insist on and have directed me to take those Bonds, as also permits for loading and unloading Small Craft if the latter be your Intention, least I should otherwise Incur the Displeasure of the populace while I am attempting to Serve the Office and Ease the navigation.[4]

Whether the new laws were eventually enforced in the Cape May region is not known. But their effect, beyond irritating the local populace, would probably have been minimal, because New Jerseyans in the region would have acted as they had previously to circumvent the law, and also because non-regional shipping was minimal. How slight this non-regional trade was is illustrated in Jacob Spicer's report on trade to the newly appointed John Hatton. Spicer, in forwarding the "Entries Inward and Clearances Southward" for 1763 and 1764, noted that his tardiness in sending records was due largely to a lack of any significant trade. He remarked that, should quarterly reports be needed, his might often be sent blank, "especially with respect to foreign vessels," which he classified as any vessel not trading by permit between the neighboring colonial ports. The total fees collected in conjunction with customs operations for a calendar year amounted to a meager £2:6:6.[5]

There is little to indicate any significant activity involving non-local maritime trade at any of the New Jersey ports during this period. Newspaper accounts for the period indicated that there was considerable local trade with Philadelphia and New York, not only from the ports of entry but from Raritan Landing, Little Egg Harbor, Barnegat, and Elizabethtown. There is little mention of the type of trade and commerce vital to the existence and development of commercial enterprises at the official ports. Indeed, the newspapers reported more vessels wrecked or floundered off the New Jersey coast than arriving either from the West Indies, from other colonies, or from Europe.[6] Local merchants continued to offer European commodities throughout the 1770s. New Jerseyans could buy Bibles, needles, looking glasses, brass chair nails, and even paint at such mercantile establishments as the Rahway store of Joseph and John Shotwell.[7] But these European items came by way of New York and Philadelphia, which not only continued to dominate New Jersey's economy but looked upon attempts by that colony to improve its economic posture—with the incorporation of Trenton in 1745, a time when New Jersey was hardly an economic competitor—as acts of commercial hostility to be countered and resisted.[8]

On the eve of the Revolution there was so little trade abroad that Governor William Franklin had to report to the earl of Dartmouth that the records kept by the customs officers

> can be of very little if any use in forming an Idea of the Quantity of our produce sent to foreign markets. New York and Philadelphia are in Reality the Commercial capitals of East and West Jersey; and almost all of the Articles we import for Home Consumption are from one or other of those Cities, of which no Entries are or can well be made at our Customs House, consequently we have no way of coming at an exact account of them.[9]

Trade to the West Indies and Madeira from New Jersey ports was quite small. It involved no more than two vessels and was carried out from Perth Amboy and perhaps now directly from New Brunswick, Raritan Landing, or similar harbors. Franklin reported in 1774 that the district of Perth Amboy included several ports.[10] Vessels that used the New Jersey ports to engage in the West Indies trade were still small sloops and schooners belonging primarily, the governor noted, to New Englanders. The few registered in New Jersey seldom returned directly to their own ports, landing their cargo instead at New York or Philadelphia. As for trade directly to Europe, there was none.[11] From all the evidence available, it appears that from the 1760s on, New Jersey's major ports languished and added little to the colony's economy.

New Jersey's economy had been hard pressed since the end of the French and Indian War. After 1763, New Jersey had experienced a serious recession. The economy had been artificially expanded during the war by great expenditures and unprecedented consumption of agricultural goods. With the coming of peace it returned to more normal levels, setting off a serious contraction in almost all economic sectors. That contraction was intensified by a chronic scarcity of all types of currency and by the withdrawal of paper money issued during the war. Merchants in Perth Amboy, Burlington, and elsewhere in the colony were confronted by the fact that as their economy was dominated by New York and Philadelphia, the colony imported from them almost all manufactured goods. What currency was in circulation tended to flow out of the colony.

In addition, New Jersey merchants faced a general deterioration of their economic well-being, a problem that confronted almost all those whose livelihood involved maritime commerce. Beginning in the 1750s, American merchants, spurred on by liberal credit policies, expanded rapidly and now found themselves overstocked and indebted to English creditors. This additional economic burden was intensified by changes in English marketing techniques that increasingly relied on a system of direct selling to the colonies through company agents and auctions. This eliminated the middleman, the local merchant.[12] The merchant class in New Jersey, as well as throughout colonial America, found itself struggling to maintain its position. Because this new marketing technique was concentrated in areas of large urban populations, even more trade was channeled to these locales; after the war this may well have made it more difficult for the lesser ports to recover.

Revolutionary Ferment and the Maritime Economy

Despite all these economic difficulties, the focus of maritime trade in the 1760s became as much political as economic, as Americans responded to what they perceived as changes in British colonial policy that went beyond Parliament's constitutional prerogatives. In an attempt to administer better and reduce the cost of its newly expanded empire, the British government enacted in this period a series of duties and taxes designed to raise revenues. Two in particular met with staunch resistance: the Stamp Act of 1765, which required a tax in the form of a stamp to be placed upon all legal documents and on commercial papers such as bills of sale, as well as dice, cards, and newspapers; and the Townshend duties of 1767, which placed a tax on the importation of paint, lead, paper, tea, and glass.[13]

Not only did these acts affect colonial shipping, they provided a focus for colonial resistance. The American response to such "tyranny" was commercial retaliation involving economic sanctions in the form of non-importation of British goods. New Jersey's port economy, in the absence of virtually all overseas imports, was little affected and subsequently could contribute little economically to this effort.

Perhaps it was this factor, as well as the absence of a large merchant community (which in other colonies helped to marshal opposition to this legislation) and newspapers that enabled Governor William Franklin to moderate local response to the Stamp Act. Both as individuals and in the legislature New Jerseyans reacted far less violently than did their neighbors. The actions that were forthcoming from the colony of New Jersey were in large part influenced by the more radical elements in New York and Philadelphia. But there was a growing radicalism in the province. For some the die had been cast, and the repeal of the Stamp Act only helped to insure that subsequent acts of Parliament would engender stronger reaction in New Jersey, with trade, commerce, and the ports a symbolic rallying point.[14]

The enactment of the Townshend duties two years later brought a renewal of non-importation policies from the American colonies. New Jersey, which before had responded mildly to parliamentary acts, now displayed a growing militancy, caused in part by a worsening economic situation that many New Jerseyans felt had been exacerbated by parliamentary action. Of immediate concern was the sudden reduction of credit and general reduction of capital occasioned by the Currency Act of 1764, which restricted the use of paper money as legal tender. This restriction hit especially hard at New Jersey farmers and small merchants, many of whom were forced to liquidate at a considerable loss. By 1768 the situation had become so grave that the New Jersey legislature demanded relief through the creation of a loan office. This atmosphere of increasing economic crisis fed the discontent that focused on the Townshend duties. Unable to participate directly in non-importation, New Jersey offered encouragement and political support to its neighbors. The legislature gave official thanks to New York and Pennsylvania for those colonies' public sacrifice in refusing to import British goods until the Townshend duties were repealed.[15]

Perhaps frustrated by their inability to act more directly, New Jerseyans were incensed at those in other colonies who acted contrary to the non-importation agreement. Newport, Rhode Island, was the target of New Jersey's wrath, but it was New York, which previously had won the accolades of the New Jersey assembly, upon whom the greatest scorn was heaped. Many in that colony, far from remaining steadfast in their resolve, had begun to trade in English goods. Those who foolishly ventured to New Jersey's shores found a hostile reception.[16] New Jerseyans' condemnation of their neighbors' trade with England was best exhibited in the aftermath of the duties' repeal. There was, at least momentarily, strong sentiment for reviving New Jersey's overseas trade through the revitalization of Perth Amboy, an action that would allow New Jerseyans to disassociate themselves from their Hudson River neighbors. But efforts to revitalize the port were soon eclipsed by more immediate economic problems, among them a second rejection of the Loan Office Act. The decision effectively ended all hope of providing a medium of exchange other than specie and further weakened New Jersey's economy.

Although New Jersey's economic and political struggles were for the most part local affairs (a battle with the governor to remove Stephen Skinner as treasurer of East Jersey for his "loss" of provincial funds; the quarrel over a legislative appropriation for quartering British troops in the colony), New Jerseyans were aware of and sympathetic to the struggle between other colonies and Parliament over the question of taxation.[17] The controversy over tea, specifically over England's right to place a tax on it in order to raise revenue, gave New Jerseyans the opportunity to express their displeasure with this policy directly. No tea consignments were due to pass through New Jersey customs. Such cargos were instead destined for merchant distributors in Boston, Philadelphia, and New York. But in 1774 the turmoil in those cities over tea sales brought the Philadelphia-bound brig *Greyhound* temporarily into the supposedly tranquil harbor of Greenwich, New Jersey.[18]

Greenwich harbor, part of the Salem-Cohansey customs district, was an active local port doing little foreign or coastwise trade. It engaged chiefly in shuttling small sloops and schooners to and from Philadelphia and the surrounding region. At Greenwich the *Greyhound's* tea was secretly unloaded and stored in a warehouse cellar for safekeeping. Tea had come to New Jersey, and its citizens, discovering its presence, seized the opportunity to do their part. While some prepared to discuss the best course of action to be taken, others dressed as Indians, and on December 22, 1774, they seized the tea as had been done earlier at Boston. They destroyed it, adding their own touch by burning the chests of tea in a huge bonfire.[19] The aftermath of this activity reflected public sentiment on the question of taxation and tea, for although attempts were made to indict several persons for the offense, no one ever came to trial.

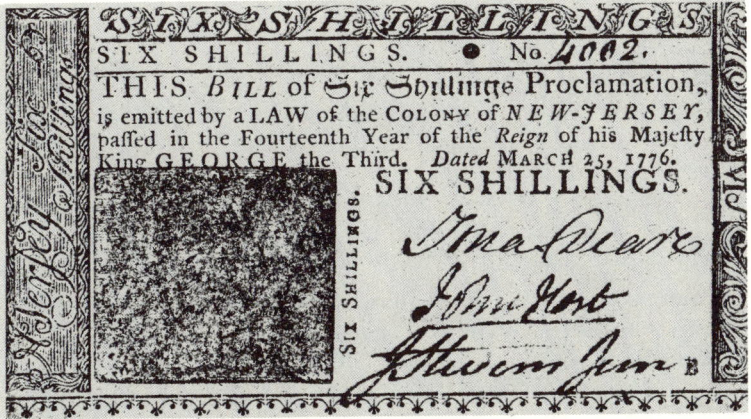

A six-shilling note, dated March 25, 1776, and signed by Jonathan Deare (1748–96), a Perth Amboy lawyer and member of the New Jersey Provincial Congress; John Hart (1711?–79), Speaker of the New Jersey Assembly and a signer of the Declaration of Independence; and John Stevens (1749–1838), Treasurer of New Jersey. NJHS

To close the New Jersey ports as a punishment for the colony's actions would have had little effect. But the British had already made an example of Boston for its Tea Party, as well as implementing some long-discussed changes to bring the Massachusetts government more closely into administrative compliance with those of other royal colonies. The result was a whirlwind of protest that led to the formation of the Continental Congress. This body turned once again to economic coercion as a means of resolving the colonies' political problems, calling upon all colonies neither to import goods from nor export goods to Great Britain. New Jerseyans responded to the call. As had been the case with the Townshend duties, careful watch was kept at the New Jersey ports and other landing places, particularly for small vessels bound from New York or Philadelphia that might be transshipping British goods. People found importing such goods or even using them were treated to public scorn, ostracism, and occasional violence, leading most to comply with the Articles of Association.[20] But this time economic pressure against Great Britain proved futile, and the events at Lexington and Concord on April 15, 1775, quickly elevated the protest to armed rebellion.

War in the Ports

The early stages of the war were fought in and across New Jersey, disrupting what little maritime commerce still remained. In July 1776, American forces camped in the vicinity of Perth Amboy. The town, as a capital of the province, had many residents who were closely tied politically or economically to the Crown, and George Washington hoped his presence would check Loyalist sentiment.[21] While Americans occupied the town, a British brig entered the harbor and exchanged fire with the Americans on shore, causing little damage but foreshadowing events to come. In November the British invaded New Jersey in force, sweeping the Continental forces from the state and forcing them to take refuge across the Delaware River. By Christmas, British forces were garrisoned in both Perth Amboy and New Brunswick.[22] The port at Perth Amboy was used by the British during this period as a staging area and supply point from which they attempted on one occasion to supply their forces via the Raritan River. It proved an ill-fated venture; the British were beaten back by American artillery. By 1777 the presence of the Continental Army once again in New Jersey forced the British to a defensive position. Six months later, the British used Perth Amboy's port facilities one last time to evacuate themselves from New Jersey's shores.[23] The port city of Burlington had experienced similar problems. Hessian troops had occupied the area for awhile, and the city had been subjected to bombardment by enemy vessels twice, though with little damage. While the British held Philadelphia the town was subjected to periodic raids.[24]

The presence of British warships and the close proximity of the enemy rendered maritime commerce impossible. But the ports and harbors were often used by privateers and raiders to strike at the British, and they often provided an avenue for supplies needed to sustain the Continental cause. In East Jersey small whaleboats working out of New Brunswick and Perth Amboy conducted raids against enemy ships, capturing both commercial and small military vessels.[25] These raids eventually became sufficiently destructive to warrant the direct attention of the British military, which launched an expedition into the New Brunswick region at the beginning of 1782, destroying the "whale boat fleet."[26]

While the British were in possession of Philadelphia, the ports at Salem and Burlington afforded the Americans little comfort. Denied those ports, New Jerseyans turned as they had so often before to the unofficial ports along the Atlantic. At Little Egg Harbor, Mullica River, Toms River, and Cape May Landing, significant privateering was being carried out in vessels ranging from whaleboats to brigantines.[27] These unofficial ports also became conduits for food and supplies, with wagons often used, as was the case with supplies for Valley Forge, to move goods into the interior. The old smugglers' route was now put to a more patriotic use.[28]

For the maritime entrepreneur, like the shipbuilding farmer, the war was at best a mixed blessing, at worst an economic disaster. A considerable number of merchants and others involved in maritime pursuits remained loyal to the Crown at the outbreak of the Revolution. They were men such as Stephen Skinner and Michael Kearny, Jr., merchants and shipowners at Perth Amboy; Bernard LaGrange, lawyer and landowner, who in partnership with his father-in-law traded out of Raritan Landing; and nearby, at New Brunswick, Arthur Scott Neilson, who managed the mercantile affairs of his uncle James Neilson (unlike his nephew, a staunch supporter of independence). All eventually came to ally themselves against the American cause. For these and other Loyalists, the rebels' control of the state after 1778, combined with, in many cases, their own direct involvement in attempting to suppress the rebellion—Stephen Skinner raised a company of New Jersey Loyalists in New York and later held the rank of major in the British Army—left most of them unwilling or unable to engage in New Jersey's maritime commerce.[29] Some merchants, most notably James Parker, a merchant, lawyer, and landowner, with strong political, economic, or family ties to the Crown, adopted a position of neutrality, withdrawing from all political and most economic activities. Parker (and many other such merchants) returned to his estate to await the outcome of the war.[30]

Merchants, landowners, and men of means who supported independence, such as the Honorable John Stevens, Colonel John Neilson (1745–1833), and William Paterson, faced the difficult task of supporting the Revolution while maintaining their own economic positions. The most successful in this regard were the merchants. Prior to the Revolution few had been involved in commerce out of their own ports. Salem had become primarily a feeder for Philadelphia, and Burlington had almost ceased to function as a port. At Perth Amboy a few merchants controlled what little trade remained. Among the few were James Neilson (d. 1783) and Richard Gibb, who conducted a shuttle trade between New Jersey and the trading centers of New England.

Lacking urban centers of their own, men like John Stevens operated through neighboring provinces, and many had business enterprises in both their own and neighboring colonies. With these avenues of commerce closed to them, they shifted their energies from peacetime activities to more hazardous speculative pursuits. Some, although committed to the cause of Revolution, were also committed to personal profit to the extent that they were willing to engage in illicit trade. They used their connections to sell the British badly needed items such as salt at more than twice its market price.

Those previously involved in maritime activities attempted to conduct trade with the Caribbean from smaller ports along the New Jersey coast. But this was extremely hazardous, and the profit was relatively small. Privateering was far more enticing. Outfitting a private war vessel commissioned by Congress to act against the commerce of Great Britain was a hazardous enterprise. The schooner *Governor Livingston*, newly built and outfitted at Bridgeton, New Jersey, at a considerable outlay of capital, made only a single voyage before being captured by a British warship.[31] Privateering also offered the potential for the highest returns, however. Many merchants were willing to accept the risk. Colonel John Neilson of New Brunswick, in conjunction with several Philadelphia merchants, outfitted the *Endeavor* to operate as a privateer in the West Indies. Thomas Leaming, Jr., a New Jersey landowner, militia officer, and son of Thomas Leaming of Cape May, was very active in privateering. By the war's end, the Philadelphia firm of A. Bunner and Company, in which Leaming was a partner, had taken over fifty vessels by privateering.[32] To minimize the capital risk in such an undertaking, the venture was often divided into shares held by as many as thirty-two persons. This was the case with Colonel Daniel Hendrickson of Monmouth County, a landowner, merchant, and retail–store owner, who held one of ten shares in the privateer ship *Love and Unity*. He further profited by acting as agent for the others in the enterprise, disposing of the captured cargos.

The disposal of captured cargos was a major source of income, and many merchants unconnected with privateering profited from the sales. By 1778 privateering had become a major enterprise for merchants. Yet New Jersey's economic livelihood continued to depend upon neighbors. Fewer than 1 percent of the vessels operating from New Jersey were registered in the state. Most had been commissioned in Philadelphia. Although New Jersey merchants were often involved in privateering ventures, most of their financing came from elsewhere. The end of the war brought the demise of this new industry, but it provided New Jersey's maritime shippers with a means of sustaining themselves.

Many merchants and shippers in the state, in order to survive economically, turned away from the sea to engage in speculation in goods and currency for profit. Such speculation often worked to the detriment of either the government or the general populace, but many justified their actions by advocating the belief that the sacrifices they made for the war should be balanced by any benefits they could accrue. John Neilson saw nothing immoral about selling salt to the government at $35 a bushel, when he had bought it for $15. Nor did men like William Paterson question their own ethics when they purchased various currencies and certificates at a deflated value and then demanded that such paper be redeemed at full value, thereby gathering a windfall profit at the expense of the citizenry.

Most merchants were glad to see the end of hostilities, for while some had become wealthy, most had been able merely to maintain some semblance of their previous economic position. In general they found the uncertainty of a wartime economy less productive than their peacetime activities. With peace at hand these merchants displayed an optimism reminiscent of an earlier age. Their vision was of a New Jersey, now part of a new nation, that would take its rightful place as a major center for trade and commerce. To accomplish this the merchants called upon the legislature in 1783 to provide an impetus to trade by declaring Perth Amboy a free port, but the legislature initially proved recalcitrant.[33] Thomas Ryerson, a New Jerseyan residing in Jamaica, having been apprised of this situation by his friend James Parker (1725–97), found it truly unfortunate that the legislature had not acted immediately at the conclusion of the peace but instead had spent years seeking a means to prevent New York and other non–New Jersey merchants from operating out of the state's ports without penalty. Ryerson found this conduct "strangely inconsistent," and the delay occasioned by it had caused the loss, he felt, of whatever advantage might have been gained by being a free port. The golden moment had slipped by as a result of legislative inaction, and he believed it was "now out of their power to recover." He foresaw that the growing need for a centralized authority would mean that Congress would be invested with the authority to levy duties, which he felt would produce an equalization among all ports and would negate any small advantage that might be gained in making Perth Amboy a free port.[34]

Attempts at Revitalization

Less than four months later the city of Perth Amboy renewed its corporate charter in the hope of taking advantage of the free-port status it sought and enticing merchants to the port through incentives. Those concerned with Perth Amboy's economic future realized that what had been true sixty-five years ago was still valid: for a port to succeed it needed "a collection of merchants together in sufficient numbers in order that the union of their forces may render them competent to great undertakings."[35] Attracting merchants to New Jersey's ports was made difficult by the rather extensive wartime damage. Middlesex County suffered perhaps more than any other New Jersey county in the war. Perth Amboy had been occupied by both armies, its population dispersed, and many of its buildings damaged or destroyed. Other harbor areas also suffered; for example, at Raritan Landing, in addition to the destruction of numerous houses, several vessels had been lost. Even more detrimental were the attitude and actions of New Jersey's commercial rivals. In a series of moves reminiscent of events a century earlier, both New York and Philadelphia, fearful that New Jersey's free-port status might afford it some commercial advantages, passed legislation placing high tariffs on goods imported from that state. It was a device intended to be used as a lever to force New Jersey to abandon its new commercial policy. The desired concentration of merchants around New Jersey's ports did not materialize. Families which had previously been engaged in maritime activities continued those endeavors. The Parker family continued into the 1800s to conduct maritime trade, but, as before, they turned primarily to the neighboring provinces to conduct business.[36]

The customs records are perhaps the best indicator of the failure of the new effort. Over an almost-four-year period beginning in 1784, Perth Amboy, most active of all of the New Jersey ports, averaged approximately fourteen entries and clearances annually, slightly less volume than at the end of the French and Indian War, when the port was barely viable. In this period, a single vessel from England and another from Madeira entered New Jersey's waters. These two vessels comprised the total overseas trade for the entire period. Some trade with the West Indies remained; Saint Eustatia was now a port of call. A comparable amount of trade now came from Nova Scotia, which replaced Boston as the focus of trade to the north. Nearly 70 percent of what little coastwise trade remained was with New York. The latter's continued domination made it appear that Perth Amboy had once again become, in part, an extension of New York shipping.[37]

New Jersey's failure to break the economic domination of its neighbors during the period of the Articles of Confederation was undoubtedly a factor in the willingness of its merchants to consider a new form of government under the Federal Constitution. The problems of New Jersey's maritime development were deep-rooted, however, and could not be easily ameliorated by governmental change, for they were in most ways self-contained. For example, in a period of fierce mercantile competitiveness, New Jersey lacked legislative and merchant leadership, and it failed to develop a viable merchant community. Furthermore, New Jersey ports had no unified role in the development of merchant shipping. New Jersey shippers' use of and growing reliance on the surrounding colonies discouraged the development of a strong local merchant class, which was necessary if the ports were to rival other colonial ports. Finally, the failure to develop urban areas made the growth of New Jersey's ports unlikely. Despite pronouncements to the contrary, most New Jerseyans never really needed or wanted a large commercial center of their own; they were content instead to be dependent economically, politically, and socially on the surrounding colonies. As a result, New Jersey's own ports failed to develop and finally ceased to function as significant channels of maritime commerce. Once again the ports lay idle for want of trade.

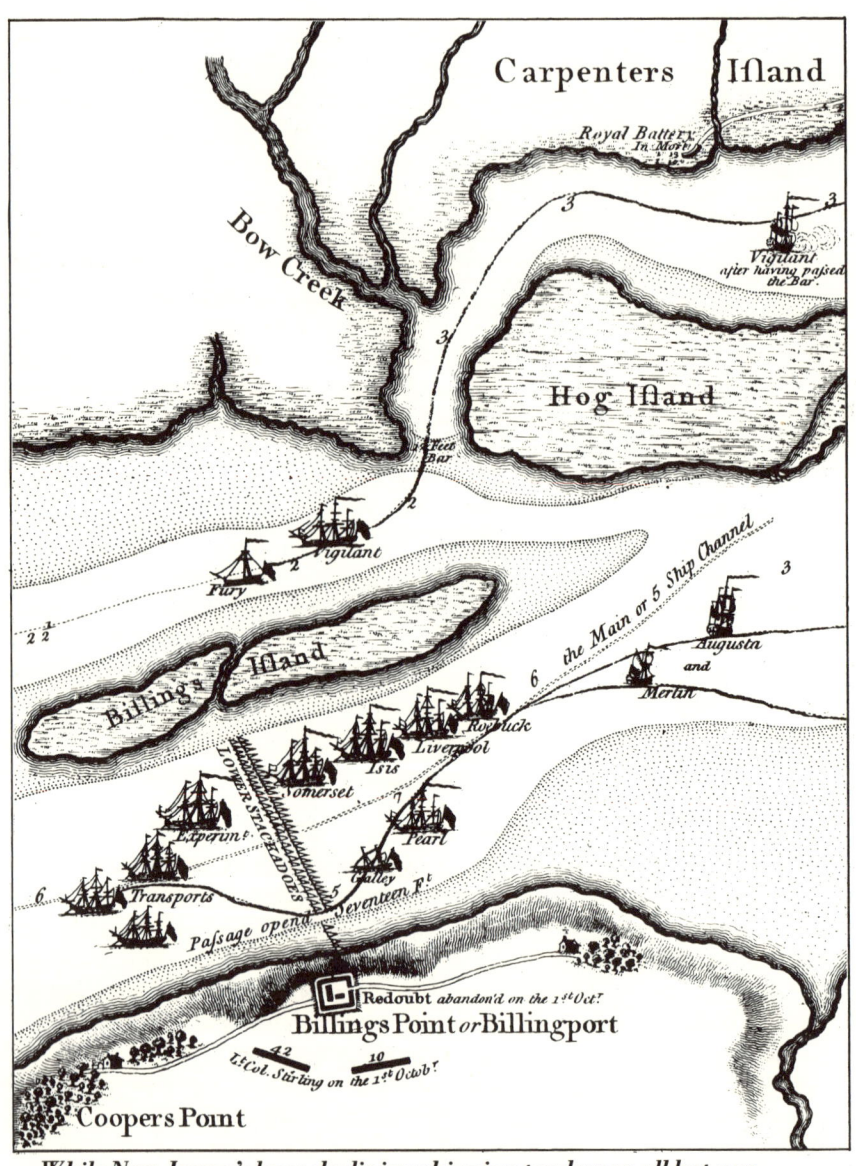

While New Jersey's long-declining shipping trade was all but nonexistent during the Revolutionary War, British naval vessels sailed, often freely, along the state's coasts and waterways. The Delaware River forts, especially, were the scene of military action in 1777 during the Philadelphia Campaign, as seen in this detail from "The Course of the Delaware River from Philadelphia to Chester . . . ," engraved by William Faden, London, 1778. NJHS.

Conclusion

NEW JERSEY'S MARITIME DEVELOPMENT was influenced by a wide variety of factors, the most important of which was its failure to develop a merchant class willing to commit the necessary resources and personal effort to New Jersey's ports over a sufficient period of time. This failure in turn was related to the colony's internal demographic and political developments. The inability of the ports to achieve sustained growth resulted less from rivals' adverse political and commercial actions than from the colony's own internal difficulties. A decentralized government dominated by diffuse farm and small town elements obviated the cohesive force needed to give focus and direction to the development of the port; such fragmentation was compounded by a heterogeneous pattern of settlement that had produced ethnic and religious enclaves.

Without general support, and faced with legislative inertia, the towns of Perth Amboy, Burlington, and Salem were rapidly surpassed by neighboring New York and Philadelphia. Once these rival harbors also controlled the functions associated with commerce—banking, marketing, insurance—rejuvenation of the New Jersey ports as major trade centers became impossible. New Jersey's own merchants, for the most part, found it economically more advantageous to work through New York or Philadelphia. New Jersey's plowmen did not have to concern themselves with the development of their own ports, for they had two alternative ports that allowed them to conduct business and commerce without appreciably changing their agrarian mode of life.

The increasingly dependent relationship between the surrounding colonies and New Jersey did, of course, accelerate the decline of New Jersey's own ports. It should be remembered, however, that contrary to common supposition, the rise of rival ports, although eventually the most overpowering factor in New Jersey's decline, was not a cause, but rather the product of the colony's unsettled development as well as the diffusion of capital and commitment by merchants for whom maritime commerce represented only one possible economic enterprise. A combination of design and default left most New Jerseyans dependent on ports other than their own.

As a result, New Jersey's maritime commerce exhibited some unique features. Port administrators, for example, retained office, for the most part, out of social and political expedience, not for the job itself. Although there were significant numbers of merchants concentrated at or near the port areas, their maritime activities were for the most part divorced from their residences. The ports were also unique, for while the general flow of commerce in and out of the colony went through the adjacent ports, neither Burlington nor Perth Amboy acted as a feeder. Instead, these ports occasionally provided an appendage to a larger pattern of trade, but they acted mostly in an independent manner. They had their own distinct regions of trade and voyage patterns, dealing in the West Indies, the coastal region, and occasionally overseas.

Because they operated as small independent ports, their activities were in some ways similar to many other ports. The commodities that passed through New Jersey's ports, although of modest volume, reflected the basically agrarian society, which in the case of New Jersey matured economically, by and large, in terms of agricultural industries and farm productivity. The latter seems to have led to the production of goods in excess of the immediate needs of the farmer, resulting in a slight surplus of capital from their sale. That such capital existed and was used to improve the standard of living, a prime consideration in evaluating economic growth, seems apparent from shipping and store records, which indicate that even in a largely rural colony, per capita income, as reflected both in imports and sales of certain types of goods, rose continually. Of even greater significance was the relative age of vessels using New Jersey ports. The relatively few years of service for all but the largest of ships indicates both rapid replacement and an expanding industry, conditions requiring the availability and expenditure of relatively large amounts of capital. Most of this capital, it appears, was generated within the colonies themselves, a significant indicator of economic growth. This and other evidence drawn from an examination of several small ports indicates strongly that while there may be some ground for debate over the question of economic growth during the colonial period, there is little doubt that real growth did occur in the maritime sector.

The areas of trade in which New Jersey was involved were predominantly coastal and at first included considerable West Indies as well as overseas trade. Over the years these areas of operations changed from the general trading patterns that encompassed all regions in the 1720s, to a more restrictive coastal and West Indies pattern in the 1740s and early 1750s, to an almost exclusively coastal pattern of trade by the 1760s. The voyage patterns followed by merchants operating from New Jersey's ports remained constant, however, in that they showed a tendency to remain within a given region and to conduct their trade with a specific location with little or no variation in the pattern. Many historians contradict this idea, but it nevertheless supports the contention that trade, especially trade involving overseas operations, was conducted primarily between entrepôts that in turn acted as points for more localized distribution and collection.

The merchants who traded from Perth Amboy also changed in composition and modes of operation as conditions at the port changed because New Jersey ports failed to develop the business facilities needed for maritime commerce. Under such circumstances merchants concentrated their efforts at other ports, leaving the trade of New Jersey's ports largely in the hands of local residents, many of whom displayed an ambivalent attitude toward their own harbors. While merchants demanded the expansion of their own facilities, they conducted much of their business, especially coastal trade, through the neighboring ports.

Over the decades the increasing tendency to trade at other ports was reflected in a continual shift at New Jersey's ports to more local commercial activities. Even these local activities required commercial facilities, however, and while some merchants were able to circumvent the need by carrying on direct trade with other merchants or firms, most shippers using the port necessarily were tied into the entrepôts of New England that provided the business services their own ports lacked. This, more than anything, accounted for that region's dominance in New Jersey's regional trade.

Even the New England trade, however, was relatively insignificant, because most New Jersey trade was conducted directly with New York or Philadelphia, either by wagon and then ferry or by boat from some local dock or landing. At first such trade was motivated by expedience, but expedience soon turned to dependence. Always short of gold and silver, New Jersey farmers made their purchases from New York and Philadelphia merchants who provided mechanisms by which they could obtain goods, either through extension of credit or, most often, by allowing them to use farm produce, especially wheat and flour, in lieu of currency. As the population increased and as farm productivity rose, there was an increasing demand for more goods and more credit. To pay for previous purchases or to make additional ones, farmers raised the level of farm income by increasing production, thus producing an almost cyclical pattern that emphasized agrarianism, retarded other economic development, and increased dependence on New York and Philadelphia.

Yet there were cost advantages in operating out of a small port. Ironically, the absence of a well-developed urban sector, a contributing factor in the decline of the port, meant lower operating costs. Among the most obvious advantages, regional specialization and narrow pattern of trade allowed for stable markets and the use of smaller vessels, which were both less costly to build and in many cases more cost effective in space utilization. Such advantages were most notable when over the decades there was an increasing tendency to move away from a broad spectrum of trading areas to a few ports in a single geographical area. Even these restricted activities, however, required some commercial facilities, and while some merchants were able to circumvent the need by carrying on direct trade with other merchants or firms, most shippers using the port were necessarily tied into the entrepôts of New England that, like New York and Philadelphia, came increasingly to provide the business services that ports such as Perth Amboy lacked. This, coupled with a growing cost advantage of regional specialization, accounted for the growing dominance of New England in New Jersey's trading pattern.

This dependency upon the commercial resources of others was disastrous for the development of maritime commerce, the ports, and much of New Jersey's manufacturing. But it was beneficial to most of the people, because it allowed them to maintain an agrarian way of life while reaping benefits from commerce and shipping. That it brought about a gradual loss of identity was of no immediate consequence or concern because of the traditional absence in the province of integrating influences. Although New Jerseyans could not have foreseen the long-range results of non-urbanization, it would not have mattered. Despite public pronouncements to the contrary, the majority of New Jerseyans never really wanted or needed a large commercial center of their own.

Conclusion

Viable maritime commerce required not only a legal port in a favorable geographical location but also a demand, popular support, support by the merchant class, and positive legislative votes. These requirements may change with time, with more emphasis on one criterion, less on another. Indeed, not all these factors had to be present in order for maritime commerce to flourish, but the absence of any single one lessened the chance of success. In New Jersey, where a number were missing, attempts to expand maritime commerce stagnated and urban areas failed to develop. New Jersey came to depend upon the well-developed commercial centers in neighboring colonies, to the extent that its own ports failed to develop and finally ceased to function as significant channels of maritime commerce. Nationhood failed to provide a catalyst to regenerate the ports. This period of turmoil simply compounded the problems of the previous half-century, and, as they had after the French and Indian War, New Jersey ports again languished in the face of unrealized potential.

Compilations from Maritime Records

1. List of Customs and Naval Officers in New Jersey

It is extremely difficult to construct a list of customs collectors and naval officers for the eighteenth century. No such list has survived, and names must be gleaned from whatever sources are available. The result, unfortunately, is that there must be inaccuracies. Dates of service are in many cases approximate. Some officials may have been neglected and others added who were deputies rather than collectors. The latter problem is the result of a failure in official correspondence to differentiate between the two, using simply the title "Collector" to designate all. With these shortcomings in mind, I have compiled the following lists:

Collector at Salem

William Fraser	1732
Andrew DeWare	1763
Francis Hopkinson	1963–64
John Hatton	1764

Collector at Burlington

John Rolfe	1710
Charles Read	1732 (?)

Collector at Perth Amboy

William Dyre	1685
Miles Foster	1687–95
Thomas Coker	1698
Charles Goodman	1699
John White	1701
Thomas Farmer	1710
Mr. Swift	1711
John Barclay	1716
John Stevens	1717
Robert Hine (King)	1722–48
John Barberie	1743–70

Naval Officer at Perth Amboy

Alexander Mackdowall	1722–30
John White	1732–34
Thomas Fox	1740–58
Jonathan Deare	1759– ?

In this idealized British view of a busy American port, merchants discuss business, dock workers unload barrels of goods, and a customs official inspects cargos. The scene is a detail from "A Map of the Most Inhabited Part of Virginia Containing the Whole Province of Maryland With Part of Pennsylvania, New Jersey and North Carolina," drawn by Joshua Fry and Peter Jefferson, engraved in Thomas Jeffreys's American Atlas . . . (London, 1776). NJHS.

2. Cost of Building the Sloop *Catharine*

	£	s	p
The Iron Cost	58	19	3
The Sail Cloth	101	16	6
The anchors	23	17	9
The Joyners	18	15	0
The Black Smyth's works	41	9	0
The Carpenter's works	270	0	0
making the Sails	27	6	6
Fixing the Rigging	6	18	6
frate [crate] for carrying The Sails	1	0	0
The Riging	102	6	8
The Blocks & pumps Sundrys	13	10	0
The Brimstone and Tar	5	8	9
two Blunder Busses	4	0	0
Sundrys	3	4	4
Sundrys at Duykink	9	18	7
To Cash paid to Capt. waiter	3	10	0
The muskets	3	10	0
To [not distinguishable] Daniel Obrien	3	19	0
To hinges for the Cabben		15	
To Diet at the widdow marsh		1	6
Hull Iron costs	58	19	3
Joyner Work	18	15	0
Black Smith	41	9	0
Carpenter	270	0	0
	389	3	3

	£	s	d
Sail Cloth	101	16	6
anchors	23	17	9
Making sail	27	6	6
fixing Rigin	6	18	6
Riggin	102	6	8
Block	13	10	0
Tar	5	8	9
Durkin	9	18	7
Cap waiter	0	10	0
Hinges	0	16	0
	295	8	3
	389	3	3
	684	11	6

Source: Ledger, Hendrickson Family Papers.

Tables Developed from the Customs and Naval Officers Records

FOR AN EXPLANATION of the data-input format for tables concerning Burlington and Perth Amboy, see James H. Levitt, "New Jersey Shipping, 1722–1764" (Ph.D. dissertation, University of Utah, 1973), pp. 249–50. A description of the three computer programs used to store, retrieve, and analyze data found in the tables is found in Levitt, "New Jersey Shipping," pp. 252–65. Thirty computer charts developed from the same data base, listing Burlington and Perth Amboy owners, masters, partners, cargos, names of vessels, and other information, are also found in Levitt, "New Jersey Shipping," pp. 267–450.

All numbers are rounded off to the nearest hundredth except when otherwise noted.

TABLE 1. Port Use at Perth Amboy, 1722–64

Year	E	C	T	Total tonnage	Mean vessel tonnage
1722*	10	8	18	813	45.167
1723	14	13	27	1,250	46.296
1724	25	20	45	1,003	22.289
1725	30	33	63	1,202	19.079
1726	68	68	136	4,460	32.794
1727*	38	35	73	2,103	28.808
1733	49	56	105	3,258	31.029
1734*	23	23	46	1,704	37.043
1740*	48	33	81	1,692	20.889
1741	37	39	76	1,841	24.547
1742*	21	16	37	574	15.514
1743	60	62	122	2,591	21.238
1744	47	48	95	2,192	23.074
1745	47	41	88	1,830	20.795
1746*	37	44	81	1,479	18.256
1747	34	50	84	1,429	17.012
1748	36	41	77	2,100	27.273
1749	31	42	73	2,383	32.644
1750	50	39	89	4,152	46.652
1751*	38	31	69	2,514	36.435
1754*	18	14	32	1,232	33.231
1755	22	17	39	1,296	33.231
1756*	13	7	20	616	30.800
1757	26	28	54	1,320	24.906
1758	11	20	31	1,016	32.774
1759	24	28	52	2,053	39.481
1763	18	19	37	1,012	27.351
1764*	10	11	21	362	17.238

Source: CO 5/1035; CO 5/1036.
Note: Records for years marked by asterisk are incomplete.
Key: E   Entered; C   Cleared; T   Total.

TABLE 2. Types of Vessels Using Perth Amboy, Selected Years

Type	1726			1745		
	E	C	% of total	E	C	% of total
Brig	—	—	—	4	3	8.0
Sloop	43	47	66.2	31	31	70.5
Schooner	4	2	4.4	9	7	18.2
Boat	—	—	—	3	0	3.4
Ship	13	11	17.6	—	—	—
Snow	6	6	8.8	—	—	—
Brigantine	2	2	2.9	—	—	—
Shallop	—	—	—	—	—	—

Type	1750			1755		
	E	C	% of total	E	C	% of total
Brig	1	2	3.4	—	—	—
Sloop	20	12	36.0	10	7	46.3
Schooner	9	8	19.1	7	8	38.5
Boat	—	—	—	—	—	—
Ship	3	3	6.7	—	—	—
Snow	6	4	11.2	1	0	2.6
Brigantine	9	8	16.9	2	2	10.3
Shallop	—	—	—	2	0	5.1

Type	1758 E	1758 C	1758 % of total	1763 E	1763 C	1763 % of total
Brig	—	—	—	—	—	—
Sloop	5	12	54.8	11	11	59.5
Schooner	6	6	38.7	4	3	18.9
Boat	—	—	—	—	—	—
Ship	—	—	—	—	—	—
Snow	0	1	3.2	1	0	2.7
Brigantine	0	1	3.2	2	2	10.8
Shallop	—	—	—	0	3	8.1

Source: CO 5/1035; CO 5/1036.

Note: The total number of items used to calculate percentages may include items left blank or unreadable items. Percents are rounded off to the nearest tenth. These account for variations in the total percentage. Partial returns for the year 1764 indicated Sloop 90.5%, Schooner 9.5%. No other type of vessel was listed.

Key: E   Entered; C   Cleared.

TABLE 3. Volume and Region of Trade, Selected Years

Burlington

Year	T I	T E	TA I	TA E	WI I	WI E	NE I	NE E	MID I	MID E	SO I	SO E	O I	O E
1732	5	5	0	1	2	3	0	1	3	0	0	0	0	0
1733	9	8	0	0	3	3	4	5	2	0	0	0	0	0
1734	3	4	0	1	0	2	0	1	3	0	0	0	0	0
1735	7	6	0	0	2	2	0	2	5	2	0	0	0	0
1736	5	5	1	2	1	2	0	1	3	0	0	0	0	0
1737	4	4	1	0	1	1	1	1	1	0	0	1	0	1
1738	3	5	0	0	1	3	0	0	2	1	0	0	0	1
1739	2	3	0	0	1	0	0	0	0	2	1	1	0	0
1740	2	2	0	0	0	0	1	2	1	0	0	0	0	0
1741	2	2	0	1	0	0	0	0	2	1	0	0	0	0
1742	2	3	0	0	0	1	1	2	1	0	0	0	0	0
1743	3	4	0	0	0	2	3	2	0	0	0	0	0	0
1744	1	1	0	0	1	1	0	0	0	0	0	0	0	0
1748	3	2	0	0	0	0	1	1	1	1	0	0	1	0

Salem

Year	T I	T E	TA I	TA E	WI I	WI E	NE I	NE E	MID I	MID E	SO I	SO E	O I	O E
1736	3	1	0	0	0	0	2	0	1	0	0	1	0	0
1737	7	9	0	1	0	1	5	7	1	0	1	0	0	0
1738	8	7	0	1	2	2	5	4	1	0	0	0	0	0
1739	7	7	1	1	1	0	5	4	0	2	0	0	0	0
1740	3	3	0	0	0	1	2	1	1	1	0	0	0	0
1741	1	2	1	0	0	0	0	0	0	1	0	1	0	0
1742	2	3	0	0	0	0	1	1	0	0	1	1	0	1
1746	0	2	0	0	0	0	0	1	0	1	0	0	0	0
1747	4	3	0	0	4	0	0	0	0	3	0	0	0	0
1749	1	1	0	0	1	0	0	0	0	1	0	0	0	0

Piscataqua

Year	T I	T E	TA I	TA E	WI I	WI E	NE I	NE E	MID I	MID E	SO I	SO E	O I	O E
1694	7	63	2	3	4	4	1	52	0	0	0	0	0	4
1695	16	105	1	0	7	11	3	91	1	0	0	0	4	3
1727	33	52	4	13	11	20	3	2	0	1	5	9	10	7
1743	61	75	5	11	17	32	4	1	0	1	13	11	22	19
1759	104	151	6	4	45	93	0	0	12	11	24	16	17	27

Sunbury

Year	T I	T E	TA I	TA E	WI I	WI E	NE I	NE E	MID I	MID E	SO I	SO E	O I	O E
1763	13	19	2	3	7	13	1	0	0	1	3	2	0	0
1764	12	16	1	2	7	11	1	0	1	1	1	1	1	1
1765	10	10	1	4	5	6	1	0	0	0	3	0	0	0
1766	11	8	0	1	7	6	0	0	0	0	4	1	0	0
1767	17	22	2	4	9	15	1	0	0	0	5	2	0	1

Key: T Total; I Import; E Export; TA Transatlantic; WI West Indies; NE New England; MID Middle Atlantic; SO Southern; O Others.

TABLE 4. Percentage of Regional Trade by Vessels Entering and Clearing Perth Amboy, Selected Years

1722–27 Area	T	E	C	1733–34 T	E	C
Transatlantic	11.3	5.4	17.5	19.6	9.6	28.8
West Indies	18.8	17.3	20.3	9.8	9.6	10.0
Coastwise	66.3	75.1	57.0	69.3	80.7	58.8
New England	48.3	52.4	44.1	41.2	46.6	36.3
Middle Atlantic	13.3	19.5	6.8	21.6	31.5	12.5
Southern	4.1	2.7	5.6	6.5	2.7	10.0
Others	0.6	0.5	0.6	—	—	—

1740–45 Area	T	E	C	1746–51 T	E	C
Transatlantic	8.4	7.7	9.2	8.2	8.8	7.7
West Indies	12.0	11.9	12.1	22.0	25.7	18.6
Coastwise	78.6	79.2	77.8	69.3	64.6	73.7
New England	60.1	62.3	57.7	50.5	50.4	50.6
Middle Atlantic	8.8	6.5	11.3	12.5	8.4	16.2
Southern	7.8	8.8	6.7	6.3	5.8	6.9
Others	1.8	1.5	2.1	—	—	—

1754–59 Area	T	E	C	1763–64 T	E	C
Transatlantic	7.0	5.3	8.8	10.3	10.7	10.0
West Indies	34.6	36.8	32.5	24.1	28.6	20.0
Coastwise	58.3	57.9	58.8	60.3	53.6	66.7
New England	41.7	40.4	43.0	41.3	39.3	43.3
Middle Atlantic	2.2	1.8	2.6	—	—	—
Southern	14.5	15.8	13.2	19.0	14.3	23.3
Others	—	—	—	—	—	—

Number of Vessels	T	E	C
1722–27	362	185	177
1733–34	153	73	80
1740–45	499	260	239
1746–51	473	226	247
1754–59	228	114	114
1763–64	58	28	30

Source: Compiled from CO 5/1035; CO 5/1036.
Key: T   Total; E   Entered; C   Cleared.

TABLE 5. Selected Samples of Voyage Patterns at Perth Amboy, 1722–27

Vessels Clearing the Port of Perth Amboy for New England, 1722–27, Arrived from the Following:

Location	#	%
New London	1	1.2
Bermuda	1	1.2
Newfoundland	1	1.2
Boston	20	25.0
New York	1	1.2
Rhode Island	49	62.0
Jamaica	1	1.2
Nevis	2	2.5
Boston and Rhode Island	1	1.2
Port Lewis	1	1.2
Delaware	1	1.2

Vessels Entering the Port of Perth Amboy from New England, 1722–27, Left for the Following:

Location	#	%
New York	1	1.1
Philadelphia	1	1.1
Antigua	2	2.3
New London	2	2.3
Bermuda	1	1.1
Boston	21	27.3
Barbados	1	1.1
Pennsylvania	1	1.1
Rhode Island	45	53.5
Virginia	1	1.1
North Carolina	5	5.9
Madeira	1	1.1
Port Lewis	1	1.1
Caleman	1	1.1

Vessels Clearing the Port of Perth Amboy for Transatlantic Crossing, 1722–1727, Arrived from the Following:

Location	#	%
Antigua	1	2.8
New York	23	63.8
Liverpool and New York	1	2.8
Isle of Man and New York	1	2.8
Rhode Island	1	2.8
Virginia	1	2.8
Madeira	1	2.8
Liverpool	2	5.6
Liverpool and the Isle of Man	2	5.6
Tenerife via Newfoundland	1	2.8
Tenerife	1	2.8
From sea in distress	1	2.8

Vessels Entering the Port of Perth Amboy from Transatlantic Crossing, 1722–27, Left for the Following:

Location	#	%
Antigua	2	13.3
New York	1	6.7
Jamaica	3	20.0
Madeira	6	40.0
Liverpool	1	5.7
Tenerife	1	5.7
Canary Islands	1	5.7

Source: CO 5/1035.

Note: Percentages are rounded off to the nearest tenth. As a result, the sum of the percentages may be slightly less or greater than 100.

TABLE 6. Tons—Guns—Men

New Jersey, 1720–40

	TA	WI	NE	MID	SO	O	ALL
Mean tons	72.29	30.04	11.49	50.52	21.26	25.43	29.24
Number of vessels	63.00	80.00	222.00	66.00	23.00	14.00	468.00
Tons to men	7.22	4.35	3.79	6.69	4.91	4.94	5.30
Tons to guns	63.70	31.35	—	35.13	37.80	178.00	53.15
Guns to men	.11	.14	—	.19	.13	.03	.10
Number of vessels	39.00	63.00	168.00	45.00	14.00	14.00	343.00

New Jersey, 1741–63

	TA	WI	NE	MID	SO	O	ALL
Mean tons	53.30	42.03	22.79	22.06	20.00	39.80	29.75
Number of vessels	64.00	126.00	289.00	79.00	60.00	15.00	633.00
Tons to men	6.18	5.96	6.00	4.17	4.61	5.42	5.54
Tons to guns	92.18	35.63	—	93.00	—	—	100.25
Guns to men	.07	.17	—	.04	—	—	.06
Number of vessels	20.00	43.00	163.00	64.00	16.00	4.00	310.00

Source: CO 5/1035; CO 5/1036.

New Jersey Registry, 1720–40

	TA	WI	NE	MID	SO	O	ALL
Mean tons	45.00	22.97	9.42	18.75	13.00	14.20	14.33
Number of vessels	5.00	37.00	100.00	8.00	13.00	5.00	168.00
Tons to men	4.17	3.72	3.08	3.81	3.05	3.23	3.39
Tons to guns	—	48.36	—	20.00	—	—	86.06
Guns to men	—	.08	—	.19	—	—	.04
Number of vessels	1.00	29.00	71.00	6.00	4.00	5.00	116.00

New Jersey Registry, 1741–63

	TA	WI	NE	MID	SO	O	ALL
Mean tons	59.93	39.77	23.54	15.35	23.67	30.25	28.67
Number of vessels	29.00	61.00	175.00	43.00	24.00	4.00	336.00
Tons to men	5.11	4.88	6.04	4.54	5.48	4.72	5.38
Tons to guns	—	68.67	—	—	—	—	306.92
Guns to men	—	.07	—	—	—	—	.02
Number of vessels	6.00	24.00	44.00	40.00	5.00	3.00	172.00

Source: CO 5/1035; CO 5/1036.

Burlington

	TA	WI	NE	MID	SO	O	ALL
Mean tons	53.57	41.03	25.48	41.03	33.33	33.33	37.13
Number of vessels	7.00	32.00	29.00	31.00	3.00	3.00	105.00
Tons to men	6.70	7.06	6.48	7.23	8.33	6.25	6.96
Tons to guns	62.50	218.83	—	70.67	—	—	129.97
Guns to men	.11	.03	—	.10	—	—	.05
Number of vessels	7.00	32.00	29.00	31.00	3.00	3.00	105.00

Salem

	TA	WI	NE	MID	SO	O	ALL
Mean tons	74.00	26.58	23.84	31.08	19.60	20.00	28.61
Number of vessels	5.00	12.00	38.00	13.00	5.00	1.00	74.00
Tons to men	8.81	4.83	6.47	5.86	5.76	6.67	6.28
Tons to guns	61.67	39.88	453.00	202.00	—	—	117.61
Guns to men	.14	.12	.01	.03	—	—	.05
Number of vessels	5.00	12.00	38.00	13.00	5.00	1.00	74.00

Source: CO 5/1035; CO 5/1036.

Piscataqua, 1727

	TA	WI	NE	MID	SO	O	ALL
Mean tons	107.06	49.52	56.40	30.00	40.00	37.94	57.32
Number of vessels	17.00	31.00	5.00	1.00	14.00	17.00	85.00
Tons to men	9.68	7.56	7.62	7.50	7.57	7.41	8.22
Tons to guns	50.56	—	—	—	—	215.00	124.92
Guns to men	.19	—	—	—	—	.03	.07
Number of vessels	17.00	31.00	5.00	1.00	14.00	17.00	83.00

Piscataqua, 1743

	TA	WI	NE	MID	SO	O	ALL
Mean tons	264.38	72.49	270.00	50.00	57.68	46.44	92.50
Number of vessels	16.00	47.00	5.00	1.00	22.00	41.00	132.00
Tons to men	13.65	9.84	13.24	8.33	9.49	7.87	10.86
Tons to guns	26.11	69.52	21.77	—	123.40	250.67	40.64
Guns to men	.52	.14	.61	—	.08	.03	.27
Number of vessels	16.00	46.00	5.00	1.00	21.00	40.00	129.00

Piscataqua, 1759

	TA	WI	NE	MID	SO	O	ALL
Mean tons	288.50	88.75	—	36.43	38.15	55.41	78.13
Number of vessels	10.00	137.00	—	23.00	40.00	44.00	254.00
Tons to men	12.65	11.05	—	9.42	9.25	12.31	11.15
Tons to guns	31.36	58.19	—	—	254.33	93.77	59.61
Guns to men	.40	.19	—	—	.04	.13	.19
Number of vessels	10.00	136.00	—	23.00	40.00	44.00	253.00

Source: CO 5/967; CO 5/968; CO 5/969.

Sunbury

	TA	WI	NE	MID	SO	O	ALL
Mean tons	95.50	50.23	61.25	30.00	55.45	63.33	57.68
Number of vessels	20.00	87.00	4.00	3.00	22.00	3.00	139.00
Tons to men	10.05	7.18	8.17	7.50	8.13	7.04	7.89
Tons to guns	—	198.18	—	—	203.33	—	286.25
Guns to men	—	.04	—	—	.04	—	.03
Number of vessels	20.00	87.00	4.00	3.00	22.00	3.00	139.00

Savannah

	TA	WI	NE	MID	SO	O	ALL
Mean tons	106.43	43.79	57.05	26.78	26.70	38.50	42.20
Number of vessels	28.00	196.00	20.00	32.00	121.00	10.00	407.00
Tons to men	10.75	6.94	9.02	4.89	5.21	6.88	6.84
Tons to guns	204.17	144.79	—	204.25	157.18	128.33	168.48
Guns to men	.05	.05	—	.02	.03	.05	.04
Number of vessels	24.00	186.00	19.00	31.00	116.00	10.00	386.00

Note: *Mean tons* are based on aggregate data, while *ratios* are developed from normalized data. Thus, each section of table 6 gives the number of vessels on which mean tons are based as well as the number of vessels from which the ratios are developed.

Key: TA   Transatlantic; WI   West Indies; NE   New England; MID   Middle Atlantic; SO   Southern; O   Others.

Source: CO 5/967; CO 5/968; CO 5/969.

TABLE 7. Types of Vessels Registered in New Jersey

1722–27		1732–64	
Type	%	Type	%
Sloop	91.5	Sloop	50.1
Schooner	6.8	Schooner	28.9
Boat	1.7	Boat	5.8
Shallop	—	Shallop	.5
Brig	—	Brig	7.3
Brigantine	—	Brigantine	4.7
Snow	—	Snow	2.4
Ship	—	Ship	.4

Note: The average size in tons (1722–27), 13.381; (1732–64), 25.966.

TABLE 8. Types of Vessels Built in New Jersey

1722–27		1732–64	
Type	%	Type	%
Sloop	89.1	Sloop	51.3
Schooner	8.4	Schooner	27.6
Boat	1.0	Boat	5.8
Shallop	—	Shallop	1.3
Brig	—	Brig	7.2
Brigantine	—	Brigantine	3.9
Snow	—	Snow	2.5
Ship	—	Ship	.4

Note: The average size in tons (1722–27), 13.849; (1732–64), 25.549.

TABLE 9. Percentage of Vessels Built and/or Registered in New Jersey, Using New Jersey

1722–27		1740–49		1755–64	
Built	Registered	Built	Registered	Built	Registered
30.2	30.2	60.3	58.8	52.1	52.1

Source: CO 5/1035; CO 5/1036. Bases on vessels using the port of Perth Amboy.
Note: Percentages are rounded off to the nearest tenth.

TABLE 10. Shipbuilding Index

Place and number	TA	WI	NE	MID	SO	O	ALL
Vessel age, Perth Amboy	3.6	3.1	3.9	5.0	3.7	4.8	3.9
Number	122.0	198.0	494.0	134.0	74.0	28.0	1050.0
Vessel age, Burlington	4.3	2.4	4.2	4.1	2.0	2.3	3.5
Number	7.0	32.0	29.0	31.0	3.0	3.0	105.0
Vessel age, Salem	1.0	4.5	6.6	5.9	3.3	4.0	5.5
Number	4.0	12.0	32.0	12.0	3.0	1.0	64.0
Vessel age, Piscataqua	6.0	3.3	7.0	10.1	5.7	4.4	4.6
Number	25.0	175.0	5.0	23.0	61.0	81.0	370.0
Vessel age, Sunbury	8.1	5.8	3.5	4.3	4.5	5.7	5.9
Number	19.0	72.0	4.0	3.0	17.0	3.0	118.0
Vessel age, Savannah	6.8	4.9	3.5	4.9	4.8	2.5	4.9
Number	23.0	142.0	14.0	27.0	106.0	10.0	332.0

New Jersey before 1740—Vessels by Age

Age and number	TA	WI	NE	MID	SO	O	ALL
Vessel age, all	3.6	3.8	4.1	5.4	4.6	7.9	4.3
Number	63.0	79.0	222.0	64.0	23.0	13.0	464.0
Vessel age, New Jersey only	2.2	2.8	4.0	1.8	3.2	7.2	3.6
Number	5.0	37.0	100.0	8.0	13.0	5.0	168.0

Tables

New Jersey after 1740—Vessels by Age

Age and number	TA	WI	NE	MID	SO	O	ALL
Vessel age, all	3.6	2.6	3.8	4.5	3.3	2.1	3.5
Number	59.0	119.0	272.0	70.0	51.0	15.0	586.0
Vessel age, New Jersey only	2.4	2.0	3.5	4.3	2.3	1.0	3.1
Number	28.0	61.0	170.0	43.0	19.0	4.0	325.0

New Jersey before 1740—Vessels by Tonnage

Weight and number	TA	WI	NE	MID	SO	O	ALL
Under 40 tons, vessel age, all	3.5	3.3	4.1	4.9	4.6	7.8	4.2
Number	13.0	65.0	220.0	34.0	21.0	12.0	365.0
Over 40 tons, vessel age, all	3.6	6.1	5.0	6.1	5.0	9.0	4.8
Number	50.0	14.0	2.0	30.0	2.0	1.0	99.0

New Jersey after 1740—Vessels by Tonnage

Weight and number	TA	WI	NE	MID	SO	O	ALL
Under 40 tons, vessel age, all	5.6	2.6	3.9	4.8	3.5	1.7	3.8
Number	18.0	68.0	232.0	59.0	48.0	7.0	432.0
Over 40 tons, vessel age, all	2.7	2.6	3.2	3.0	.03	2.4	2.8
Number	41.0	51.0	39.0	11.0	3.0	8.0	153.0

Piscataqua, 1743—Vessels by Age

Age and number	TA	WI	NE	MID	SO	O	ALL
Vessel age, all	6.0	3.4	7.0	—	4.6	4.4	4.4
Number	16.0	39.0	5.0	—	17.0	33.0	110.0
Vessel age, New Hampshire only	4.6	3.4	5.3	—	4.6	4.5	4.1
Number	9.0	33.0	3.0	—	16.0	26.0	87.0

Piscataqua, 1759—Vessels by Age

Age and number	TA	WI	NE	MID	SO	O	ALL
Vessel age, all	8.2	3.3	—	10.1	6.4	4.6	4.8
Number	6.0	125.0	—	23.0	39.0	43.0	236.0
Vessel age, New Hampshire only	2.0	3.3	—	10.3	6.5	4.0	4.7
Number	1.0	107.0	—	20.0	36.0	30.0	194.0

Piscataqua, 1743—Vessels by Tonnage

Weight and number	TA	WI	NE	MID	SO	O	ALL
Under 40 tons, vessel age, all	—	1.5	—	—	7.9	6.3	6.4
Number	—	2.0	—	—	8.0	16.0	26.0
Over 40 tons, vessel age, all	6.0	3.5	7.0	—	1.4	2.5	3.8
Number	16.0	35.0	5.0	—	7.0	17.0	80.0

Piscataqua, 1759—Vessels by Tonnage

Weight and number	TA	WI	NE	MID	SO	O	ALL
Under 40 tons, vessel age, all	—	5.4	—	9.5	7.1	5.9	7.1
Number	—	5.0	—	11.0	23.0	14.0	53.0
Over 40 tons, vessel age, all	8.2	3.2	—	10.6	5.3	4.0	4.2
Number	6.0	119.0	—	12.0	16.0	29.0	182.0

Source: CO 5/709; CO 5/710; CO 5/967; CO 5/968; CO 5/969; CO 5/1035; CO 5/1036.

Key: TA   Transatlantic; WI   West Indies; NE   New England; MID   Middle Atlantic; SO   Southern; O   Others.

TABLE 11. Master/Vessel Relationship

Perth Amboy, All Vessels, 1722–64

Master owner		Master not owner	
#	% of total vessels	#	% of total vessels
519	41.9	813	57.6

Perth Amboy, Vessels of New Jersey Registry, 1722–64

Master owner		Master not owner	
#	% of total vessels	#	% of total vessels
366	46.0	428	53.8

Number and Percentage of Master-owned Vessels, Perth Amboy, Selected Years

Master owner			Master not owner		
Year	#	% of total vessels	Year	#	% of total vessels
1733	48	45.7	1749	29	39.7
1734	11	47.8	1750	48	53.9
1740	39	48.1	1751	31	44.9
1741	29	38.2	1754	14	43.8
1742	22	59.5	1755	23	59.0
1743	54	44.3	1756	13	65.0
1744	28	29.5	1757	28	51.9
1745	22	25.0	1758	11	35.5
1746	16	43.2	1759	10	19.2
1747	38	45.2	1763	12	32.4
1748	28	36.4	1764	8	38.1

Burlington, All Vessels, 1732–48

Master owner		Master not owner	
#	% of total vessels	#	% of total vessels
63	59.9	42	40.1

Source: CO 5/1035; CO 5/1036.
Note: Percentages rounded off to nearest tenth.

TABLE 12. Types of Ownership of Vessels Using Perth Amboy

Types of Ownership of All Vessels Using Perth Amboy, 1722–27

1		2		3		4		5		6		CO	
#	%	#	%	#	%	#	%	#	%	#	%	#	%
182	50.0	102	28.1	32	8.8	11	3.0	2	0.5	—	—	31	8.4

Types of Ownership of Owner-Master Vessels Using Perth Amboy, Selected Years

Year	1		2		3		4		5		6		CO	
	#	%	#	%	#	%	#	%	#	%	#	%	#	%
1741	10	34.5	17	58.6	2	6.9	—	—	—	—	—	—	—	—
1745	9	40.9	11	50.0	—	—	—	—	—	—	—	—	2	9.1
1747	13	42.2	23	60.5	1	2.6	—	—	—	—	—	—	1	2.6
1750	11	22.9	24	50.0	6	12.5	3	6.3	2	4.2	1	2.1	1	2.1

Types of Ownership of All Vessels Using Perth Amboy, Selected Years

Year	1 #	1 %	2 #	2 %	3 #	3 %	4 #	4 %	5 #	5 %	6 #	6 %	CO #	CO %
1733	28	26.7	43	41.0	19	18.1	7	6.7	1	1.0	—	—	6	5.7
1734	20	43.5	11	23.9	8	17.4	2	4.3	—	—	—	—	5	10.9
1740	32	39.5	43	53.1	5	6.2	—	—	—	—	1	1.2	—	—
1741	35	46.1	33	43.4	5	6.6	1	1.3	—	—	1	1.3	—	—
1742	18	48.6	16	43.2	2	5.4	—	—	—	—	1	2.7	—	—
1743	44	36.1	55	45.1	—	—	—	—	—	—	—	—	22	18.0
1744	38	40.0	42	44.2	—	—	—	—	—	—	—	—	15	15.8
1745	36	40.9	34	38.6	4	4.5	—	—	3	3.4	—	—	9	10.2
1746	40	49.4	30	37.0	1	1.2	—	—	—	—	—	—	9	11.1
1747	44	52.4	32	38.1	1	1.2	—	—	—	—	—	—	7	8.3
1748	26	33.8	30	39.0	3	3.9	3	3.9	—	—	—	—	15	19.5
1749	25	34.2	25	34.2	5	6.8	—	—	2	2.7	—	—	14	19.2
1750	19	21.3	34	38.2	16	17.0	9	10.1	8	9.0	1	1.1	2	2.3
1751	26	37.7	27	39.1	9	13.0	1	1.4	3	4.2	1	1.4	2	2.9
1754	15	46.9	12	37.5	1	3.1	—	—	—	—	—	—	4	12.5
1755	11	28.2	18	46.2	6	15.4	—	—	—	—	—	—	4	10.3
1756	6	30.0	13	65.0	1	5.0	—	—	—	—	—	—	—	—
1757	10	18.5	39	72.2	1	1.9	—	—	—	—	1	1.9	3	5.6
1758	6	19.4	21	67.7	4	12.9	—	—	—	—	—	—	—	—
1759	12	23.1	22	42.3	12	23.1	2	3.8	—	—	—	—	4	7.7
1763	14	37.8	12	32.4	6	16.2	4	10.8	—	—	—	—	1	2.7
1764	13	61.9	5	23.8	2	9.5	—	—	—	—	—	—	1	4.8

Source: CO 5/1035; CO 5/1036.

Key for tables 12 and 13: 1–6 Number of individuals owning a portion of vessel; CO Seven or more individuals, or specification of company ownership in records; # Number of vessels; % Percentage of total vessels.

Abbreviations

CSFP
  Calendar of the Stevens Family Papers. Calendars of Manuscript Collections in New Jersey. 2 vols. vol. 1: 1664–1750; vol. 2: 1751–74. (Newark, N.J., 1940).

CO 5/709; CO 5/710
  Customs and Naval Officers Records for the Georgia Ports. Partial Records for Savannah, 1752–65, and Sunbury, 1762–67. Public Record Office, London.

CO 5/967; CO 5/968; CO 5/969
  Customs and Naval Officers Records for the New Hampshire Port. Partial Records for Piscataqua, 1694–1759. Public Record Office, London.

CO 5/1035
  Customs and Naval Officers Records for the New Jersey Ports. Partial Records for Perth Amboy, 1722–54; Burlington, 1732–48; and Salem, 1736–40. Public Record Office, London.

CO 5/1036
  Customs and Naval Officers Records for the New Jersey Ports. Partial Records for Perth Amboy, 1750–64. Public Record Office, London.

CO 5/975
William Frazer (Collector). A List of Trading Vessels that have Entered and Cleared out of the Port of Salem and Cohansey in New Jersey in the Western Division of New Jersey from June 24, 1736 to June 24, 1749. Public Record Office, London.

Lewis Morris Papers
Lewis Morris, *The Papers of Lewis Morris, Governor of the Province of New Jersey, from 1738 to 1746.* Collections of the New Jersey Historical Society, vol. 4 (New York, 1852).

NJA
Archives of the State of New Jersey; binding title, New Jersey Archives series 1. (Newark, N.J., 1880–1917). Specific volumes indicated in notes.

NJHS
New Jersey Historical Society, Newark, New Jersey. Specific collections cited in notes.

NJHS Proceedings
Proceedings of the New Jersey Historical Society. A Magazine of History, Biography and Genealogy. Specific volumes cited in notes.

Rutgers
Special Collections, Rutgers University Library, New Brunswick, New Jersey. Specific manuscript groups cited in notes.

Notes

Introduction

1. Entries for 1741, CO 5/1035.
2. Ibid.
3. W. Woodford Clayton, ed., *History of Union and Middlesex Counties, New Jersey* (Philadelphia, 1882), p. 613.
4. Thomas C. Barrow, *Trade and Empire: The British Customs Service in Colonial America, 1660–1783* (Cambridge, Mass., 1967), p. 280.
5. CO 5/967; CO 5/968; CO 5/709; CO 5/710; CO 5/969.
6. See in particular: Bernard Bailyn, *The New England Merchant in the Seventeenth Century* (Cambridge, Mass., 1955); Virginia D. Harrington, *New York Merchants on the Eve of the Revolution* (New York, 1935); William F. Baxter, *The House of Hancock: Business in Boston, 1724–1775* (Cambridge, Mass., 1945); James B. Hedges, *The Browns of Providence Plantations: Colonial Years* (Cambridge, Mass., 1952).
7. CO 5/1035; CO 5/1036; CO 5/975.
8. A case is the entire entry as it appears in CO 5/1035 and CO 5/1036.
9. Gary M. Walton, "Colonial Tonnage Measurement: A Comment," *Journal of Economic History* 36 (1967):392–97; John J. McCusker, "Colonial Tonnage Measurement: Five Philadelphia Merchant Ships as Samples," *Journal of Economic History* 36 (1967):82–91.

Chapter 1

1. Jacob M. Price, "Economic Function and the Growth of American Port Towns in the Eighteenth Century," *Perspectives in American History* 8 (1974):128–38.
2. Darrett B. Rutman, *Winthrop's Boston: Portrait of a Puritan Town, 1630–1649* (Chapel Hill, N.C., 1965), pp. 23–40; Carl Bridenbaugh, *Cities in the Wilderness: The First Century of Urban Life in America, 1625–1742* (London, 1938), pp. 34–35; Price, "Economic Function," p. 149.
3. Price, "Economic Function," pp. 128–38. For an even higher estimate of the number engaged in maritime activity, see Gary B. Nash, *The Urban Crucible: Social Change, Political Consciousness, and the Origins of the American Revolution* (Cambridge, Mass., 1979), pp. 387–91.
4. Bridenbaugh, *Cities in the Wilderness*, pp. 7–8.
5. Ibid., p. 32.
6. Rutman, pp. 241–52; Bridenbaugh, *Cities in the Wilderness*, pp. 30–35, 178; Michael Kammen, *Empire and Interest: The American Colonies and the Politics of Mercantilism* (New York, 1970), pp. 4–8.
7. Price, "Economic Function," pp. 143–45.
8. Randolph J. Vecoli, *The People of New Jersey* (Princeton, N.J., 1965), p. 1–31.
9. "A Brief Account of the Province of New Jersey in America Published by the Present Proprietors. . . ," in Samuel Smith, *The History of the Colony of Nova Cæsaria, or New Jersey: Containing An Account of Its First Settlement, Progressive Improvements. The Original and Present Constitution, and other Events to the Year 1721. With Some Particulars Since; and a Short View of Its Present State* (Burlington, N.J., 1765), p. 542.
10. "Proposal by the Proprietors of East-Jersey, in America, for the Building of a Town on Amboy Point. . . ," in Samuel Smith, pp. 543–44.
11. In this connection, see Bailyn, *New England Merchants*.
12. New York's Governor Edmund Andros originally claimed sovereignty over the right to collect customs but then went on to issue a proclamation against the Eastern Division "Forbidding not only Carteret but all acting under him to exercise any jurisdiction," in effect making East Jersey almost totally dependent upon New York. J. A. Doyle, *English Colonies in America*, vol. 4: *The Middle Colonies* (New York, 1907), pp. 391–93.
13. West Jersey, which had not suffered the hectic readjustment of landownership, was not immune from Andros's actions. Andros made no attempt to claim sovereignty over West Jersey, but he demanded that duties be laid on all imports and exports involving that region and that such revenue as was realized be paid to the duke. This would in effect have destroyed not only commerce but settlement as well, for, as William Penn pointed out, to require duty on goods needed for stocking a new colony would discourage investment and settlement. Doyle, p. 391.
14. Ibid., pp. 415–17; William A. Whitehead, *East Jersey under the Proprietary Governments* (Newark, N.J., 1875), p. 89.
15. Doyle, p. 391.
16. Nicholas Murray, *Notes Historical and Biographical concerning Elizabeth-Town: Its Eminent Men, Churches and Ministers* (New York, 1941), p. 11.
17. Whitehead, *Proprietary Governments*, pp. 203–6.

18. Ibid., pp. 195–98.
19. Francis B. Lee, *New Jersey as a Colony and as a State*, 4 vols. (New York, 1902–1903), 1:272–73.
20. Bridenbaugh, *Cities in the Wilderness*, pp. 42–43, 52, 185–86.
21. David M. Ellis et al., *A History of the State of New York* (Ithaca, N.Y., 1973), pp. 32–34.
22. Lee, 1:193.
23. Governor Robert Hunter to the Lords of Trade with Act of the New Jersey Assembly, 8 April 1717, *NJA*, 4: *Administrations of Governor Robert Hunter and President Lewis Morris, 1709–1720*, p. 293.
24. Richard P. McCormick, *New Jersey from Colony to State, 1609–1789* (Princeton, N.J., 1964), pp. 56–59.
25. *NJA*, 4:11–12. See also the footnote.
26. Irving S. Kull, *New Jersey: A History*, 6 (New York, 1930–32), 1:204.
27. "Petition to the King from the Representatives of the Province of New Jersey, 9 January 1728," in Samuel Smith, pp. 421–23.
28. Ibid.; Petition to the King from the New Jersey Assembly, 4th 5 mo [July], 1730, *NJA*, 5: *Administrations of Governor Burnet, Governor Montgomerie, President Lewis Morris, Governor Cosby, President Anderson and President Hamilton, 1720–1737*, pp. 270–73. Both petitions contain the same phrasing.
29. An Address to the King from the Council and Representatives of New Jersey— Thanking him for Giving New Jersey a Separate Governor," *NJA*, 6: *Administrations of Governor Lewis Morris, President John Hamilton and President John Reading, 1738–1747*, pp. 58–59.
30. Patricia U. Bonomi, *A Factious People: Politics and Society in Colonial New York* (New York, 1971), p. 70. See in particular her explanatory footnote on Lewis Morris's "Dialogue Concerning Trade."
31. McCormick, pp. 63–72.
32. Governor William Burnet to the Lords of Trade, 1 August 1721, *NJA*, 5:11.
33. Lewis Morris to the duke of Newcastle, 18 October 1740, *Lewis Morris Papers*, p. 121.
34. This and other statistical data are drawn from a number of sources, among them the U.S. Bureau of the Census, *Historical Statistics of the United States: Colonial Times to 1970* (Washington, D.C., 1970), pp. 1180–81; William Douglass, *A Summary, Historical and Political of the First Planting, Progressive Improvement and Present State of the British Settlement in North America*, 2 vols. (Boston and London, 1755), 2; CO 5/1035; CO 5/1036.
35. "A Brief Account," in Samuel Smith, pp. 541–51.
36. Hubert Schmidt, *Rural Hunterdon: An Agricultural History* (New Brunswick, N.J., 1945), pp. 12–13; Wheaton J. Lane, *From Indian Trail to Iron Horse* (Princeton, N.J., 1939), p. 6.
37. Lane, *From Indian Trail to Iron Horse*, pp. 60–73.
38. Samuel Smith, pp. 485–88.
39. William E. Schermerhorn, *The History of Burlington, New Jersey* (Burlington, N.J., 1927), p. 35.
40. George DeCou, *Burlington: A Provincial Capital. Historical Sketches of Burlington, New Jersey and Neighborhood* (Philadelphia, 1945), p. 95; Evan M. Woodward and John F. Hageman, *History of Burlington and Mercer Counties, New Jersey, with Biographical Sketches of Many of Their Pioneers and Prominent Men* (Philadelphia, 1883), p. 124.
41. Joseph W. Dally, *Woodbridge and Vicinity: The Story of a New Jersey Township*

(Madison, N.J., 1967), p. 107.
42. Gawen Lawrie to the Proprietors, 2 March 1684, in William Whitehead, *Contributions to the Early History of Perth Amboy* . . . (New York, 1856), pp. 7–9.
43. John O. Raum, *A History of New Jersey*, 2 vols. (Philadelphia, 1877), 1:146.
44. Whitehead, *Proprietary Governments*, pp. 394–95, 203–4; *Early History of Perth Amboy*, p. 296.
45. Petition sent by Merchants of Perth Amboy and incorporated in part into the preamble of the charter obtained from Governor Robert Hunter, 24 August 1718, in William C. McGinnis, *History of Perth Amboy, New Jersey, 1651–1948*, 4 vols. (Perth Amboy, N.J., 1958–60), 1:35.
46. Schmidt, p. 5.
47. A census taken in 1726 shows a total white population of 29,861. Twelve years later a similar census listed the population as 43,338. *NJA*, 6:244.
48. Schmidt, pp. 11–12.
49. Wheaton J. Lane, "Water Transportation in Colonial New Jersey," *NJHS Proceedings* 53 (1935): 77–89.
50. Carl R. Woodward, *Ploughs and Politicks: Charles Read of New Jersey and His Notes on Agriculture* (New Brunswick, N.J., 1941), p. 57–58.
51. Whitehead, *Early History of Perth Amboy*, pp. 297–302.
52. Douglass, p. 283.
53. Roger T. Trindell, "The Ports of Salem and Greenwich in the Eighteenth Century," *New Jersey History* 86 (1968): 202.
54. Ibid.
55. "Philo-Patria to Mr. Americanus," 8 March 1758, in McGinnis, 2:38.
56. Hedges, pp. 41–46.
57. Harrington, pp. 253–54.
58. Ibid., p. 52; Arthur L. Jensen, *The Maritime Commerce of Colonial Philadelphia* (Madison, Wis., 1963), pp. 132–42.
59. Governor Thomas Dongan's "Report to the Committee of Trade on the Province of New York, 22 February 1687," in E. B. O'Callaghan, *The Documentary History of the State of New York* (Albany, N.Y., 1849), p. 151.
60. John Watts to Gedney Clarke, 30 March 1762, *Letter Book of John Watts, Merchant and Councillor of New York, 1 January 1762–22 December 1765* (New York, 1928), pp. 31–32.
61. Larry R. Gerlach, "Customs and Contentions: John Hatton of Salem and Cohansey, 1764–1776," *New Jersey History* 89 (Summer 1971): 70.
62. Arthur D. Pierce, *Smugglers' Woods* (New Brunswick, N.J., 1960), pp. 6–16.
63. Gerlach, pp. 62–92.
64. Council of New Jersey to Governor Lewis Morris, [n.d.] January 1744/5, *NJA*, 6:225.
65. Donald L. Kemmerer, "A History of Paper Money in Colonial New Jersey, 1668–1775," *NJHS Proceedings* 74 (1956):107–44.
66. Whitehead, *Early History of Perth Amboy*, p. 302.

Chapter 2

1. Bridenbaugh, *Cities in the Wilderness*. See especially chapter 6, pp. 175–205.
2. Price, "Economic Function." pp. 128–37; James F. Shepherd and Gary M. Walton, *Shipping, Maritime Trade, and the Economic Development of Colonial North America* (Cambridge, Mass., 1972).
3. Marc Engal, "The Economic Development of the Thirteen Colonies, 1720 to 1775," *William and Mary Quarterly* 32 (1975): 190–222.
4. Shepherd and Walton, *Maritime Trade*, p. 64.
5. Gary M. Walton and James F. Shepherd, *The Economic Rise of Early America* (Cambridge, Mass., 1979), p. 107.
6. Samuel Smith, pp. 116–21.
7. Whitehead, *Early History of Perth Amboy*, p. 89.
8. "A Memorial of the State of the Case of the Proprietors of East New Jersey," *NJA*, 2: *1687–1703*, p. 172.
9. Problems associated with the enforcement of the Navigation Acts, such as those experienced by William Dyre, customs collector for East Jersey, in 1685, proved detrimental to their relationship with the Crown. In his initial attempts to enforce the Navigation Acts, Dyre was frustrated by the courts of East Jersey. The local judiciary not only found against him in a judgment involving his seizure of a vessel for violating the acts, but imprisoned Dyre for a period of time in an attempt to collect court costs. The collector protested to London. This, added to the growing complaints and similar accusations, may well have been what led the proprietors to surrender the government to the Crown. Shortly thereafter, New Jersey was incorporated into the dominion of New England but was returned to the proprietors in a restoration of government during the reign of William and Mary (Preston W. Edsell, ed., *Journal of the Courts of Common Right and Chancery of East New Jersey, 1683–1702* [Philadelphia, 1937], pp. 133–39).
10. O'Callaghan, 1:151.
11. Copy of Coker's commission to be collector at Perth Amboy, *NJA*, 2:130.
12. The Commissioners of the Customs order to Mr. Randolph about port of Perth Amboy, *NJA*, 2:178.
13. Order of Council, directing the payment of all duties to the Governor of New York, by vessels trading in Hudson's River, *NJA*, 2:200.
14. To the Right Honourable the Lords of Council of Trade and Foreign Plantations, *NJA*, 2:308–9.
15. Govr Bass, His Proclamation ab^t ye Ports of ye Jerseys, *NJA*, 2:227–28.
16. The Humble Petition of the Proprietors of the Province of East Jersey in America [1698], *NJA*, 2:255–56.
17. Ibid.
18. Memorial of the Proprietors of East Jersey to the Lords of Trade 1699, *NJA*, 2:259–63.
19. Earl of Bellomont to the Lords of the Treasury, *NJA*, 2:341–42; Instructions from Queen Anne to Lord Cornbury, 16 November 1702, ibid., pp. 513–14.
20. Lord Cornbury to the Lords of Trade, 7 June 1707, *NJA*, 2:230–32.
21. McCormick, pp. 40–42.; Thomas F. Gordon, *The History of New Jersey* (Trenton, N.J., 1834), pp. 38–39.

22. John W. Barber and Henry Howe, *Historical Collections of the State of New Jersey* (New York, 1844), p. 25.
23. Schermerhorn, p. 35.
24. Whitehead, *Early History of Perth Amboy*, p. 295.
25. Governor Dongan's Report to the Committee on Trade on the Province of New York, 22 February 1687, in O'Callaghan, 1:160.
26. Ibid.
27. *Boston News-Letter*, 3 September to 10 September 1705, in *NJA*, 11: Part 2, *Extracts from American Newspapers, Relating to New Jersey, 1704–1739*, p. 11.
28. *Boston News-Letter*, 25 June to 2 July 1705, *NJA*, 11:9–10.
29. *Boston News-Letter*, 24 June to 1 July 1706, 1 July to 8 July 1706, 8 July to 15 July 1706, and 5 August to 12 August 1706, *NJA*, 11:17–18; *Boston News-Letter*, 9 June to 16 June 1707, ibid., pp. 22–23.
30. *Boston News-Letter*, 23 April to 26 April 1705, *NJA*, 11:6; *Boston News-Letter*, 21 May to 28 May 1705, ibid., p. 8; *Boston News-Letter*, 16 July to 23 July 1705, and 27 August to 3 September 1705, ibid., p. 10; *Boston News-Letter*, 19 November to 26 November 1705, and 4 March to 11 March 1705–6, ibid., p. 14; *Boston News-Letter*, 12 May to 19 May 1707, and 26 May to 2 June 1707.
31. Lord Cornbury to the Lords of Trade, 1 July 1708, *NJA*, 3:336–37.
32. Speech of Lord Cornbury to the Assembly of New Jersey, 7 April 1707, *NJA*, 3:167.
33. Bridenbaugh, *Cities in the Wilderness*, p. 204.
34. *Boston News-Letter*, from Monday, 7 January to Monday, 14 January 1712, *NJA*, 11:31.
35. Ibid., pp. 27, 32–33.
36. Ibid., pp. 39–41, 43.
37. Ibid., p. 38.
38. *NJA*, 4:276.
39. McGinnis, 1:38.
40. Governor Hunter's Speech to the Assembly, 19 April 1718, *NJA*, 4:364.
41. *Boston News-Letter*, from 18 October to 25 October 1714, *NJA*, 11:38.
42. Ibid.
43. Ibid.
44. Stuart Bruchey, *Roots of American Economic Growth, 1607–1861* (New York, 1968), pp. 21–28.
45. See table 1, this book.
46. Francis Burke Brandt, *The Majestic Delaware, the Nation's Foremost Historic River* (Philadelphia, 1929), pp. 97–101.
47. See table 1, this book.
48. See table 2, this book.
49. See table 1, this book.
50. See table 1, this book.
51. See table 2, this book.
52. The period 1748–50 shows an increase in both tonnage and vessel size, indicating apparent growth. See table 1, this book.
53. See table 1, this book.
54. See table 1, this book.
55. See table 2, this book.
56. See table 1, this book.

57. Douglass, p. 394; Cerinda W. Evans, *Some Notes on Shipbuilding and Shipping in Colonial Virginia* (Williamsburg, Va., 1957), p. 8.
58. See table 1, this book.
59. See table 2, this book.
60. See table 1, this book.
61. For example, William Fraser, collector at Salem, reported no entries from 1750 to 1751. CO 5/1035.
62. See table 3, this book.
63. See table 3, this book.
64. See table 3, this book. Douglass, p. 394.
65. CO 5/1035.
66. Ibid.
67. *Proposals for Traffick and Commerce, or Foreign Trade in New Jersey, in Answer to that Upbrading Question Why Should Not We Have Trade, As All Other The [sic] Plantations* [N.p., n.d.], p. 6.
68. Ibid., pp. [5], 3.
69. Ibid., pp. 4–[5], 3.
70. Ibid., pp. 4, 6.
71. Minutes of the Assembly, 27 January 1719, New Jersey Assembly Minutes, State Library Archives and History Bureau, Trenton, N.J.
72. Lewis Morris to the duke of Newcastle, 2 June 1732, *NJA*, 5:315.
73. Whitehead, *Early History of Perth Amboy*, p. 302.
74. Aaron Leaming and Jacob Spicer, eds., *The Grants, Concessions and Original Constitutions of the Province of New Jersey* (Philadelphia, 1732), pp. 25, 342, 390, 409, 432, 446.
75. Ibid., pp. 131–32.
76. Ibid., pp. 220–21, 222.
77. *An Ordinance for Regulating and Establishing Fees Within This His Majesty's Province of New Jersey* (Philadelphia, 1724), p. 13.
78. Samuel Nevill, comp., *The Acts of the General Assembly of the Province of New Jersey, from the Year 1703 . . . to the Year 1752 . . .* (Philadelphia, 1752), 1:338.
79. Governor William Franklin to the earl of Dartmouth, 28 March 1774, *NJA*, 10: *Administration of Governor William Franklin, 1767–1776*, 442.
80. A Flour Act was passed in 1714 and repealed in 1716/17; it was passed again in 1723 (William Bradford, comp., *The Acts of the General Assembly of the Province of New Jersey, from the Time of the Surrender of the Government to the Fourth Year of the Reign of King George the Second* [Philadelphia, 1732], pp. 78, 161).
81. Leaming and Spicer, *Grants, Concessions and Constitutions*, p. 25. The crisis soon passed, for this act was repealed shortly after its enactment.
82. Ibid., pp. 129, 343–44; Bradford, pp. 23, 72. This act of January 1716 contained such typical modifications as the discontinuing of the duty on hogshead staves, "being found by Experience to be Prejudicial to the Inhabitants of this Province" (Nevill, 1:285–90).
83. Carl Magnus, ed. and trans., "Pastor Wrangel's Trip to the Shore," *New Jersey History* (Spring 1969):12–13; 24–25.
84. Richard Pares, *Yankees and Creoles: The Trade between North America and the West Indies before the American Revolution* (Cambridge, Mass., 1956), pp. 38–39.

85. Leaming and Spicer, *Grants, Concessions and Constitutions*, p. 508.
86. Ibid., pp. 317–18.
87. Ibid., p. 508.
88. Bradford, pp. 164–66. This act was passed on August 13, 1725.
89. Nevill, 1:445.
90. Ibid., p. 446.
91. Leaming and Spicer, *Grants, Concessions and Constitutions*, pp. 117–18.
92. Bradford, p. 164. This was the apparent reason for the enactment of the 1725 law. The problem seems to have been a continual one, for the legislature, in March of 1774, reiterated the need for wholesome pork and enacted a still more stringent law (Samuel Allinson, comp., *Acts of the General Assembly of the Province of New Jersey, 1720–1776* [Burlington, N.J., 1776], p. 450).
93. Nevill, 1:446–48. This act, passed in 1751, went into effect on March 1 of the following year. Its provisions were to be enforced only for a period of two years following its implementation.
94. Ibid., p. 448.
95. Whitehead, *Early History of Perth Amboy*, p. 298.
96. For an examination of regulatory actions of colonial government, see Richard B. Morris, *Government and Labor in Early America* (New York, 1965).
97. Lane, "Water Transportation in Colonial New Jersey," p. 79.
98. *The New York Gazette, Revived in the Weekly Post Boy*, 4 April 1748; *The New York Weekly Post Boy*, 11 November 1745; *New York Gazette*, 19 May 1740; *The Pennsylvania Gazette*, 4 June 1744; *The New York Weekly Post Boy*, 26 August 1745; *The Pennsylvania Gazette*, 21 May 1745, *NJA*, 12:437, 283, 27, 223, 272, 256–57, and others.
99. Dally, p. 107.
100. Richard Pitts Powell, "Transportation and Travel in Colonial New Jersey," *NJHS Proceedings* 16 (1931):287.
101. Whitehead, *Early History of Perth Amboy*, pp. 270–71.
102. Lane, *From Indian Trail to Iron Horse*, p. 61.
103. Kull, 1:295.
104. The area known as Inians Ferry became the chartered city of New Brunswick in 1730.
105. Lane, "Water Transportation in Colonial New Jersey," pp. 17–18.
106. Peter O. Wacker, *The Musconetcong Valley of New Jersey: A Historical Geography* (New Brunswick, N.J., 1968), pp. 133–34. See also in this context: Peter O. Wacker, "Preliminary View of the Possible Association between Cultural Background and Agriculture in New Jersey during the Latter Part of the Eighteenth Century," *Proceedings of the Eleventh Annual Meeting of the New York–New Jersey Division, Association of American Geographers* 4 (May 1971); and Alex Dobrowski, "New Brunswick as a Port between 1800 and 1900" (unpublished paper, Department of Geography, Rutgers University, 1970).
107. Lane, *Indian Trail to Iron Horse*, p. 60.
108. Journal of Janeway and Broughton, General Merchants, 16 June 1737–1845, Rutgers.
109. John P. Wall, "New Brunswick of Over a Century Ago," *NJHS Proceedings* 7 (January 1922):35–36.
110. Harrington, pp. 221–22.
111. Lane, *Indian Trail to Iron Horse*, p. 61.
112. Dr. Alexander Hamilton, quoted in William H. Benedict, "New Jersey As It Appeared to Early Observers and Travellers," *NJHS Proceedings* 5 (July

1920):160.
113. Adolph B. Benson, ed., *Peter Kalm's Travels in North America* (New York, 1937), 1:122.
114. Kull, 1:295; Lane, "Water Transportation in Colonial New Jersey," pp. 17–19.
115. Dr. Johann David Schoepf, quoted in Benedict, "New Jersey As It Appeared to Early Observers," pp. 164–65.
116. Discussion with Dr. Peter O. Wacker, Department of Geography, Rutgers University, 19 January 1972. See also Wacker, "A Preliminary View."
117. Schmidt, pp. 33, 42.
118. Anderson, pp. 11–13.
119. Discussion with Dr. Peter O. Wacker.
120. Ibid. Nowhere is this more graphically presented than in the population density maps created by Herman R. Friis, "A Series of Population Maps of the Colonies and the United States, 1625–1790," *Geographical Review* 30 (1940):463–70.
121. Gordon, pp. 40–41.
122. Ibid.
123. CO 5/1035.
124. This was a very real problem, for the deep freeze was usually a result of the dominance of a high-pressure ridge. Warmer weather and the subsequent breaking up of the ice in the river usually came as a low-pressure area forced out the high and in the process brought rain or snow and high winds.
125. Harold Fisher Wilson, *The Jersey Shore: A Social and Economic History of the Counties of Atlantic, Cape May, Monmouth and Ocean* (New York, 1953), p. 148.
126. Jacob Leaming to John Hatton, 11 September and 7 and 19 November 1764, Jacob Spicer Papers, MG 59, NJHS; William Nelson, ed., *The New Jersey Coast in Three Centuries* (New York, 1902):1, 437–38.
127. Lane, *Indian Trail to Iron Horse*, pp. 415–16.

Chapter 3

1. Thomas C. Barrow, *Trade and Empire: The British Customs in Colonial America, 1660–1783* (Cambridge, Mass., 1967), p. 270.
2. For detailed examination of the purpose and evolution of these statutes see: O. M. Dickerson, *The Navigation Acts and the American Revolution* (New York, 1951); Lawrence A. Harper, *The English Navigation Laws: A Seventeenth Century Experiment in Social Engineering* (New York, 1939).
3. Charles M. Andrews, *The Colonial Period of American History* (New Haven, Conn., 1938):4, 163.
4. Alfred S. Martin, "The Kings Customs, Philadelphia, 1763–1774," *William and Mary Quarterly* 5 (April 1948):202–3.
5. CO 5/1035 and/or CO 5/1036. Vessel information—arrivals, departures, cargo, size, type, and other pertinent information noted in this chapter—are drawn from these listings.
6. Andrews, *Colonial Period*, 4:196–97.

7. CO 5/1035; CO 5/1036.
8. CO 5/1035.
9. *An Ordinance for Regulating and Establishing Fees*, pp. 62–63.
10. Nevill, p. 350.
11. CO 5/1035.
12. Andrews, *Colonial Period*, 4:173.
13. Ibid, pp. 207–8.
14. Lords of Trade to the King—with a Draft of the Instructions to Lewis Morris as Governor of New Jersey, *NJA*, 6:13–15.
15. Lords of Trade to Governor Lewis Morris, 3 July 1745, *Lewis Morris Papers*, pp. 256–57.
16. Governor Jonathan Belcher to Board of Trade, 20 January 1749/50, *NJA*, 8:381.
17. William Fraser to the Lords of Trade, 2 February 1750/51, *NJA*, 8:587; see also note on that page.
18. Jacob Spicer to John Hatton, 7 November 1764, Jacob Spicer Papers.
19. Governor William Franklin to the Lords of Trade, 8 February 1764, *NJA*, 9:402–4.
20. Barrow, p. 74.
21. Woodward, *Ploughs and Politicks*, pp. 54, 62, 224.
22. Archibald Douglas Turnbull, *John Stevens: An American Record* (New York, 1928), pp. 1–16; *CSFP*, 1:vii; McGinnis, 1:35.
23. John Stevens to Richard Stevens, 28 April 1712, Stevens Family Papers, MG 409, NJHS.
24. John Barclay, Collector, Port of Perth Amboy, 23 October 1716, *CSFP*, 1:14.
25. Account of Wheat Seized by John Stevens Collector and Delivered into Assembly, 3 May 1722, State Library Archives and History Bureau, Trenton, N.J.
26. Ibid.
27. From 10 October 1766 to 17 October 1767, for example, no fines or forfeitures were recorded at any of the New Jersey ports (Public Records Office, Treasury Papers, 1/452:47).
28. Caleb Heathcote, Surveyor General, Northern District, to John Stevens, 20 April 1717, Stevens Family Papers.
29. Andrews, *Colonial Period*, 4:204–7.
30. Barrow, p. 267.
31. Andrews, *Colonial Period*, 4:204–5.
32. Honorable John Stevens of New York to Scott and Pringle, 10 March 1770, Stevens Family Papers.
33. CO 5/1035.
34. Woodward, *Ploughs and Politicks*, p. 37.
35. Ibid., pp. 10–11; Fisher, pp. 60–61.
36. *An Ordinance for Regulating and Establishing Fees*, pp. 62–63.
37. Andrews, *Colonial Period*, 5:180–81, 204.
38. Ibid.
39. Gerlach, p. 70.
40. Barrow, pp. 160–85.
41. Aaron Leaming's Diary, 14 November 1775, The Historical Society of Pennsylvania, Philadelphia.

Chapter 4

1. See tables 1 and 3, this book.
2. CO 5/1035.
3. See table 4, this book.
4. Ibid.
5. Ibid.
6. Ibid.; CO 5/1035.
7. CO 5/1035.
8. Ibid.; see table 4, this book.
9. CO 5/1035.
10. See table 4, this book; CO 5/1035.
11. CO 5/1035.
12. CO 5/1035; CO 5/1036; see table 4, this book.
13. See table 4, this book; CO 5/1036.
14. Ibid.
15. See table 4, this book.
16. CO 5/1035.
17. See table 4, this book; CO 5/1035.
18. Ibid.
19. Ibid.
20. James C. Connolly, "Slavery in Colonial New Jersey and the Causes Operating against Its Extension," *NJHS Proceedings* 14 (April 1929):181–202.
21. CO 5/1035.
22. Ibid.
23. See table 3, this book; CO 5/1035.
24. Ibid.
25. Ibid.
26. CO 5/1035; CO 5/1036; CO 5/975.
27. See, for example, William A. Fairburn, *Merchant Sail*, 6 vols. (Center Lovell, Maine, 1945–55)1:195–96; Harrington, pp. 164–66.
28. Hedges, chapters 2–8.
29. This system has been used with considerable success by William I. Davisson and Lawrence J. Bradley in preparing "New York Maritime Trade: Ship Voyage Patterns, 1715–1765," *New-York Historical Quarterly* 55 (October 1971):309–17.
30. See table 5, this book.
31. William I. Davisson, "The Philadelphia Trade" (abstract), *Western Economic Journal* 3 (1965):310–11; Davisson and Bradley, "New York Maritime Trade," pp. 309–17.
32. Ibid.
33. Barrow, p. 269.
34. Bridenbaugh, *Cities in the Wilderness*, p. 33
35. John L. Carvin, "Portsmouth and the Piscataqua: Social History and Material Culture," *Historical New Hampshire* 26 (1971):6–8.

36. Compiled from table 3, this book.
37. CO 5/967.
38. Ibid.; see table 3, this book.
39. Ibid.
40. Compiled from table 3, this book.
41. Barrow, p. 268.
42. Bridenbaugh, *Cities in the Wilderness*, pp. 34, 179–180; Roger T. Trindell, "Transportation Development and the Hinterland Piracy: An Example for Colonial North America," *Journal of Transportation History* 7 (November 1966): 205–16.
43. See table 3, this book.
44. See table 6, this book.
45. CO 5/967; CO 5/968; CO 5/969.
46. Carvin, pp. 9–13.
47. Ibid.
48. Ibid.; CO 5/1035; CO 5/1036; tables 3 and 4, this book.
49. See table 1, this book; CO 5/967; CO 5/968; CO 5/969.
50. CO 5/967; CO 5/968; CO 5/969.
51. See table 3, this book.
52. Ibid.
53. See table 6, this book; CO 5/969.
54. See tables 6 and 7, this book.
55. CO 5/967; CO 5/968; CO 5/969.
56. See chapter 6, this book.
57. See table 3, this book.
58. Ibid.
59. CO 5/967; CO 5/968; CO 5/969; CO 5/1035; CO 5/1036; CO 5/709; CO 5/710.
60. Ibid.
61. Even the briefest perusal of the papers of the Parker and Stevens families for this period indicates the overwhelming involvement with land sales, purchases, rentals, and other land transactions. Stevens Family Papers; Parker Family Papers, MG 18, NJHS.

Chapter 5

1. McCusker, "Colonial Tonnage Measurement," pp. 82, 85n; George F. Dow, *The Sailing Ships of New England* (Salem, Mass., 1928), p. 12.
2. Ibid.
3. For work currently being done in this area by economic historians, see Gary M. Walton, "Sources of Productivity Change in American Colonial Shipping, 1675–1755," *Economic History Review* 20 (1967):67–68; and Walton, "A Measure of Productivity Change in American Colonial Shipping," *Economic History Review* 21 (1968):268–82; McCusker, "Colonial Tonnage Measurement"; Shepherd and Walton, *Maritime Trade*; Walton and Shepherd, *The Economic Rise of Early*

America, chapter 5; D. Ball and Gary Walton, "Agricultural Productivity Change in 18th Century Pennsylvania," *Journal of Economic History* 36 (March 1976):102–7.
4. Carl C. Cutler, *The Important Types of Merchant Sailing Craft* (Mystic, Conn., 1930), pp. 6–7.
5. For examples, see CO 5/1035 and CO 5/1036.
6. The manner in which vessels were rigged, and the relationship of rigging and design to the use of the craft, are amply explained in a number of works. Among them are: Howard I. Chapelle, *The History of American Sailing Ships* (New York, 1935); and Edgar L. Bloomster, *Sailing and Small Craft Down the Ages* (Menasha, Wis., 1940); and William A. Baker, *Colonial Vessels* (Barre, Mass., 1962).
7. Vessels registered at Burlington and Salem were, as represented in the port records, insignificantly few. Perth Amboy records show only two Burlington-registered craft in the period covered; the New Jersey fleet consisted almost wholly of vessels registered at Perth Amboy.
8. See table 2, this book.
9. See table 9, this book.
10. See table 7, this book.
11. Ibid.
12. CO 5/1035; CO 5/1036.
13. Jensen, pp. 1–23.
14. See table 9, this book.
15. Ibid.
16. See table 7, this book.
17. CO 5/1035; CO 5/1036.
18. Ibid.; see table 7, this book.
19. See table 10, this book.
20. Ibid.; CO 5/1035.
21. See table 10, this book.
22. Ibid.
23. Ibid.
24. Ibid.
25. Ibid.
26. See tables 10 and 6, this book.
27. See table 10, this book.
28. Ibid.
29. Ibid.
30. Ibid.
31. Ibid.
32. CO 5/1035; CO 5/1036.
33. Chapelle, *American Sailing Ships*, pp. 7–8.
34. Letters, both public and private, as well as pamphlets, stressed the abundance of timbers and the possibility of their use for shipping. See "A Brief Account of the Province of East Jersey in America . . . ," and letters from T. Rudyard, S. Groome, Gawen Lawrie, John Barclay, and Arthur Forbes, in Samuel Smith, pp. 166–79, 539.
35. John Barclay, Arthur Forbes, and Gawen Lawrie to the Scotts Proprietors, 26 March 1683, in Samuel Smith, pp. 179–89.

36. Lord Cornbury to the Lords of Trade, New York, 1 July 1708, *NJA*, 3:336–37.
37. Simeon J. Crowther, "The Shipbuilding Industry and the Economic Development of the Delaware Valley, 1681–1776" (Ph.D. diss., University of Pennsylvania, 1970), p. 54.
38. Ibid., p. 79.
39. Ibid., p. 89.
40. Ibid., p. 141.
41. See table 9, this book; CO 5/1035.
42. Robert Hunter, Governor of New Jersey, to the Secretary, 14 November 1715; Lewis Morris, President of the Council of New Jersey, to the Lords of Trade, 21 November 1719, *NJA*, 4:223, 443.
43. CO 5/1035.
44. Leaming and Spicer, *Grants, Concessions and Constitutions*, pp. 129, 343–44; Bradford, pp. 23, 72.
45. CO 5/1035; CO 5/1036.
46. Barber and Howe, pp. 107–8.
47. Chapelle, *American Sailing Ships*, p. 8.
48. Crowther, p. 127.
49. CO 5/1035.
50. Crowther, p. 18.
51. Walton and Shepherd, *Economic Rise*, pp. 125–28.
52. Shepherd and Walton, *Maritime Trade*, pp. 73–75.
53. Ibid., p. 74, 196.
54. See table 6, this book.
55. Ibid.
56. Ibid.
57. Ibid.
58. Ibid.
59. Ibid.
60. Ibid.
61. Shepherd and Walton, *Maritime Trade*, p. 76.
62. Ibid.; see table 5, this book.
63. See table 10, this book.
64. See table 8, this book.
65. Ibid.
66. Crowther, pp. 132–33; 152.
67. Lee, 1:203.
68. CO 5/1035.
69. See table 8, this book.
70. CO 5/1035.
71. Schermerhorn, p. 305.; *New York Weekly Post Boy*, 12 November 1744, *NJA*, 12:241.
72. Letter from Colonel Daniel Cox, 31 May 1722, *NJA*, 5:39.
73. Wacker, *Musconetcong Valley*, p. 141; Nelson, 1:436.
74. Nelson, 1:13; Byron Fairchild, *Messrs. William Pepperell, Merchants at Piscataqua* (Ithaca, N.Y., 1954), p. 142.
75. *Boston Evening-Post*, 23 January 1749; *New York Weekly Post Boy*, 10 December 1744; both in *NJA*, 12:512, 244.
76. Chapelle, *American Sailing Ships*, p. 26.
77. *New York Gazette, Revived in the Weekly Post Boy*, 10 April 1749; *Boston Weekly*

News-Letter, 18 March to 25 March 1742; both in *NJA*, 12:527–28, 120.
78. *New York Weekly Journal*, 7 April 1740; *American Weekly Mercury*, 29 April to 6 May 1742; *New York Weekly Post Boy*, 12 January 1747; *Boston Weekly Post-Boy*, 5 March 1750; *New York Gazette, Revived in the Weekly Post Boy*, 2 April 1750; *New York Gazette, Revived in the Weekly Post Boy*, 31 December 1750; all in *NJA*, 12:20, 127, 331, 612–13, 598–99, 583, 618.
79. *Boston Weekly News-Letter*, 7 August to 14 August 1740; *Boston Evening-Post*, 11 August 1740; *New York Gazette, Revived in the Weekly Post Boy*, 20 July 1747; *Boston Evening-Post*, 27 July 1747; *Boston Weekly News-Letter*, 23 June 1748; all in *NJA*, 12:48–49, 371–72, 452–54.
80. This is graphically demonstrated by the yearly appearance of newly built vessels in Perth Amboy waters as reflected in CO 5/1035; CO 5/1036.
81. Crowther, pp. 132–33, 152; A brig, snow, or ship ranged in cost from £1,100 to £3,500.
82. See entries, April through December 1726, in CO 5/1035.
83. See table 11, this book.
84. CO 5/1035; CO 5/1036.
85. See table 11, this book.
86. See table 6, this book. Masters of vessels and others similarly involved often shared ownership of the vessels on which they served, and many were prosperous and well educated enough to have left wills for the disposal of their personal estates. As a category, mariners appear to have been comparatively significant. From 1670 to 1750 they constituted slightly over 5 percent of those whose occupations were mentioned in wills. From their wills it is apparent that mariners often invested their maritime earnings in real estate and businesses such as breweries. That a few purchased slaves suggests that many were affluent. Evidence in wills indicates that at least in one county (Gloucester) mariners were among the wealthiest men; the value of their personal estates exceeded that of all others.

    While mariners often invested their profits in non-maritime enterprises, it is also evident that other tradesmen and farmers owned shares in sloops, whaleboats, shallops, and all manner of sailing craft. Such personal effects as ship carpenter tools indicate that many of these people also prospered by building and repairing those same vessels that New Jersey mariners sailed. Clearly, maritime commerce played an important role both directly and indirectly in the local economy of New Jersey (Harry B. Weiss, *The Personal Estates of Early Farmers and Tradesmen of Colonial New Jersey, 1670–1750* [Trenton, N.J., 1971], pp. 39, 48, 51, 52, 89, 90).
87. See table 11, this book.
88. Throughout the colonial period, professional seamen provided only a small nucleus of the overall profession. (Pares, *Yankees and Creoles*, pp. 18–19.)
89. *American Weekly Mercury*, 28 March 1723, *NJA*, 11:69.
90. *American Weekly Mercury*, 27 June to 4 July 1723, *NJA*, 11:72; *Boston Weekly Post-Boy*, 31 March 1740; *New-York Evening Post*, 14 November 1748; *Boston Evening-Post*, 23 January 1749; all in *NJA*, 12:19, 311, 497, 512, 592–93.
91. Pares, *Yankees and Creoles*, pp. 20–21.
92. Walton, "Productivity Change in American Colonial Shipping," pp. 67–68.
93. *American Weekly Mercury*, 1 January 1722, *NJA*, 11:67; *Pennsylvania Gazette*, 31 March 1743, *NJA*, 12:176.
94. See table 6, this book; CO 5/1035. As few as four people could handle a large

schooner or brig to Madeira.
95. See table 6, this book, comparing the tons, guns, and men for an extended period for vessels at New Jersey ports; it indicates no decisive change in relationship of men to tons. Similar comparisons of larger vessels (one by Walton, "Productivity Change in American Colonial Shipping") show a reduction of the size of crews from the beginning of the century to the end.
96. Kammen, *Empire and Interest*, chapter 1. Herbert E. Krooss and Charles Gilbert, *American Business History* (Englewood Cliffs, N.J., 1972), pp. 43–44.
97. Harper, *The English Navigation Acts*, pp. 242–74. See also "The Effect of the Navigation Acts on the Thirteen Colonies," in Richard B. Morris, ed., *The Era of the American Revolution* (New York, 1959), pp. 3–39; Louis M. Hacker, *The Triumph of Capitalism* (New York, 1940), pp. 145–70.
98. Dickerson, passim.
99. Gary M. Walton, "The New Economic History and the Burdens of the Navigation Act," *Economic History Review* 24 (November 1971): 533–42.
100. Robert P. Thomas, "A Quantitative Approach to the Study of the Effects of British Imperial Policy on Colonial Welfare," *Journal of Economic History* 25 (December 1965): 615–38.
101. Gary M. Walton, "The Burdens of the Navigation Acts: A Reply," *Economic History Review* 26 (December 1973):687–88; Peter D. McClelland, "The Cost to America of British Imperial Policy," *American Economic Review, Papers and Proceedings* 59 (May 1969):370–81.
102. Peter D. McClelland, "The New Economic History and the Burdens of the Navigation Acts: A Comment," *Economic History Review* 26 (November 1973):679–86; Joseph Reid, "On Navigating the Navigation Acts with Peter McClelland," *American Economic Review* 60 (December 1970):949–55; and a reply by McClelland, pp. 956–58.
103. Stuart Bruchey, *The Roots of American Economic Growth* (New York, 1968), pp. xiii–xxv; Herman E. Krooss, "The Influence on America of British Imperial Policy," *American Economic Review* 59 (1969):384–85; David J. Loschky, "Studies of the Navigation Acts: New Economic Non-History," *Economic History Review* 26 (November 1973):689–91. A contrary argument is advanced by Joseph Reid, "Economic Burden: Spark to the Revolution?" *Journal of Economic History* 38 (March 1978):81–100.
104. Kull, pp. 229–33, 292–93.
105. CO 5/1035; CO 5/1036.
106. Ibid.
107. Ibid.
108. Ibid.
109. Ibid.; Andrew W. Leake, Account Book, 1756–66, MG 118, NJHS.
110. Somewhat scarce were imports destined for use in early manufacturing. Cargo manifests show grindstones for milling or anchors, anchor stores, and ship rigging for the shipbuilding industry. But these items reflected a natural expansion of existing conditions, not a substantial change that heralded expansion or development in this largely agrarian colony (CO 5/1035, CO 5/1036).
111. Ibid.
112. Ibid.
113. Ibid.
114. Ibid.
115. Ibid.

116. Ibid.
117. Merchants and others to the Lords of Trade, 24 May 1723, *NJA*, 5:68–69.
118. CO 5/1035.
119. William Burnet to the Lords of Trade, 8 September 1721, *NJA*, 5:21–22; Lewis Morris to the duke of Newcastle, 2 June 1732, *NJA*, 5:314–15; Jonathan Belcher to the Lords of Trade, 28 December 1754, *NJA*, 8:82–83.
120. Ibid.; Lewis Morris to the Lords of Trade, 15 December 1742, *Lewis Morris Papers*, p. 156.
121. Census of the Province of New Jersey Anno 1726, *NJA*, 5:164; Number of people in New Jersey taken in 1737/38 and 1745, *NJA*, 6:242–44.
122. Ibid.
123. Andrew W. Leake, Account Book.
124. CO 5/1036.

Chapter 6

1. Harrington, p. 58; Jensen, p. 11.
2. Those merchants were John Johnston, Thomas Gordon, John Hamilton, George Willock, John Barclay, William Eier, John Stevens, William Hodgson, William Frost, Henry Berry, John Sharp, Thomas Turnbull, Andrew Redford, and Alexander Walker (McGinnis, 1:135).
3. CO 5/1035.
4. The merchants who signed the "Certificate of Perth Amboy Merchants of the Value of New Jersey Bills in December 1726" were Andrew Johnston, Fenwick Lyell, William Williamson, Henry Neale, Andrew Cooper, Michael Kearney, Charles Dunster, Samuel Alting, Ebenezer Lyon, Alexander Mackdowell, Heron Putland, Joseph Bonnett, John Stevens, and Joseph Ogdens (*NJA*, 5:154–55).
5. CO 5/1035.
6. Cornelius Vermeule, "Early Transportation in and about New Jersey," *NJHS Proceedings* 9 (April 1924):106–24; *New-York Gazette, and the Weekly Mercury*, 22 November 1773, *NJA*, vol 29: *Documents Relating to the Colonial History of the State of New Jersey*, edited by William Nelson succeeded by A. Van Doren, *Tenth Volume of Extracts from American Newspapers Relating to New Jersey, 1773–1774* (Paterson, N.J., 1917), p. 106.
7. General Store Accounts, Hendrickson Family Papers, 1750 (1753), Special Collections, Rutgers University Library, New Brunswick, N.J.
8. Will of Daniel Hendrickson, 16 November 1727, Hendrickson Family Papers.
9. Accounts of the sloop *Catharine*, Hendrickson Family Papers.
10. Accounts of the *Catharine*; A Copy of Orders for Captain Patrick Boyle from, Daniel Hendrickson, Hendrickson Family Papers.
11. Accounts of the *Catharine*; "Invoice of Sundreys Shipped on Board the Sloop *Catharine* . . . Bound to Kingston Jamaica," 3 November 1752, Hendrickson Family Papers.
12. Accounts of the *Catharine*; A copy of letter to Mr. Daniel Hendrickson from West and Cook, 25 December [n.d.], Hendrickson Family Papers.
13. Accounts of the *Catharine*; Ledger page dated 15 March 1752, Hendrickson

Family Papers.
14. Patrick Boyle to Daniel Hendrickson, Curaçao, 13 March 1753, Hendrickson Family Papers.
15. Owners of the sloop *Catharine* to Stephen Skinner, entries for 1763 and 1764, Hendrickson Family Papers.
16. Bill of sale from Daniel Hendrickson to James Van Brankle, 18 July 1753, Hendrickson Family Papers.
17. Account with West and Cook from 15 July 1752 to 30 March 1754; invoice for goods shipped aboard the *Jersey*, Hendrickson Family Papers; Holmes Family Papers, Special Collections, Rutgers University Library, New Brunswick, N.J.
18. Sloop *Charming Betty*, Special Collections, Rutgers University Library, New Brunswick, N.J.
19. *Charming Betty*, entries from December 1730 to January 1730/31.
20. Ibid.
21. The Hendrickson Family Papers are full of the same kind of initialing system.
22. *Charming Betty*, entries from 1731 at Cape Fear.
23. Ibid., entries from December 1730 to January 1730/31.
24. Ibid., entry for 2 June 1731.
25. Ibid., entry for 19 October 1732.
26. Crowther, p. 10.
27. Krooss and Gilbert, *American Business History*, p. 51.
28. Ibid.
29. Besides being high sheriff, Elisha Parker was a justice of the peace and a member of the governor's council (Clayton, *History of Union and Middlesex*, p. 557; McGinnis, 3:73–75).
30. McGinnis; Anne Young Zimmer, "Minutes of Elisha Parker, 1748–1750: Economic Mirror of a Transition Period" (master's thesis, Wayne State University, 1964), pp. 58-66.
31. Zimmer, p. 85.
32. CO 5/1035.
33. Whitehead, *Early History of Perth Amboy*, p. 72.
34. CO 5/1035.
35. Wheat received from tenants in Sussex County, Parker Family financial records, 1686–1790; Account Book for 1791; even at this late date payment in produce was still taking place as entry notes hogs in lieu of cash, Parker Family Papers.
36. Parker Family financial records, 1686–1790, Parker Family Papers. See especially James Parker's account book, 1753 in James Parker's Diary, MG 287, NJHS.
37. Stuart Bruchey, "Success and Failure Factors: American Merchants in Foreign Trade in the Eighteenth and Early Nineteenth Century," *Business History Review* 32 (1958):276–78.
38. James Parker's account book for 1753, Parker Family financial records, 1686–1790, Parker Family Papers.
39. *NJA*, 11:83; Vermeule, p. 110.
40. Log of the Ship *Catherine*, in Ship's Log Collection, MG 49, NJHS.
41. Ibid.
42. CO 5/1035.
43. Ibid.; log of the *Catherine*.
44. Log of the *Catherine*.

45. CO 5/1035; CO 5/1036.
46. *NJA*, 11:83n.
47. Andrew Johnston was married to one of the Van Cortlands; John Parker's son married Catherine Alexander, daughter of James Alexander, a prominent New York lawyer. The Parkers' close connection with the Alexanders is revealed by their reliance on that family after John Parker's death. James Parker studied law under Alexander, and Elisha married one of the daughters (Zimmer, pp. 3, 61–62, 88–89).
48. McGinnis, 3:75.
49. CO 5/1035.
50. Zimmer, p. 61.
51. Arthur H. Cole, "The Tempo of Mercantile Life in Colonial America," *Business History Review* 33 (1959):282–84, 290.
52. CO 5/1035; CO 5/1036.
53. Ibid.
54. Harrington, p. 52.
55. CO 5/1036.
56. Harrington, pp. 134, 295.
57. CO 5/1036.
58. Harrington, p. 154.
59. John Watts to James Neilson, 1 February 1762 (*Letter Book of John Watts*, pp. 19–20).
60. John Watts to Henry Cruger, 10 May 1763 (*Letter Book of John Watts*, pp. 140–41)..
61. Sales for the *Little David*, July 1753; Account of David Johnston and James Parker at Saint Croix, 20 January 1752; Listing of current accounts of Mr. James Parker and Company at Kingston in Jamaica, 1–13 April 1752; Invoice from Saint Croix, 19 April 1752; John Smyth to De Lancey Robinson and Company, 5 February 1763; Statement of Accounts, Parker Family Papers.
62. Ibid.
63. John Stevens to Richard Stevens, Philadelphia, 7 July 1746; Stevens Family Papers.
64. CO 5/1035.
65. General Account of loading and fitting the brig *Molly*, Richard Stevens master, for Antigua, January 1742, Stevens Family Papers.
66. Ibid.; CO 5/1036.
67. John Stevens to Scott, Pringle and Scott, 3 November 1742, Stevens Family Papers.
68. Moses Rolfe to Richard Stevens, 26 October 1739, Stevens Family Papers.
69. John Stevens Day Book for 1760, Stevens Family Papers.
70. Ibid.
71. *CPSF*, 1:vii-viii.
72. Ibid., p. viii.
73. Ibid., passim.
74. James Parker to Henry Livingston in Jamaica, 18 May 1751, Parker Family Papers.
75. John Stevens to [Mr.] Pringle, 20 April 1742, Stevens Family Papers.
76. John Stevens to Mr. Scott, Pringle and Scott, 3 November 1742, Stevens Family Papers.
77. John Stevens to Mr. Richard Jeneway, 27 May 1741; John Stevens to Traitas

and Santos, 12 March 1743; Bill of loading enclosed to Madeira, 20 December 1743, Stevens Family Papers.
78. Scott, Pringle and Scott to John Stevens, 11 May to 6 July 1746, Stevens Family Papers.
79. Ibid.
80. John Stevens to Richard Jeneway, 10 December 1743, Stevens Family Papers.
81. Willing and Caldwall to John Stevens, 24 August 1750; John Stevens to William Alexander [Lord Stirling], 8 March 1749; *CPSF*, 1:171, 129.
82. John Stevens to Pringle, 20 April 1742, Stevens Family Papers.
83. Shipping bills, June 1741, Stevens Family Papers.
84. Account for 16 June 1741; see also in this regard account of Richard Stevens, captain on the Brig *Catherine*, 11 May 1746, Stevens Family Papers.
85. Insurance form 10 May 1742, Stevens Family Papers.
86. John Stevens to Richard Jeneway, 5 October 1744, Stevens Family Papers.
87. [John Stevens] to Mr. Godfrey Malbone, 13 January 1743, Stevens Family Papers.
88. Account of Richard and John Stevens, January to March 1743, Stevens Family Papers.
89. John Stevens to Scott, Pringle and Scott, 3 November 1742, Stevens Family Papers.
90. Ibid.
91. Scott, Pringle and Scott, 11 May 1746, Stevens Family Papers.
92. Ibid.
93. Ibid.
94. [Richard Stevens] to John Stevens, 25 September 1747, Stevens Family Papers.
95. [John Stevens] to Mr. Peter Mourque, 27 May 1741, Stevens Family Papers.
96. Account Book of John Stevens, 1745–50, Stevens Family Papers.
97. John Stevens to Scott, Pringle and Scott, 3 November 1742, Stevens Family Papers.
98. Bruchey, "Success and Failure," pp. 280–82.
99. Andrew and Lewis Johnston to John Stevens, 1 September 1739, Stevens Family Papers.
100. William Byam to John Stevens, 8 July 1749; Reade and Livingston to John Stevens and Company, 25 March 1750; Reade and Livingston to John Stevens and Company, 5 October 1750, *CPSF*, 1:136, 161, 174.
101. Reade and Livingston to John Stevens, 6 October 1750, *CPSF*, 1:174.
102. William Byam to John Stevens, 8 July 1749; Henry Steers to John Stevens, 7 July 1750; Henry Steers to John Stevens, 18 September 1750, *CPSF*, 1:136, 167, 173.
103. Reade and Livingston to John Stevens and Company, 5 October 1750, *CPSF*, 1:174; Brome and Barons to John and Richard Stevens, 22 December 1752, *CPSF*, 2:34.
104. John Stevens to John Terrill, 26 December 1751; John Terrill to John Stevens, 31 December 1751, *CPSF*, 2:30.
105. CO 5/1036.
106. An Act for the Relief & Discharge of Richard Stevens from all Demands against him for any debt contracted before the Sixteenth day of February 1767, Parker Family Papers.
107. Ibid.

Notes

108. Stephen DeLancey to John Parker, 25 February 1739, Parker Family Papers. The requestor, James Johnston, was the son of James Johnston, who married Eliza Parker, daughter of Elisha Parker, and often dropped the *t* from the spelling of his name.
109. James Johnston to James Parker, 25 June 1764, Parker Family Papers.
110. CO 5/1035.
111. William H. Benedict, *New Brunswick in History* (New Brunswick, N.J., 1925), pp. 26–28.
112. CO 5/1035.
113. Robert T. Thompson, *Colonel James Neilson: A Business Man of the Early Machine Age in New Jersey, 1784–1862* (New Brunswick, N.J., 1940), pp. 6–7.
114. Ibid.
115. CO 5/1035.
116. Ibid.
117. Ibid.
118. Morris R. Smith, *The Burlington Smiths: A Family History* (Philadelphia, 1877), 65–103.
119. CO 5/1035.
120. Albert Cook Myers, ed., *Hannah Logan's Courtship* (Philadelphia, 1904), pp. 20–38; DeCou, pp. 111–12.
121. Morris R. Smith, p. 100.
122. CO 5/1035.
123. Myers, pp. 1–59. See also Frederick B. Tolles, *Meeting House and Counting House* (New York, 1963).
124. Morris R. Smith, p. 127–29.
125. CO 5/1035.
126. Ibid.
127. Morris R. Smith, p. 127.
128. CO 5/1035; CO 5/975; manuscript page, 29 December 1757, Spicer Papers.
129. Diary, 30 March 1761, Spicer Papers.
130. Diary, 4 June 1761, Spicer Papers.
131. CO 5/1035.
132. Diary, 1 March 1760, 30 March 1761, Spicer Papers.
133. Diary, 11 March 1755, 27 November 1756, expenses for the year 1758, Spicer Papers.
134. Rules to Observe in Trade, Spicer Papers.
135. Diary, 16 July 1761, expenses for the year 1758, Spicer Papers.
136. Rules to Observe in Trade, Spicer Papers.
137. Burlington, 17 June 1745, Spicer Papers.
138. Jacob Spicer to Mr. Abel James, 22 August 1755, Spicer Papers.
139. Diary, 5 July 1761, Spicer Papers.
140. Ibid.
141. John R. Stevenson, "Samuel Spicer and His Descendants. With Some Notice of the Early Settlement of Camden and Cape May Counties, New Jersey," *NJHS Proceedings* 13 (January 1894): 41–58.
142. See tables 12 and 13, this book.
143. See table 12, this book.
144. In 1722, the sloop was owned jointly by John Heard and Andrew Johnston; the following year Johnston dropped out of the partnership for a voyage and then returned (CO 5/1035).

145. CO 5/1035.
146. Ibid.
147. Even a brief perusal of the owner relationships makes this apparent (CO 5/1035).
148. See table 12, this book.
149. Ibid.
150. Baxter; Hedges; Harrington.

Chapter 7

1. Jacob Spicer to John Hatton, 7 November 1764, Spicer Papers.
2. Jacob Spicer to John Hatton, 19 November 1764, Spicer Papers.
3. Ibid.
4. Ibid.
5. Spicer to Hatton, 7 November 1764.
6. *NJA*, vols. 24 and 25:passim.
7. Harry B. Weiss, *Trades and Tradesmen of Colonial New Jersey* (Trenton, N.J., 1965), pp. 63–64.
8. Kull, p. 260.
9. Governor William Franklin to the earl of Dartmouth, 28 March 1774, *NJA*, 10:442.
10. Ibid.
11. Ibid.
12. Marc Engal and Joseph Ernst, "An Economic Interpretation of the American Revolution," *William and Mary Quarterly* 29 (January 1972):3–32.
13. James H. Levitt, *New Jersey's Revolutionary Economy*, New Jersey's Revolutionary Experience, vol. 9 (Trenton, N.J., 1975), pp. 5–6.
14. Ibid., pp. 6–9
15. Raum, p. 386.
16. Fisher, pp. 429–31.
17. John T. Cunningham, *New Jersey: America's Main Road* (New York, 1966), pp. 82–89.
18. W. I. Lincoln Adams, "New Jersey's Tea Party," *NJHS Proceedings* 10 (April 1925):168–70; Pierce, pp. 139–43.
19. Ibid.
20. Fisher, pp. 452–56.
21. J. P. Wall and Harold E. Pickersgill, *History of Middlesex County, New Jersey* (New York, 1921), pp. 378–79; McGinnis, pp. 52–55, 56–61.
22. Ibid.
23. Ibid.
24. Schermerhorn, pp. 72–80.
25. Benedict, *New Brunswick*, pp. 127–28.
26. John Taylor to Governor Livingston, 30 January 1782, Miscellaneous MSS, MG 25, NJHS.
27. Lewis T. Stevens, *The History of Cape May County* (Cape May, N.J., 1897), pp. 210–12.

28. Ibid.
29. E. Alfred Jones, *The Loyalists of New Jersey: Their Memorials, Petitions, Claims, etc. from English Records*. Collections of the New Jersey Historical Society, vol. 10 (Newark, N.J., 1927), pp. 115, 152, 196.
30. Charles W. Parker, "Shipley: The Country Seat of a Jersey Loyalist," *NJHS Proceedings* 16 (April 1931):117–18.
31. Ruth Cook Brown, comp., *Early Shipbuilding Particularly in South Jersey* (Greenwich, N.J., n.d. [c. 1965] for the Cumberland County Historical Society), p. 3.
32. Lewis T. Stevens, p. 184; Benedict, *New Brunswick*, pp. 128–29.
33. McCormick, p. 162; Kull, p. 260.
34. Thomas Ryerson to James Parker, 6 July 1785, Parker Family Papers.
35. Whitehead, *Early History of Perth Amboy*, p. 56.
36. Peter Kemble, Gouveneur and Kemble, New York to James Parker, 9 February 1787; Cortland Parker, West Indies, for account of Leman and Scott, 19 June 1799; Account book of the sloop *Elisa*, 1785–86; James and Cortland Parker insurance forms, 1784–1803; Insurance forms, 1805; James and Cortland Parker concerning the schooner *Ceres*, going to Saint Thomas, 17 June 1805, Parker Family Papers.
37. Whitehead, *Early History of Perth Amboy*, pp. 303–4.

Bibliographical Note

CENTRAL TO THIS STUDY of port activity in the eighteenth century were the British customs records for the ports of Perth Amboy, Burlington, and Salem found in the Public Record Office, London; they are available on microfilm as CO 5/1035, CO 5/1036, and CO 5/975. Similar records for Piscataqua, New Hampshire (CO 5/967, CO 5/968, CO 5/969), and for Sunbury and Savannah, Georgia (CO 5/709, CO 5/710), were also useful for a comparative approach.

Other excellent sources for the study of maritime history are the manuscript holdings of the New Jersey Historical Society, in Newark. The Parker Family Papers (MG 17), the Stevens Family Papers (MG 409), and the Jacob Spicer Papers (MG 59) are invaluable to an understanding of the routine of colonial merchant life. Also useful are the Society's Ship Logs Collection (MG 49); numerous account books, most notably that of Andrew W. Leake (MG 118); the Smith Family Papers; and the William A. Whitehead Papers (MG 77), which contain much of the original materials and references used in Whitehead's preparation of *East Jersey under the Proprietary Governments* (Newark, N.J., 1875) and *Contributions to the Early History of Perth Amboy . . .* (New York, 1856).

The Special Collections of the Rutgers University Library, in New Brunswick, is also an excellent source for manuscripts on New Jersey maritime development. The Hendrickson Family Papers, which contain materials on the operation of the sloop *Catharine* and related merchant activities, are particularly valuable. The account book of the sloop *Charming Betty*, the journal of Janeway and Broughton, General Merchants, and the papers of the Holmes and Neilson families are also worthy of note.

Aside from these two major holdings, other materials are found in the manuscript collections of the State Library, in Trenton, and in the Historical Society of Pennsylvania, which houses the Aaron Leaming Diaries and also considerable materials on prominent West Jersey individuals and families.

Printed source materials are invaluable for a study of New Jersey's ports. Of outstanding value is the series *Archives of the State of New Jersey*, series 1, 1–30 and series 2, 1–5 (Newark, N.J. 1880–1917). In addition there are numerous compilations of laws, contemporary histories, and pamphlets that extol the benefits of settlement in New Jersey or discuss the advantages and problems associated with trade and commerce. Among the more useful are *Acts of the General Assembly of the Province of New Jersey, 1702–1776* (Burlington, N.J., 1776), compiled by Samuel Allinson; *The Acts of the General Assembly of the Province of New Jersey . . .* (Philadelphia, 1732), compiled by William Bradford; and *The Grants, Concessions and Original Constitutions of the Province of New Jersey* (Phildelphia, 1732), edited by Aaron Leaming and Jacob Spicer.

Excellent histories for this period are Samuel Smith's *History of the Colony of Nova-Cæsaria, or New Jersey . . .* (Burlington, N.J., 1765), and William Douglass's *Summary, Historical and Political of the First Planting, Progressive Improvement, and Present State of the British Settlement in North America*, vol. 2 (Boston, 1755). To help provide a sense of the times see Andrew Burnaby's *Travels Through the Middle Settlements in North America in the Years 1750 and 1760* (Burlington, N.J., 1775); Peter Kalm's *Travels in North America*, vol. 1 (New York, 1937), edited by Adolph B. Benson; and *Proposals for Traffic and Commerce, or Foreign Trade in New Jersey in Answer to That Upbrading Question. Why Should Not We Have Trade, As All Other the* [Sic] *Plantations* [N.p., n.d.].

Secondary sources for a study of New Jersey and its colonial ports are more plentiful. A good overview of New Jersey and the evolution of its ports might well begin with Richard P. McCormick's work, *New Jersey from Colony to State, 1609–1789*, revised edition (Newark, N.J., 1981) and his *Experiment in Independence, New Jersey in the Critical Period, 1781–1789* (New Brunswick, N.J., 1950). The political development of the colony is described in Jacob E. Fisher's old but still valuable *New Jersey as a Royal Province, 1738–1776* (New York, 1911) and in Donald L. Kemmerer's *Path to Freedom: The Struggle for Self-Government in Colonial New Jersey, 1703–1776* (Princeton, N.J., 1940).

The influence of geography upon the nature of settlement is discussed in Peter O. Wacker's *Musconetcong Valley of New Jersey, A Historical Geography* (New Brunswick, N.J., 1968) and his *Land and People: A Cultural Geography of Pre-Industrial New Jersey: Origins and Settlement Patterns* (New Brunswick, N.J., 1975).

Still valuable are the old multi-volume works on specific regions. The *History of Union and Middlesex Counties, New Jersey . . .* (Philadelphia, 1882), edited by W. Woodford Clayton, and *The New Jersey Coast in Three Centuries* (New York, 1902), edited by William Nelson, are good examples.

Information directly related to New Jersey's ports and commercial centers is to be found in William H. Benedict's *New Brunswick in History* (New Brunswick, N.J., 1925); William E. Schermerhorn's *History of Burlington, New Jersey* (Burlington, N.J., 1927); Henry H. Bisbee's *Burlington Story* (Burlington, N.J., 1952); George Decou's *Burlington, A Provincial Capital . . .* (Philadelphia, 1945); William C. McGinnis's *History of Perth Amboy, New Jersey, 1651–1958*, 4 vols. (Perth Amboy, N.J., 1958–60); and Roger T. Trindell's "Ports of Salem and Greenwich in the Eighteenth Century," *New Jersey History* 86 (Winter 1968):199–214. Works on the growth and development of neighboring colonies include Thomas J. Archdeacon's *New York City, 1664–1710: Conquest and Change* (Ithaca, N.Y., 1976), and Arthur L. Jensen's *Maritime Commerce of Colonial Philadelphia* (Madison, Wis., 1963). For a general understanding of the evolution of ports and urban centers one might consult Carl Bridenbaugh's solid if slightly dated *Cities in the Wilderness: The First Century of Urban Life in America, 1625–1742* (London, 1938) and *Cities in Revolt: Urban Life in America, 1743–1776* (New York, 1955).

These works are complemented by more recent works such as Jacob M. Price's "Economic Function and the Growth of American Port Towns in the Eighteenth Century," *Perspectives in American History*, no. 8 (1974):123–86, which provides more current information and theories on the process of urban growth. Other more general works that explore the economic character of this period are J. W. Crowley's *This Sheba Self: The Conceptualization of Economic Life in Eighteenth-Century America* (Baltimore, 1974); Gary B. Nash's *Urban Crucible: Social Change, Political Consciousness, and the Origins of the American Revolution* (Cambridge, Mass., 1979); and James F. Shepherd and Gary M. Walton, *Economic Rise of Early America* (Cambridge, Mass., 1979).

Also helpful in this regard are Marc Engal's "Economic Development of the Thirteen Colonies, 1720–1775," *William and Mary Quarterly* 32 (April 1975):190–222; and Michael Kammen's *Empire and Interest: The American Colonies and the Politics of Mercantilism* (New York, 1970).

A sense of how small ports operated in the eighteenth century may be gleaned from Thomas C. Barrow's *Trade and Empire: The British Customs Service in Colonial America, 1660–1783* (Cambridge, Mass., 1967); Larry R. Gerlach's "Customs and Contentions: John Hatten of Salem and Cohansey, 1763–1776," *New Jersey History* 89 (Summer 1971):69–92; Alfred S. Martin's "The Kings Customs, Philadelphia, 1763–1774," *William and Mary Quarterly* 5 (April 1948):201–16; and Carl R. Woodward's *Ploughs and Politicks: Charles Read of New Jersey and His Notes on Agriculture, 1715–1774* (New Brunswick, N.J., 1941).

The various patterns of trade and the complexity of maritime commerce are noted in James B. Hedges's *The Browns of Providence Plantations: Colonial Years* (Cambridge, Mass., 1952); Byron Fairchild's *Messrs. William Pepperell, Merchants at Piscataqua* (Ithaca, N.Y., 1954); and in two works by Richard Pares on the West Indies trade, *War and Trade in the West Indies, 1739–1763* (Oxford, 1936), and *Yankees and Creoles: The Trade between*

North America and the West Indies before the American Revolution (Cambridge, Mass., 1956). An outstanding article that uses computer technology to trace shipping patterns is William I. Davisson and Lawrence Bradley, "New York Maritime Trade: Ship Voyage Patterns, 1715-1765," *New-York Historical Society Quarterly* 55 (October 1971):309-17.

For an introduction to shipbuilding and design, Howard I. Chapelle's *History of American Sailing Ships* (New York, 1935) is useful. The development of the Navigation Acts and the question of their effectiveness is taken up by Oliver M. Dickerson in *The Navigation Acts and the American Revolution* (New York, 1951) and in Lawrence A. Harper's *English Navigation Laws: A Seventeenth Century Experiment in Social Engineering* (New York, 1939). The controversy these works engendered is discussed in Peter D. McClelland's "Cost to America of British Imperial Policy," *American Economic Review, Papers and Proceedings* 59 (May 1969):370-81, and in Gary M. Walton's "Economic History and the Burdens of the Navigation Acts," *Economic History Review* 24 (November 1971):533-42. A highly interpretive work and one that provides a good summary of the changes in maritime technology and trade is James F. Shepherd and Gary M. Walton, *Shipping, Maritime Trade and the Economic Development of North America* (Cambridge, Mass., 1972).

At the center of all maritime activity was the merchant. The most successful colonial merchants operated within family networks, a phenomenon treated in Bernard Bailyn's *New England Merchant in the Seventeenth Century* (Cambridge, Mass., 1955) and "The Atlantic in the Seventeenth Century," *Journal of Economic History* 13 (Fall 1953):378-87. A work previously noted, James B. Hedges's *The Browns of Providence Plantations*, and Virginia D. Harrington's *New York Merchants on the Eve of the Revolution* (New York, 1935) are also worth consulting.

The activities of New Jersey merchant families are not as well known, but Archibald D. Turnbull's *John Stevens: An American Record* (New York, 1928) and Robert T. Thompson's *Colonel James Neilson: A Business Man of the Early Machine Age in New Jersey, 1784-1862* (New Brunswick, N.J., 1940), chapters 1 and 2, are useful, as is Morris R. Smith's *Burlington Smiths: A Family History* (Philadelphia, 1877). Two articles provide considerable insights into merchant life: Stuart Bruchey's "Success and Failure Factors: American Merchants in Foreign Trade in the Eighteenth and Early Nineteenth Centuries," *Business History Review* 32 (Autumn 1958):272-92, and Arthur J. Cole's "The Tempo of Mercantile Life in Colonial America," *Business History Review* 33 (Autumn 1959):277-99.

Merchant life was considerably disrupted by the coming of the American Revolution. The breakdown of the relationship between England and her colonies and in particular the growing strife in New Jersey are examined in Larry R. Gerlach, *Prologue to Independence: New Jersey and the Coming of the American Revolution* (New Brunswick, N.J., 1976). The coming of the war, the economic disruption resulting from a war of attrition, and the economic industries engendered by it are discussed in Leonard Lundin's *Cockpit of the Revolution: The War for Independence in New Jersey* (Princeton, N.J., 1940) and Arthur D. Pierce's very readable *Smugglers' Woods* (New Brunswick N.J., 1960), with detailed chapters on the development of the salt works along the New Jersey coast and on privateering. Works on the general economic life of New Jersey during this period include Edward A. Fuhlbruesse's "Abstract of New Jersey Finances during the Revolution," *Proceedings of the New Jersey Historical Society* 55 (July 1937):167–90; David L. Cowen's "Revolutionary New Jersey, 1763–1787," *Proceedings of the New Jersey Historical Society* 71 (January 1953):1–23; and James H. Levitt's *New Jersey's Revolutionary Economy*, New Jersey's Revolutionary Experience, vol. 9 (Trenton, N.J., 1975).

Levitt's work involved the use of the computer to develop quantitative data on New Jersey's ports; for those interested in pursuing this methodology, good starting points are Thomas H. Crowley's *Understanding Computers* (New York, 1967) and Edward Shorter's *Historian and the Computer: A Practical Guide* (Englewood Cliffs, N.J., 1971). The use of personalized data bases for the study of history is explained in James H. Levitt and Claude LaBarre's "Building a Data Base from Historical Archives," *Computers and the Humanities* 9 (March 1975):77–82; the various uses of quantification in history are explained in an excellent work edited by Robert P. Swierenga, *Quantification in American History: Theory and Research* (New York, 1970).

Index

Accounting. *See* Maritime bookkeeping
Acton, William, 110, 112
Agriculture, 16, 17, 104, 105, 116. *See also* names of specific agricultural commodities
Albany (sloop), 94
Alexander, Elizabeth, 123
Alexander, James, 119, 123, 207n.47
Alexander family, 119
Andros, Edmund, 15, 23, 190n.12–13
Anne and Elizabeth (sloop), 2
Anne and Judith (schooner), 96
Anne and Sarah (ship), 96
Antigua, 60, 64, 71, 116, 171, 172

Barbados, 31, 60, 64, 70, 71, 116, 171
Barberie, John, 54, 160
Barclay, John, 52, 53, 160
Barnegat, N.J., 141
Basse, Jeremiah, 25, 36
Baxter, W.T., 117
Beef, 37, 38, 61, 105
Beer, 105
Belcher, Jonathan, 51
Belfast (snow), 133

Bellomont, earl of. *See* **Coote,** Richard
Bermuda, 171
Betty and Salley (snow), 122
Blain, James, 2
Bland, Elias. *See* Elias Bland and Company
Blanding, Bryand, 1
Board of General Proprietors of the Eastern Division of New Jersey, 6, 7, 10, 24
Borden, Jeremiah, 2
Boston, 8, 61, 71, 72, 74, 80, 89, 116, 171
Boyle, Patrick, 108, 109
Branford, William, 94
Bread, 104, 105
Bridgeton, N.J., 148
Brigantines, 79, 119
Brigs, 76, 79, 80, 82
Broughton. *See* Janeway and Broughton
Bruchey, Stuart, 101
Brunswick of East Jersey (sloop), 138
Brunswick (sloop), 131
Burlington, N.J., 13, 14, 15; Geography, 42; Master/vessel relationship, 183;

Merchant-shippers, 133, 134; Port decline, 17, 18, 32, 34, 43, 44, 65, 106, 139; Port personnel, 47, 54, 55, 159; Port recordkeeping, 50, 51; Port status, 24, 26, 45; Shipbuilding, 87, 93; Shipmasters, 97; Trade routes, 64; Vessel age, 83; Vessel tonnage, 175; Volume and region of trade, 167
Burnet, William, 106
Burnet of New York (snow), 117
Burroughs, William, 110, 111, 112
Byam, William, 129
Byllings, Edward, 10

Callender, Joseph, 134
Callender, Robert, 138
Callender, William, 134, 138
Campbell, Anne, 52
Campbell, John, 52
Canada, 71, 73, 74, 151, 171
Canary Islands, 27, 59, 74, 96, 172
Cape May, N.J., region, 44, 135, 139, 140, 147
Cargo trends, 102–6
Cargos. *See* specific names of commodities
Carteret, George, 10, 26
Carteret, Philip, 11, 23
Catharine (sloop), 108, 109, 161–62
Catherine (brig), 122, 125, 126, 127, 128
Catherine (ship) 117, 118
Charles (sloop), 138
Charleston, S.C., 74
Charming Betty (sloop), 110, 111, 112
Cider, 63, 105
Cloth, 103
Coastal trade, 58, 66, 99, 133, 155
Cohansey, N.J. *See* Salem-Cohansey Customs District
Coker, Thomas, 24, 160
Colden, Cadwallader, 19
Commission merchants, 123–30
Computers and historical research, 163, 217
Cooper's Ferry, N.J., 43
Coote, Richard (earl of Bellomont), 24, 25, 26
Corn, 127

Cornbury, Lord. *See* Hyde, Edward
Cosby, William, 13
Council of Proprietors of the Western Division of New Jersey, 6, 7, 10, 24
Cox, William, 131
Cruger, Henry, Jr., 121
Cunningham, Waddell, 120
Curaçao, 60, 122
Currency Act (1764), 144
Customs administration, 46, 48; Port personnel and, 47, 49, 54, 55, 56, 57, 159; Port recordkeeping and, 49, 50

Dairy products, 63
David, Solomon, 1
De Ware, Andrew, 159
Deare, Jonathan, 145, 160
Delaware, 171
Delaware River, 14, 15, 18, 26, 42, 43, 97, 94; forts, 152
Delight (sloop), 121
Dickerson, Oliver M., 100, 101
Dolphin of Rhode Island, 49
Dolphine (sloop), 136
Dongan, Thomas, 11–12, 19, 23
Dove (sloop), 135, 138
Durham boats, 94
Dutch settlers, 86
Dutch West India Company, 11
Dyre, William, 160, 193n.9

Eagle of Amboy (snow), 117, 138
Eagle (sloop), 116
East Jersey Proprietors. *See* Board of General Proprietors of the Eastern Division of New Jersey
Egg Harbor, N.J., 37, 42, 43, 44, 135
Eier, William, 53
Elias Bland and Company, 93
Elizabeth, N.J., 23, 141
Elizabeth (ship), 122, 129
Elizabethtown, N.J. *See* Elizabeth, N.J.
Engal, Marc, 22

Factors. *See* Commission merchants
Farmer (captain), 117, 118
Farmer, Thomas, 160
Farmers, 16, 17, 44, 88, 153, 156
Fayal, 27

Index

Ferries, 44, 52
Fishermen, 94
Flour, 38, 61, 104, 105, 125
Fogel, Robert, 101
Forester, Miles, 27, 160
Fox, Thomas, 160
Franklin, William, 36, 51, 141, 142, 143
Fraser, George, 98, 138
Fraser, William, 98, 159
French and Indian War (1755–63), 63, 81
Friends, Society of, 12, 17, 108
Funchal (brig), 122, 125, 129

General stores, 41, 106, 149
Gibb, Richard, 133, 148
Good Resolution (sloop), 2
Goodman, Charles, 160
Gordon, Thomas, 16
Governor Livingston (schooner), 148
Greenwich Tea Party (1774), 145
Greg, Cunningham, and Company, 120
Greyhound (brig), 145
Griffen (ship), 26
Groome, Samuel, 86–87

Hacker, Louis M., 100
Hamilton, Alexander (doctor), 41
Hancock, Thomas, 120
Hanna (sloop), 52, 53
Hanse, John, 138
Hardware, 102, 103, 106
Harper, Lawrence, 100, 101
Hart, John, 145
Hatton, John, 55, 56, 140, 141, 159
Heard, John, 209n.144
Hendrickson, Daniel, 108, 109, 110, 149
Hester (ship), 25, 26, 28
Hides, 63
Historiography, 21, 22, 100, 101, 117
Hopkinson, Francis, 159
Hudson River, 14
Hude, Jacob, 131
Hunter, Robert, 12, 31
Hyde, Edward (Lord Cornbury), 26, 30

Inians, John, 40

Inians Ferry, 40, 196n.104
Insurance, marine, 125
Iron, 102, 103, 125
Isle of Man, 172

Jamaica, 60, 108, 109, 171, 172
James, Abel, 136
James (duke of York), 10, 11
Janeway and Broughton, 41
Jeffry, George, 72
Jeneway, Richard, 125
John and Anne (ship), 93
John and Mary of Perth Amboy (sloop), 48, 49, 116
Johnston, Andrew, 137, 207n.47; Owner of sailing vessels, 107, 125, 129, 209n.144; Partner of John Parker, 115, 116, 117, 129
Johnston, David, 120, 121
Johnston, James, 115, 130, 138
Johnston, Jennette, 115
Johnston, John, 16
Johnston, John (doctor), 115
Johnston, Lewis, 125, 129
Johnston family, 72
Joseph and Betty (snow), 96

Kalm, Peter, 41
Katy (brig), 121
Kearney, Michael, 107, 147
King, Robert Hine, 160

Leake, Andrew W., 106
Leaming, Thomas, Jr., 149
Leaming, Thomas, Sr., 149
Leaterland, James, 1
Lisbon, 125, 126
Little David (sloop), 120, 121
Little Egg Harbor, N.J., 88, 139, 141, 147
Liverpool, 59, 67, 172
Livingston, Henry, 124
London, 59
Long Ferry Tavern (Perth Amboy, N.J.), 114
Lords of Trade, 50, 51, 87
Love and Unity (ship), 149
Low, Cornelius, 107, 108
Low family, 41

Loyalists, 147–48
Lumber, 37, 86, 105

Mackdowall, Alexander, 49, 55, 160
Madeira, Perth Amboy, N.J., and, 27, 59, 60, 67, 118, 122, 123, 124, 126, 127, 142, 171, 172; Piscataqua, N.H., and, 70; Wine trade, 27, 59, 70, 122, 124, 126, 127, 128, 129
Manesly, Joseph, 96
Manufactured goods, 99, 103, 106, 142
Maria (sloop), 110
Maritime bookkeeping, 111–12, 116, 117
Maritime partnerships, 137–38
Marlborough (privateer), 94
Martha (flyboat), 26
Martha (sloop), 129
Mary (ship), 93
Mary and Ann (sloop), 2
Mary and Catherine (brigantine), 117
McClelland, Peter, 101
Merchant-shippers, 107–10; Commission merchants and, 123–30; Financial difficulties, 130–31; Maritime partnerships, 137–38; Use of New York, 119–23; Use of Philadelphia, 121, 122, 134, 135, 136; Versatility, 113, 115–18. *See also* Maritime partnerships
Mercury (snow), 93
Middletown, N.J., 94, 98
Molasses, 18, 70, 96, 104, 116
Molly (brig), 122
Molly (shallop), 98
Money. *See* Paper money
Monmouth County, N.J., 108
Morris, Lewis, 13, 50–51
Mullica River, 147
Muscovado sugar. *See* Sugar

Naval officers, 55, 159
Navigation Acts, 7, 45, 46, 50, 99–102, 193n.9
Neilson, Arthur Scott, 147
Neilson, James, 121, 131, 133, 147, 148
Neilson, John (colonel), 148, 149
Neilson family, 75
Nevis, 171
New Brunswick, N.J., 40, 41, 108, 115, 132, 142; Merchant-shippers, 131, 133; Revolutionary War in, 146, 147
New England, Burlington, N.J., and, 64; Coastal trade, 31, 80; Perth Amboy, N.J., and, 58, 61 63, 90, 171; Piscataqua, N.H., and, 70; Regionalized trade,, 67, 68. *See also* Boston; Rhode Island
New Jersey, Assembly, 11, 12; Geography, 14, 17, 19, 39, 40, 42, 43; Governor's Council, 12; Legislature, 34, 35, 36, 37
New York, N.Y., 7, 10, 19, 22, 89, 171, 172; Commercial dominance, 17, 20, 27, 28, 119–23, 142, 153–57; Commercial policy, 8, 11, 23, 25, 36, 81; Geography, 39; Maritime development, 11, 12, 14; Merchant-shippers, 117, 118
New London, Conn., 171
Newbridge, N.J.; 88
Newbury, N.H., 69
Nicholls, Richard, 10
North Carolina, 171

Oake, Jacob, 131
Oake, William, 126
Ogden, John, 2
Ogden, Samuel, 2
Oysters, 118

Paper money, 20, 145
Paris, Peace of (1763), 100
Parker, Elisha, 53, 115, 124
Parker, Elizabeth, 115
Parker, James (1725–97), 119, 120, 121, 123, 124, 130, 207n.47
Parker, John (1693–1732), Life, 113–15; Maritime Partnerships, 137, 138; New York mercantile firm, 119; Partner of Andrew Johnston, 115, 116, 117, 129; Supercargo, 2
Parker, John (younger), 117, 124
Parker Castle (Perth Amboy, N.J.), 114, 115
Parker family, 3, 72, 73, 75, 121, 131, 151
Paterson, William, 148
Peel, Oswall, 138
Penn, William, 15, 190n.13
Pepperell, William, 72

Index

Perth Amboy, N.J., 9, 10, 13, 14, 96, 114, 144, 164; Charter (1718), 16, 107; Duty-free port, 23, 25, 150; Merchant-shippers, 113–18; Exports, 104, 105; Geography, 42; Imports, 104, 105; Master/vessel relationship, 183; New York and, 119–23; Port decline, 17, 32, 33, 106, 139; Port personnel, 47, 50, 160; Port recordkeeping, 49, 50, 51; Port status, 24, 26, 45; Revolutionary War in, 146, 147, 150; Seal, 16, 31; Shipbuilding, 87, 93; Slave trade, 117, 118; Trade routes, 58, 59, 60, 64, 67, 169–70, 171; Types of ownership of vessels, 184–85; Vessel age, 83, 84, 85; Vessel tonnage, 89, 90, 91, 92; Vessel types, 32, 81, 82, 84, 165–66

Philadelphia, 7, 22, 64, 94, 116; Commercial dominance, 8, 17, 19, 20, 34, 43, 134, 135, 136, 142, 153–57; Maritime development, 11, 14; Smuggling, 19

Pierce, Joshua, 72

Pine Barrens, 42

Pinks, 79

Pirates, 98

Piscataqua, N.H., Shipbuilding, 187; Trade routes, 69–75; Vessel age, 83, 84, 85, 181–82; Vessel tonnage, 89, 90, 92, 176; Volume and region of trade, 168

Pitt, William, 19

Pork, 37, 38, 61

Port administration. *See* Customs administration. *See also* specific names of ports

Port Lewis, 171

Portsmouth, N.H., 69

Portugal, 27, 59. *See also* Lisbon; Madeira

Privateering, 29, 30, 32, 149

Puritans, 9, 10

Quakers. *See* Friends, Society of

Queen Anne's War (1702-13). 29, 30

Rahway, N.J., 108, 141

Randolph, Edmund, 24

Raritan Bay, 14, 15

Raritan Landing, N.J., 40, 41, 108, 141, 142, 147, 150

Raritan River, 14, 15, 39, 40, 41, 117, 133

Read, Charles, 50, 51, 54–55, 56, 159

Reade and Livingston, 129

Reading, John, 35

Reed, Joseph, 117, 118, 119

Regionalized trade, 66–69

Revolutionary War, Delaware River forts, 152; Navigation Acts and, 100, 101, 102; War in the ports, 146–50

Rhode Island, 61, 72, 74, 80, 82, 106, 116, 136, 171

Robinson, Beverly, 120, 121

Rolfe, John, 159

Rum, 18, 104, 105, 116

Ryerson, Thomas, 150

Sailing vessels, Age, 82–85; Cargo capacity, 77, 78, 92; Crews, 89–92, 95–99; Trade routes and, 79, 80, 82, 99; Types, 76, 79, 80, 93, 99, 165–66, 178, 179. *See also* Cargo trends; Shipbuilding

Sailors, 95–99, 203n.86

Saint Christopher, 60

Saint Eustatia, 151

Salem, N.J., Merchant-shippers, 133, 135, 136; Port decline, 17, 32, 34, 139; Port personnel, 47, 159; Port status, 26, 45; Vessel age, 83; Vessel tonnage, 175; Volume and region of trade, 167

Salem-Cohansey Customs District, 45, 139, 140

Salley (brig), 120

Samuel (brig), 1

Savage, Joseph, 136

Savannah, Georgia, 81, 177

Schooners, 76, 80, 82, 93, 133

Scott, Pringle and Scott, 124, 125, 127

Seahorse, 122

Shield, 26

Shipbuilding, 86–89, 99; Design and costs, 92–95, 161–62; Vessel age, 180–82

Shipmasters, 95–99

Ships, 76, 79, 80, 94

Ships. For types of sailing vessels in general, *see* Sailing vessels

Shipwrecks, 94, 97, 98
Shotwell, Henry, 108
Shotwell, James, 108
Shotwell, John, 141
Shotwell, Joseph, 141
Shrewsbury, N.J., 88
Skinner, Stephen, 144, 147, 148
Slave trade, 96, 105, 106, 117, 118
Sloops, 76, 80, 93, 99, 133
Smith, Daniel, 133
Smith, John, 134
Smith, Richard, Jr., 134
Smith, Samuel, 133
Smith family, 3, 34, 64, 73, 133, 134
Smuggling, 18, 19, 20
Snows, 79, 82, 119
Southern colonies, 64, 71, 75, 84, 99
Speedwell of New York (sloop), 49
Spicer, Jacob, 44, 135, 136, 139–41
Spicer, John 51
Stacy, Mahlon, 27
Stamp Act (1765), 143
Stelle, Caleb, 96
Stelle, Isaac, 138
Stevens, John (ca. 1682–1737), 16, 51, 52–54, 160
Stevens, John [Honorable] (1715–92), 54, 137, 148, Importer of Madeira wine, 59, 124–27, 128, 129; Shipping from New York and Philadelphia, 122, 123; Use of commission agents, 124–27, 128, 129
Stevens, John (1749–1838), 145
Stevens, Richard, 122, 125, 127, 128, 129
Stevens family, 3, 72, 73, 75, 121, 122
Sugar, 96, 104, 116
Sunbury, Georgia, 74, 84, 168, 177
Swan (sloop), 121

Tariffs, 35, 37, 143, 144
Taverns, 114
Tea, 144
Tenerife, 59, 60, 172
Thomas, Robert P., 101
Tom, John, 97–98
Toms River, N.J., 147
Townsend's Inlet, N.J., 135
Townshend Duties (1767), 143, 144
Trade routes. *See* Coastal trade; New England; Regionalized trade; Sailing vessels, Trade routes and; Transatlantic trade; Triangular trade; West Indies. *See also* specific ports and areas
Transatlantic trade, 57–58, 172. *See also* specific ports and areas
Triangular trade, 66
Tritons Prize (warship), 29
Two Brothers (sloop), 2
Two Friends (brig), 122

Utrecht, Treaty of (1713), 30

Van Brankle, James, 110
Van Cortland family, 119
Van Dam, Anthony, 120
Van Horn, Cornelius, 117, 118, 119
Vanderhoven, Johannes, 53
Vincent, Samuel, 96
Virginia, 171, 172

Walton, Gary, 101
Watts, John, 19, 120, 121
West Indies, 18, 29, 123, 128, 142, 155; Boston and, 8; Burlington, N.J., and, 15, 66, 134; Imports from New Jersey, 26–27, 60; Perth Amboy, N.J., and, 60, 61, 71, 72, 90, 91, 116, 128, 129; Piscataqua, N.H., and, 71, 72; Vessels sailing to, 82, 90, 91. *See also* Antigua; Barbados; Curaçao; Jamaica; Saint Christopher; Saint Eustatia
West Jersey Proprietors. *See* Council of Proprietors of the Western Division of New Jersey
Whaling, 113, 147
Wheat, 37, 104, 105, 116, 118, 125
White, John, 160
Whitehead, William A., 38
William of Perth Amboy (sloop), 98
Willing Mind, 26
Winants, Peter, 1, 2
Winants, Vinant, 2
Wine, 70, 103, 104, 116, 118, 122, 123, 124, 125, 126, 127, 128
Woodbridge, N.J., 40, 108, 115
Woodbridge (sloop), 116
Wrangel, Carl Magnus, 42

York, N.H., 69